LOCKERBIE

LOCKERBIE

A Father's Search for Justice

Jim Swire and Peter Biddulph

BIRLINN

This edition first published in 2024 by
Birlinn Limited
West Newington House
10 Newington Road
Edinburgh
EH9 1QS

www.birlinn.co.uk

Reprinted 2025

First published in 2021 by Birlinn Ltd as
The Lockerbie Bombing: A Father's Search for Justice

ISBN 978 1 78027 920 6

Designed and typeset by Hewer Text UK Ltd, Edinburgh

For Flora and all who seek Truth

Contents

Authors' Note   ix
Preface   xi

Introduction   xv
Family Life   xxv

Into a New Existence   1
Two 'Guilty' Men?   53
The Trial   123
A Desperate Appeal   175
Concealed Evidence, False Evidence   185
Libya Destroyed, a Deathbed Farewell   215
Truth Will Find a Way   229
Spring 2021: Aftermath   239
Epilogue   241

Notes   243
Acknowledgements   255
Index   257

Authors' Note

THE WITNESSES WHO appear in this account from Chapter 12 onwards are only a selection. They appear because their evidence is central to the prosecution case.

Preface

It was Autumn 1999. The Lockerbie bombing had taken place eleven years earlier and was persistently in the news, sometimes even lead item on serious TV channels. Prominent throughout was a Dr Jim Swire, a tall, precisely spoken middle-aged man with a shock of white hair, described privately by some in the media as 'the presenter's dream'. His ability to compress a complex issue into twenty seconds was much admired.

There was something about all this I found puzzling. Why had no book been published? Where was that writer, that prominent journalist stepping in to explain events, ask questions, lead the reader into an understanding of Jim Swire, his family, his tragedy, his deep mourning, his world-famous campaign for something I did not yet understand?

I telephoned Jim. He seemed pleased at my interest and invited me to his home, a lovely semi-mansion on the edge of the quiet town of Bromsgrove in Worcestershire. There I was introduced to his wife, Jane, who, with kind eyes and a gentle smile, checked me out to calculate if I could be trusted. Why, I wondered? Only years later, as my knowledge of Jim and his family grew, did I learn that from one year after the bombing he had been regarded by the British Foreign Office and intelligence services as a 'person of interest', and that he and members of his Lockerbie support group were being carefully monitored.

Within days of my first working meeting with Jim, my instincts told me that here was a hero challenging a cover-up on an international scale, created by several governments and aided by their intelligence services. And that that the various elements of this extraordinary story might one day merge to become the theme of an important film or TV drama.

When friends ask me why it took almost thirty years to complete this book, my explanation is complex. For year after year following the Lockerbie trial and appeal, new evidence has been unearthed. And as each new significant item emerged, we re-wrote a chapter, or even added an entire section. The most important new information came in John Ashton's book *Megrahi: You Are My Jury – The Lockerbie Evidence*, published in 2012. This demonstrated, using conclusions reached by prominent scientists, that the most significant piece of evidence on which Abdelbaset al-Megrahi's guilty verdict was founded – a tiny fragment from an electronic circuit board – was false. Manufactured by unknown persons and most definitely not emanating from Libya or used by Megrahi. (We describe this in detail in our chapter 'The Truth Will Out'.)

Draft of the book followed draft: first person present, first person past, third person present then past. New information was examined for relevance, then discarded, with red herrings occasionally emerging from the FBI and CIA or the Crown Office of Scotland, only to disappear into the sands of Libya. We were alerted to several huge skips in a New York back street said to contain thousands of files dumped after the closure of Pan Am that would expose the truth behind the Lockerbie bombing. All proved to be a wasteful and expensive tale of nothing.

Jim and I decided we needed a good agent. One morning I was watching Richard Branson's mother, Eve, on BBC Breakfast. Hmm, I wondered. Might I also write her story? Perhaps a foolish idea. I wandered through the BBC's telephone system and reached the TV studio. 'Could I speak to Eve Branson?' A daring request. Never mind. On a return phone call came a rich, cultured voice: 'I am Richard Jeffs. Eve Branson asked me to call you. How can I help?' Since that day Richard has been a calming and wise voice throughout our journey to today.

Meanwhile, a friend was watching from afar – Oskar Slingerland, a man interested in the possibilities of a film based on our book. He rapidly set up a company, Lockerbie Productions, and over dinner Jim and I signed our first contract.

And now our book has become something special in the world of TV. Several major companies have taken us on an exciting journey culminating in the creation of a five-part television series. Actors considered among the greatest of the current generation – Colin Firth and Catherine McCormack – play Jim and wife Jane.

Whilst the book and the film tell Jim's story up to a certain point, even today new information regarding some of the original trial evidence, and the inner workings of the electronically driven bomb which destroyed Pan Am 103 are being explored by expert friends. These may reveal further weaknesses in the prosecution case. Might it be possible that Jim Swire's search for the truth has not yet ended?

Peter Biddulph
November 2024

Introduction

THIS BOOK IS partly the story of over thirty years of my life. Although of course it centres on the aftermath of the Lockerbie disaster, I believe it also has to be set in some autobiographical context. How could initial faith in the establishment take thirty years to convert into distrust towards all those touched by that addictive drug we call power?

One of my most vivid memories of early life comes from 1940 when I was five, crossing the Atlantic in a convoy, my father having been recalled to Britain after running the British garrison in Bermuda on the outbreak of war. He was an officer in the Royal Engineers and a man of principle of whom I was already deeply in awe. He and my mother Otta (née Tarn), and my elder sister Flora, were listening to words of defiance from Winston Churchill, speaking over the ship's Tannoy: England would never surrender. What made it so memorable was that they were totally absorbed by that defiant and powerful rhetoric; it cut them off from the reality around them. I think that if a torpedo had chosen that moment to strike, they would have stayed exactly where they were to the end.

My parents had married late in their thirties and were steeped in the mores of the late Victorian era. In our households there were two communities, upstairs and down. Parents inhabited the 'drawing room', and we children were sent to fraternise with them with brushed hair and on best behaviour for an hour in the evening.

Once we were back in the UK, my father, Colonel Roger Swire, was away most of the time fighting WWII. I believe his psyche had been forever altered by his experience of the 'Great' War – as a young Royal Engineer subaltern aged seventeen he was sent on a horse and with a sabre to the trenches, winning a MC and Bar, but witnessing the mayhem of machine-gun bullets churning the mud of the parapets and sometimes the flesh of his men. One of the worst experiences seems to have been when playing tennis behind the lines with his best friend, the friend was shot dead on court by a sniper. None of these things would he ever mention himself. Meanwhile, Otta had to run the family on her own and apply the discipline that the Colonel would have required.

Looking back later, I wonder what it cost him to teach me to use a gun in Skye, or what memories were evoked for him when he and I used to go out onto the moors there in winter with lengths of wire to repair the phone lines blown off their poles by storms.

When the family settled into Orbost House in Skye in 1947, one of my regular tasks was to trim the wicks and clean the chimneys of the ordinary paraffin lamps, and to fill and pump up the tanks of the Tilley pressure-driven lamps which alone were powerful enough to light an entire space the size of the drawing room. The hiss of a Tilley and the smell of methylated spirit with which they had to be pre-warmed remain with me still.

It was necessary to ensure that any smell of spilled paraffin was scrubbed off me, and this was always achieved by our nanny, Louisa Macdonald, a Skye lady. She loved my elder sister Flora and myself like a mother and had been with the family from my sister's birth. Both my grandmothers had come from Skye, and it was because of our family's long association with the island that she was recruited from there. She had started with us when our family was billeted at number twenty-four the Cloisters in Windsor Castle, where my sister and I were born. 'Louie' had been with us in Bermuda, braved the Atlantic with us, and had lived to see and love our own children too. Like me, she was hugely in awe of the Colonel.

Sent down to England from the age of seven to stay in the best boarding schools, I think I was being prepared to take on the mantra of a leader. But the role did not fit; I felt I had neither the self-confidence nor the ambition.

School holidays were spent roaming the hills of Skye, bringing home meat and fish for the table. During term time Nanny, who had bought herself a shotgun, made up for shortages in my absence. No doubt my long-isolated hunting treks over the Skye moors, and fishing trips in my homemade single-seat canoe, reinforced my shyness.

National Service as a second-lieutenant in the Royal Engineers in Archbishop Makarios's terrorist infested but beautiful island of Cyprus and in Port Said in the Suez crisis taught me about *esprit de corps*, plastic explosives, the workings of bombs, the sadness, madness and loss of war, and also about the shapes of organised religion and the power of the financial might of America.

After that came three lovely years reading geology in Cambridge where, on 21 June 1960, I met a delightful young trainee teacher, Jane, and on 16 December 1961 we married: a ceremony which forever transformed my life for the better. Jane is brave, tough and loving. Somehow she knew, twenty-seven years later, after Flora's murder, that my campaign was at least in part my way of coping with the loss.

From 1960 I enjoyed my job as a TV technician in the BBC; electronics had been a major hobby, and 'Auntie' reinforced that with a professional training course. But when I finally did decide to read medicine, which meant initial years of penury, Jane backed my decision.

The arrival of our first child, Flora, changed the world for us. Flora was everything a first-born could possibly be. Even on the breast as a baby her eyes were looking around, weighing up her people and her world, full of fun and curiosity, bursting with energy. Soon she had a sister, Cathy, and then a brother, William, and we were a fortunate and happy family. Flora's clever hands gave her skills in many hobbies including dressmaking.

Flora had a lovely voice and became an accomplished pianist and skilled guitar player, winning diplomas at music festivals. I vividly remember her singing to her own guitar when she was about ten in a croft house in Skye, with the croft's budgerigars twittering in time to her beat, all of us crammed in around the peat fire. Having worked at the BBC I was into recording, but I still can barely listen now to that cosy evening ceilidh with young Flora singing '*I dreamed the world had all agreed to put an end to war . . .*', and the words of love and appreciation that her fresh skills had evoked.

Later, Flora decided to study medicine, and I have fond memories of discussions between us about diseases old and new. Like most medical students she went through phases of believing that she had one of the diseases being studied. Once she became worried about a deeply coloured spot on one of her toes: was it a malignant melanoma? After close examination and a few giggles it was clearly not, but she being Flora I had to explain why I was sure that it was not.

There is no bond stronger than that between a mother and her child, and it shines through what Jane has written about those happy years before Flora's murder. Jane's words evoke the spirit of Flora as no others can; to read them blurs my eyes with tears.

Breaking the embargo against families being allowed to see the victims' bodies, I arranged to visit the Lockerbie ice rink after the disaster, where our lovely Flora's body had been thoughtfully arranged for me. She had received fatal injuries when the bomb exploded almost under her feet and the fuselage ripped apart at 31,000 feet, throwing her body into the screaming, freezing dark. She had landed on a green Scottish hillside, but her face had been so distorted by impact that I had to make sure it was indeed her body. The pathologist moved the sheet from over her feet, and there on her toe was the same dark mark which she and I had examined years before.

Mrs Thatcher attended the memorial service in Lockerbie. To us was read the story of the restoring to life of Lazarus. I suppose the vast majority of us there were agnostics, unable honestly to decide what, if anything, follows this life. For me it was a wildly inappropriate choice of reading, for the one thing we could not be granted was the return of our lost loved ones to be with their families again.

Within a month of the disaster I obtained a detailed warning from West Germany, received by the UK Government in October 1988, several weeks before the Lockerbie attack. It described the design and function of a series of improvised explosive devices (IEDs) built into domestic tape recorders and the like. It explained how they would always give a plane around thirty-five minutes of flight time before exploding, being fully automated.

I was also able to access a 'warning about this warning' sent on to Heathrow security by the UK Department of Transport just before the night of the Lockerbie attack. In it the Heathrow people were told: 'Any item about which a searcher is unable to satisfy himself/herself must, if it is to be carried in the aircraft, be consigned to the aircraft hold.' The crass stupidity of this advice took my breath away, demolishing my faith in those who had been charged with the protection of our families. An early target for me became the improvement of aviation security, but the system proved arrogantly resistant to criticism, aided by Margaret Thatcher's refusal to allow an enquiry.

On 21 December 1988 just such a bomb was duly loaded into the hold of our Flora's aircraft at Heathrow. It exploded after thirty-eight minutes of flight at 31,000 feet over Lockerbie, just as the German police warning had predicted.

Was the failure of Margaret Thatcher's government to act on that precise warning from Germany part of the reason why they denied us any inquiry? We do not of course know, for Lockerbie files remain sequestered now beyond even the thirty-year time limit. If you read Lady Thatcher's tale *The Downing Street Years* you will find that there is no mention of Lockerbie. Indeed, you will find she claims on page 449 that following her support for the USAF bombing of Tripoli and Bengazi in April 1986, the aftermath was that 'the much vaunted Libyan counter-attack could not and did not take place . . . There was a marked decline in Libyan sponsored terrorism in succeeding years.'

Are we to assume then that 1988 was not a 'succeeding year' to 1986? Or could it be that she knew all along that the tale of Libya being responsible for the Lockerbie bombing was false?

It was Alphonse Marie Louis de Prat de Lamartine, statesman in France's Second Republic, who wrote of how 'absolute power corrupts the best natures'. Perhaps power had already corrupted one of England's most illustrious prime ministers? Could the 'Iron Lady' have steeled her heart against allowing even the parents of terrorist victims to know the truth about why no meaningful effort had been made to protect their children? Students who wish to study such a terrible possibility may gain insight from *The Importance of Being Awkward*, the biography of that late and much missed redoubtable defender of truth, Tam Dalyell MP.

In November 1991 indictments were issued against two Libyans over the Lockerbie bombing. Up until the end of the Zeist trial, in January 2001, I had managed to cling to the belief that the authorities were indeed genuinely seeking the killers of the innocent. The unfolding 'evidence' in the court finally convinced me otherwise.

Those ten years from 1991 to 2001 had been pivotal for me. They started with my taking my courage in both hands and going, accompanied only by a single Arab journalist Nabil Nagameldin, to see that much dreaded dictator Muammar Gaddafi, with only the most rudimentary idea of whether I would be taken hostage or even shot on sight. Another terrible test as you will read, for my beloved Jane.

As time passed, I met with my now long-term friend Robert Black QC, FRSA, FRSE, FFCS, ILTM, Professor Emeritus of Scots Law at the University of Edinburgh. His concern, like mine, was to find a way to get the accused to trial under Scots law, for the plane had crashed in Scotland. Besides, I felt sure that if the accused were to be tried in America they would receive the death penalty. I remember that my idea of law professors was that they would probably be smartly dressed in dark suits with polished shoes and briefcases, so I was slow in identifying the professor for the first time at the airport, in his jeans and with a backpack slung over his shoulder. He has dispelled many imaginary cobwebs from my mind since then. His company has been one of the great tonics that keeps our search for truth going. There have been so many other friends too. His was the original idea for the nature of the Zeist trial; we travelled together promoting this, and our intent was to find a solution for the refusal of Colonel Gaddafi to allow a trial under US, Western or international law.

It says a great deal for the integrity of the professor that when the trial was over he said, upon meeting the convicted Abdelbaset al-Megrahi in prison in Scotland, 'As a result of today's meeting I am satisfied that not only was there a wrongful conviction, but the victim of it was an innocent man. Lawyers, and I hope others, will appreciate this distinction.'

I found to my amazement that I could talk to people like Colonel Gaddafi, though he was a man of deep mood swings. On one visit the Colonel was almost mute (he could speak excellent English normally, but was in pain and was sulking). The professor and I found ourselves cooped up with him in a tiny tent in the desert behind Sirte, and we knew him well enough by then that his armed guards had been dispensed with. He would say nothing. What to do? I tried the schoolboy trick of pretending to look furtively under the folding table, and when the Colonel asked what I was doing, I said I was checking that

Monica Lewinsky was not hiding there. Mercifully he did not get out his gold-plated automatic but guffawed with laughter. After that we could and did talk.

You will read how the trial progressed and how, in January 2001, the verdict of guilty was given against al-Megrahi, and how the last vestiges of my faith in the integrity of the official search for the perpetrators evaporated.

After many years running the British Empire we have evolved all sorts of subtle ways of concealing truth when it is inconvenient for government to admit failure. Supposedly even these subtle secrecies are limited by a 'thirty-year rule'; but now we sail into a future where up to fifty Lockerbie documents are sequestered from public view well beyond that thirty-year limit with no explanation as to why. There seems no sign of conscience or even knowledge of right and wrong. My daughter and all those who died with her deserve better; it is as though their deaths simply did not matter.

But as Victor Hugo wrote, 'Life is a flower and love is the honey.' Flora cannot die from the earth for she will always be honey in our hearts, and I prefer to remember with her those many who sympathised with our needs and tried to help. Bless you all.

Destroyed is the respect and awe I used to feel towards authority. Was it for these deceits that men like my father fought and very nearly died for our country? Of course decent men remained, such as the late Tam Dalyell, 'Father of the House' of Commons. He did his utmost to assist when few others would listen. Douglas Hurd, as foreign secretary, recorded in Cabinet minutes that he regarded our bereaved-relatives' group as responsible people who should be kept informed. But probably the most forthright adviser was the late great Nelson Mandela; he warned us that 'No one country should be complainant, prosecutor and judge.'

There seems no doubt now that Lockerbie was a revenge attack for the destruction by two US missiles some five months earlier of an Iranian airbus with 290 innocents aboard. In the cemetery where those victims lie, the fountain runs with blood-red water; I think it runs to tell us that too much human blood has been spilt. That water flows for Flora too, and Truth, Justice and Forgiveness are the healers, never hatred nor revenge.

I have, dear Flora, done my best to discover why you had to die. I know that you and I have discovered truth where others have not. That has to be our warm, shared knowledge. It will be for others now to see to it that our country learns that it must protect its young people properly and relate the truth, with honesty, to its citizens. Nelson Mandela also once said, 'When a man has done what he considers to be his duty to his people and his country, he can rest in peace.' I wish, Flora, that at some point during the richly rewarding life you were denied, I could have introduced you to him. He too would have tasted the honey.

Jim Swire
April 2021

Family Life

THE TERRIBLE EVENTS that took place on Pan Am 103 in the sky above Lockerbie just after 7 p.m. on 21 December 1988 tore our hearts in two. A terrorist bomb, loaded into the hold of our daughter's aircraft at Heathrow Airport, exploded after thirty-eight minutes of flight. We knew at once that this was not something we would ever 'get over' and that life would never be the same.

Flora was on the eve of her twenty-fourth birthday. She was born on 22 December 1964, some three years after our marriage in December 1961 (Jim and I having met in Cambridge in 1960 where he was about to take a degree in Natural Sciences at Trinity College, and I was at Homerton College training to be a teacher). At the time of her birth, Jim had recently made a career switch, abandoning his work as a BBC television engineer to become a trainee doctor at Birmingham University's Medical School, and we lived in a rented flat in Edgbaston. The winter of that year was harsh and snowy, and quite a challenge for all, but baby Flora took it in her stride, after a few short months alert to everything. In the spring she could sit up in the garden to enjoy the company of friends in this leafy area of Birmingham. Next door lived three-year-old Louise, known by Flora as 'best friend Weeze', a trusty chum and playmate from their first acquaintance, and surely there is nothing sweeter to a busy mother's ears than the sound of happy children playing.

In September 1967 we moved to the Worcestershire village of Blackwell, agreeably situated in the Lickey Hills between the village of Barnt Green and the town of Bromsgrove. Our second daughter, Catherine Mary Jane, was on her way, and was born on 23 December at the Queen Elizabeth Hospital, where Jim worked as a Senior House Officer on the Professorial Unit under the distinguished consultant physician Professor Melville Arnott. His job was challenging and hard, requiring him to stay at the hospital whenever on call. Thus, in our early months living in Blackwell, some ten miles to the south, I was often alone with the children. Paternity leave was unheard of. Occasionally I wished I had someone to reassure me or advise, but perhaps it was as well that there was no time for self pity as I now had two small children utterly dependent on me for every hour of daily care. And so life was busy and exhausting for both Jim and me.

Some five years later our lives had eased to a satisfactory pace. In January 1972 our son William arrived, and soon after his birth Jim took the significant step of leaving hospital medicine to join a GP practice in Bromsgrove. To have at last sufficient income and free time for a stable family life was a joy. It meant that I could devote myself entirely to our beloved children whose well-being and education meant so much to us.

Our new life arranged itself well. We were able to double the size of the house, enabling each child to have their own bedroom, plus a spare room for my mother to use when visiting from her home in Spain. One of the best features was a half-acre rear garden full of apple and pear trees, giving cascades of white blossom in the spring and barrow loads of fruit in the autumn. At the end of the garden was a wooden shed which Jim equipped with bunk beds should the children choose to sleep with their friends for an overnight 'adventure'. Flora, by then aged twelve, emerged as the self-styled proprietor, imposing strict rules for its use, together with charges for a night's stay, and extra penalties and charges for any misuse or breakages. In spite of her strict rules our children soon developed a growing circle of friends from the neighbourhood. All in all it was a happy time, and in 1983 we were fortunate to purchase Caspidge House, a large home just to the north of Bromsgrove.

Flora was now at school and proving herself to be an able and industrious student. School days are not always as much fun as some would have us believe, but Flora always appeared to be happy, with plenty of time left for hobbies, making things with her clever hands, and for her music and singing. Piano exams were taken and passed with distinction; she earned herself first prize certificates and a silver cup for singing with her guitar in local music festivals; she took the main part of the little sweep in Benjamin Britten's opera performed by her school in 1976; sang in the choir of our local Methodist church; won first prize in a French speaking competition at Birmingham University; and showed herself gifted in many spheres, not least at sewing and dressmaking. After saving her pocket money for more than a year she became the proud owner of a Husqvarna sewing-machine and was to design and, astonishingly, make a whole wardrobe of clothes for herself. Her schoolwork was broadened and enhanced, rather than hindered, by these extra activities. Her Maths teacher invited her to join the Maths Club, held on Saturday mornings at the University. There she joined other young people from all over Birmingham with high mathematical ability to play number games and puzzles, a skill which amazed all of us. She finished her school days at King Edward's High School with high grades in Maths, Physics and Chemistry at A level, and won an Upper Sixth Form Prize and a Physics prize. Afterwards a group of sixth formers, boys and girls, joined Flora and our family for a week on the Isle of Skye, where energetic swimming and walking was followed by evenings of wild card games. It was a good time to be young and full of fun.

In her last year of school her entry to medical school had to be negotiated. The final choice was Nottingham, where her friend Geoff Marston had also been offered a place, and the pair started their course in the autumn of 1983. For her first year Flora stayed in Derby Hall, purpose built for undergraduates in the University Park. She plunged headlong into university life with eagerness and verve – very soon she and a friend, Lisa, were designing and making their own party clothes for the Medics Ball, and special fancy-dress costumes for the witch and her cat for Halloween celebrations. She joined a madrigal group, played a leading role in the University Dramatic Society's production of *Don Juan*, joined in a race to get to Paris and back for charity, and assembled a throng of male admirers along the way. Apart from all this there was physiology and anatomy to be studied, and time spent at the dissecting table. Always able to be single-minded, she amazed her friends by being able to withdraw and concentrate completely on her medical studies in the library, only to emerge with enough energy and joie de vivre to drink everyone else under the table. This legendary reputation was even remarked upon in the University's Medic's Year Book of 1986. Finally her hard work rewarded her with a degree of Bachelor of Medical Sciences with first class honours, and Jim and I, along with other proud parents, attended the congregation for the conferment of her degree on 10 July 1986.

Such praiseworthy success brought Flora to the attention of her professors at the medical school and an invitation arrived for her to join Professors Marsden and Birmingham in a programme of research in the Department of Physiology and Pharmacology at the Nottingham Queen's Medical Centre. A philosophy doctorate in the middle of her current medical course seemed to her interesting, but she knew there was still a three-year clinical course to be completed. The medical course was lengthy without these extra years, so her response was not immediately and unequivocally positive. A good deal of nail biting went on when she came home for holidays at Bromsgrove, but eventually she agreed to join the research project. The title was 'Effects of two H1-receptor antihistamines on event-related potentials (ERPs) and psycho-motor performance'. (A project rather above the heads of the rest of us!) Flora informed us that it was to do with the measurement of the effects of sedatives on memory and attention.

Throughout the first year of her PhD, Flora worked in the laboratories at the Queen's Medical Centre, and took her turn at teaching medical students. Both Professor Marsden and Professor Birmingham regarded her as a future doctor of exceptional promise, and when she was offered a further opportunity to do research at the prestigious Institute of Neurology in Queen Square, London, under Dr Martin Halliday, they encouraged her to accept.

In London her project was on Alzheimer's disease, comparing the records of brainwaves through electrodes on the scalps of patients with those of healthy volunteers. Both Jim and I were entreated to take part and enjoyed the experience of having our brainwaves measured according to our ability to respond to the correct visual stimuli. Also doing research at the same hospital were Hart Lidov, an attractive young American doctor, and Dr Gabriella Turano from Italy. Both became Flora's firm friends. It was not long before Flora and Hart became romantically attached and, when he had to go back to his department at Harvard University, Flora went to stay with him and to meet his parents. Cathy too was hoping to visit America with her at some point and even thought about buying a ticket to travel on Flora's Pan Am 103 plane. With a promise to Hart that she would return shortly before Christmas 1988 to celebrate her twenty-fourth birthday with him, Flora returned to London to write up her thesis.

As the year 1989 approached we looked forward to family celebrations through Christmas and into the New Year that would be wonderful, light-hearted and convivial. Our children and home were 'safe', a comfortable retirement beckoned. All was settled, vivid and happy. None of us could suspect the disaster that lay ahead.

True to her promise to Hart, Flora booked a flight to New York with Pan Am for the evening of 21 December 1988. At New

York she intended to transfer to a flight for Boston, arriving in time to celebrate her birthday the next day. But at three minutes past seven on the evening of the 21st a terrorist bomb ripped her plane apart. Our darling Flora and 269 others were killed.

She was a rare spirit with an irrepressible sense of humour and that special vibrant energy that always characterises the truly great. And truly great we think she would have become if only she had been allowed to live. She had all the right ingredients: a good intelligence, boundless energy, and most of all a warm and loving heart with her feet planted firmly on the ground. When the dreadful news of the crash came through on the television, with the images of burning buildings in the little town of Lockerbie, there are no words which can adequately describe our paralysing shock, fear, grief and devastating sadness. So much is there a need for the Floras of this world and we, her family, needed her too. Over the past thirty years we, her parents and Cathy and William, have each missed her in our own individual and unique ways, finding space within the family for each other to mourn. Jim's channelling of all his emotional energy into a campaign to find the truth and hold governments to account has been his recipe for survival and, as this book reveals, he has searched tirelessly and single-mindedly for knowledge of the political events that led to the outrage. He travelled widely, visiting Malta, Germany, France, Sweden, the United States and Libya in this cause. He has sought to tighten up the lax airline security systems that were in place to allow the bombing to occur. At times I and the children have found such an extroverted media campaign quite hard to cope with. We all shared feelings of loss and grief, each in our own ways. For me the who, why, where and how questions have seemed almost irrelevant when faced with the loss of a person so precious that at times life itself seemed almost insupportable.

Jane Swire
April 2021

Into a New Existence

Chapter 1

I SETTLE INTO my study chair and it creaks in sympathy; a long day in surgery, an avalanche of anxious patients. In these pre-Christmas days, time and the affairs of man brook no prisoners. Along the passageway our kitchen echoes with the rattle of cooking as Jane prepares a comforting meal. Beyond the wood and fields, across our tiny town of Bromsgrove, driven by a north wind, mid-winter drizzle sweeps down along the high street, below the twinkle of Christmas lights, where folks busily gather in last-minute presents.

Our teenage son, William, is somewhere, impossible to find in this rambling old home, Caspidge House. Four days ago was our wedding anniversary and tomorrow comes the twenty-fourth birthday of our first-born daughter, Flora, by now on her way to America courtesy of Pan Am Airways. Our second-born daughter, Cathy, waved her goodbye at Heathrow and is homeward bound somewhere on the M40.

My eyes are tiring. I struggle to focus on what will be a Christmas calendar constructed from a dozen photographs, each a happy memory. I'll assemble them in some kind of order to create a series of Christmas-card sized pages, then I'll print off a dozen sets as presents for the family. My thoughts wander across a photo of the mother of a girl who worked as a house-maid for my parents on the Isle of Skye – a wrinkled old woman, firm and stalwart, born and died in the Western Isles, her face tanned and leathered by seventy Hebridean summers and winters.

Suddenly Jane shouts something I can't make out. She chokes and struggles with more words. Slowly I understand: 'There's a plane down, an airliner'. The world rocks on its axis. I blunder into the sitting room and stand transfixed before the television.

'A Pan American jumbo jet with more than two hundred and fifty people on board has crashed tonight in the Scottish Borders. It hit a petrol station in the centre of the town of Lockerbie. Police say there are many casualties.'

Paralysed with dread, we watch the little town of Lockerbie burn. TV cameras pan across destroyed streets then cut to the glowing gable ends of a bungalow, a chimney standing above a crushed wall, the roof gone, flames and sparks showering heavenward, images that will return to me day and night until I die.

I wrap my arms around Jane's shoulders. Her arms hang by her side as if dislocated. We stand in a tableau drawn with hard, black lines. The scent of a mother's hair drifts upwards, her face just below my chin. Against me her heart thuds with a quick, regular beat, an icy fear that only a mother can know when her child is in danger.

The emergency contact numbers flashing on the TV screen are all engaged. Within minutes we are on an evil merry-go-round, I'm switching the phone from ear to ear, searching for a voice that might understand my incoherence.

'Is Flora on the flight? Is Flora on the flight? Tell me!'

Jane starts to shuffle backward and forward like an imprisoned animal. I dial and dial, the skin of my fingers growing sore, but still no answer. Flora's face fills my brain, the room grows cold around us. Suddenly Cathy's car crunches along the drive and she stumbles in. We embrace in silence.

Midnight. Five hours have passed. The emergency numbers are all still engaged. Are ghoulish tricksters ringing the numbers to block us out? Finally I discover the direct route. 'Hello, is that JFK airport, the Pan Am desk? Why can't you tell me? Why with all your damn computers can't you say whether my child is on the plane?'

'Sir, I can't.' Fighting for self-control the Pan Am lady puts down the phone, her desk besieged by panicking relatives and hysterical media.

We sit, holding hands, constantly switching TV channels until all close down; then on the radio the BBC World Service, each bulletin adding more death. We turn the radio off and wait.

Suddenly the phone rings. Pan Am New York is calling. The passenger list has been checked. Flora MacDonald Margaret Swire was on the plane, no survivors, no point in going to Heathrow, no point in doing anything. My daily toil in surgery and hospital has made me all too familiar with death, and yet how I need in the depths of this night to see her, to know the truth of it all. I force myself to imagine her walk, her hair, her face, her laughter. As the plane cracked open beneath a starry sky and a 500mph wind impacted, what did she see and hear and feel? How long was she conscious? Was there time for a single thought before death came? Has she been disfigured, dismembered? My body shudders uncontrollably as the questions encircle us like hungry demons.

Soon grey dawn claws into our sleeplessness. The first day of a new existence passes, and then another. Friends telephone, then visit. What can they say? In the street a few folks we've known for years see us from a distance and cross to the other side of the road to avoid us. Two hundred and seventy murders in a split second, parents, sons, daughters, children, babes in arms, entire families on the plane and in the town of Lockerbie. Death on such a scale terrifies, people cannot comprehend it. Relatives visit and hug, unafraid to touch. Others shake hands as if across a room and murmur, 'Let us know if you need help.'

As the first days of our new existence pass by, unknown to us and far to the north, the townspeople of Lockerbie silently watch as vans pass in procession towards the town's municipal ice rink. In time we will learn that the collected bodies and body parts would not fit into Lockerbie hospital's tiny mortuary. Thus, the ice rink, so often echoing with the laughter of children, is now filled with silence and simple wooden pallets upon which rest the dead, each covered by a white sheet, each queuing for dissection seeking evidence of cause. My daughter! Have they found her? I know well the process of a post-mortem, know well each bloody detail. And until that is done, and checked and rechecked, and is complete and written down and all confirmed, heart's closure of the grave will remain denied.

Television crews swarm across the tiny Scottish town. In close focus, repeated often in news reports, Prime Minister Margaret Thatcher and her entourage walk amid the bodies and debris. As a northern wind flicks her blonde hair back and forth she stands powerless as American search teams locate and remove 'sensitive' material. At her shoulder walks the American ambassador. For all present it is a devastating experience, a memory that will surely stay with them throughout their lives. And yet, in her memoirs,[1] to be published but six years in the future, she will not only fail to describe the trauma of her visit, she will not even mention the word *Lockerbie*.

* * *

To add to our suffering and that of all the families who are part of the Lockerbie disaster, the cruelty of events grows daily. News reports claim that Flora's flight was destroyed by a bomb and that two weeks before the crash an anonymous telephone caller warned that a bomb would be placed on a Pan Am plane flying from Frankfurt to the USA. The US State Department passed the warning to government embassies, airlines and Interpol. Passengers were not told. Washington claims that the warning came from an anti-PLO Abu Nidal Group. Some embassy staff flew to London direct from Moscow and other European cities in order to avoid Frankfurt. When asked why passengers were not told, a Pan Am spokesman said: 'It is the airline's policy not to discuss publicly any threat to the airline.' For the first time in my life the word 'publicly' has become significant.[2]

In spite of this, both London and Washington say no specific warning was received. Why the word 'specific'? In the background are rumours that South African President Pik Botha and his team cancelled their Pan Am 103 flight just before boarding.[3] It was a Boeing 747-100, named *Maid of the Seas*, capable of seating more than 500 passengers; yet Flora's plane was carrying only 243. Did many other would-be passengers cancel because of the warning? The papers are full of news that Iran, Syria and the Popular Front for the Liberation of Palestine General Command (the PFLP-GC) did it. The *Daily Express* claims that a passenger, Khaled Jafaar, was a US Drug Enforcement Agency (DEA) courier. He carried the bomb on board thinking he was carrying a controlled delivery of drugs. The information was said to come from 'sources' within the FBI and Scotland Yard.

We find ourselves surrounded by a special kind of loneliness; Jane presses me to eat, but it proves almost impossible, just enough to stay alive. I do not go to work, I'm not sure I'll ever work again. What remains of Flora lies somewhere in Scotland and that is all that matters. Reporters flood to our front door, it is impossible to know who is who. We share a long twisting drive with a neighbour farmer that ends with our gravelled frontage and garden. Again and again the reporters and strangers brave the narrowness, the bracken and thorns, trudge across the gravel and ring our doorbell. At first we find a way to reply to them politely, sympathetically. It's a comfort, like putting on the kettle and making tea. But soon the story develops a sinister momentum. We have become just names and pictures, things. To the world's media Flora no longer matters. Are camera teams camped out around every bereaved home, poking their lenses into every sad face? We send every reporter

away and I slam my oldest car across the end of the drive to
stop them all.

David Johnston, a Scottish journalist, says he's discovered
that FBI agents were quickly on the scene, wandering the hills
looking for something of which they will never tell. Tam
Dalyell MP is speaking out about something he hasn't yet
defined; journalists speculate, moving the story onward to
more murder. The facts will prove even more sinister. A source
with trusted intelligence contacts claims that within fifty
minutes of the crash – even allowing for delays in confirmation that an airliner crash had occurred – an Arctic-
camouflage-white helicopter with a postcard size image of
the Stars and Stripes on its tail-rotor boom was scrambled
from the secret US Navy Seal base at Machrihanish on the
Mull of Kintyre. Its instructions were primarily to search for
the suitcase of Charles McKee, leader of a CIA team returning from Beirut.[4] Inside the case were top secret documents so
sensitive that the United States government will impose a
total ban on all mention of it.

Two United States intelligence agencies are already deep into
their own style of investigation. The FBI made their presence
widely known by their search of the Lockerbie hills within two
hours of the bombing. The Central Intelligence Agency too are
there but in the background. Their Middle Eastern structures
have been in place for decades and will prove highly useful. The
CIA Lockerbie team is led by a Vincent Cannistraro, a long-
experienced agent.

Jane confesses to feeling shredded, imprisoned by anguish
and grief. Cathy and William offer what comfort they can
muster from their own deep sorrows. All watch, powerless to
help, as my numbness warms to a kind of anger. A policeman
arrives.

'Do you know where Flora's dental records are kept, do you
have information that will identify her, do you . . ., do you . . .?'

The Lockerbie police come again and take us through it all.

A Bromsgrove constable tries to ask us the same questions. We tell him, 'We've said all we're going to say, so please go away.'

The Lockerbie police come yet again: 'Do you know where . . . Do you know what . . . Do you know if . . .?'

We tell it all again and for a time all goes silent. What else do they need? The word 'murder' echoes around the world; every broadcast, every news article. Each time I hear it my spine tingles. I've always understood the word to be something singular, an act performed against one person, someone you know; I've never believed it can be the killing of rows of faces sitting in aircraft seats.

For you who read these words, I suspect that few have ever witnessed a single murder. During 1988, however, almost 600 murders were committed within the Lockerbie framework. Five months before the bombing of Flora's plane, an airbus carrying 290 pilgrims to Mecca was blown from the sky by the USS *Vincennes*. The names of the first group will never be known in Western media circles since the Iranian nation did not at the time possess the technology to record and publicise them. Only their families hold their memories in the form of photographs and memorabilia. We Western nations, in matters of war always correct, lawful and civilised, have widely published the names of our dead. We ask you therefore, to pause for a while to witness an image of the murder of 270 human beings in a single half minute, and reflect on the existence of a parallel Iranian list of persons whom we will never see or know, their names now deep in the sediments of the history of war.

The dead of Pan Am 103 and the town of Lockerbie:

John Michael Gerard Ahern, 26, Rockville Centre, N.Y. **Sarah Margaret Aicher**, 29, London, England. **John David Akerstrom**, 34, Medina, Ohio. **Ronald Ely Alexander**, 46, New York, N.Y. **Thomas Joseph Ammerman**, 36, Old Tappan, N.J. **Martin Lewis Apfelbaum**, 59, Philadelphia, Pa. **Rachel Marie Asrelsky**,

21, New York, N.Y. **Judith Ellen Atkinson**, 37, London, England. **William Garreston Atkinson**, 33, London, England. **Elizabeth Nichole Avoyne**, 44, Croissy-sur-Seine, France. **Jerry Don Avritt**, 46, Westminster, Calif. **Clare Louise Bacciochi**, 19, Warwickshire, England. **Harry Michael Bainbridge**, 34, Montrose, N.Y. **Stuart Murray Barclay**, 29, Farm Barnard, Vt. **Jean Mary Bell**, 44, Berkshire, England. **Julian MacBain Benello**, 25, Brookline, Mass. **Lawrence Ray Bennet**, 41, Chelsea, Mich. **Philip Bergstrom**, 22, Forest Lake, Minn. **Alistair David Berkley**, 29, London, England. **Michael Stuart Bernstein**, 36, Bethesda, Md. **Steven Russell Berrell**, 20, Fargo, N.D. **Noelle Lydie Berti**, 40, Paris, France. **Surinder Mohan Bhatia**, 51, Los Angeles, Calif. **Kenneth John Bissett**, 21, Hartsdale, N.Y. **Diane Anne Boatman-Fuller**, 35, London, England. **Stephen John Boland**, 20, Nashua, N.H. **Glenn Bouckley**, 27, Liverpool, N.Y. **Paula Bouckley**, 29, Liverpool, N.Y. **Nicole Elise Boulanger**, 21, Shrewsbury, Mass. **Francis Boyer**, 43, Toulosane, France. **Nicholas Bright**, 32, Brookline, Mass. **Daniel Solomon Browner** (Bier), 23, Parod, Israel. **Colleen Renee Brunner**, 20, Hamburg, N.Y. **Timothy Guy Burman**, 24, London, England. **Michael Warren Buser**, 34, Ridgefield Park, N.J. **Warren Max Buser**, 62, Glenrock, N.J. **Steven Lee Butler**, 35, Denver, Colo. **William Martin Cadman**, 32, London, England. **Fabiana Caffarone**, 28, London, England. **Hernan Caffarone**, 28, London, England. **Valerie Canady**, 25, Morgantown, W.Va. **Gregory Capasso**, 21, Brooklyn, N.Y. **Timothy Michael Cardwell**, 21, Cresco, Pa. **Bernt Wilson Carlsson**, 50, New York, N.Y. **Richard Anthony Cawley**, 43, New York, N.Y. **Frank Ciulla**, 45, Parkridge, N.J. **Theodora Eugenia Cohen**, 20, Port Jervis, N.Y. **Eric Michael Coker**, 20, Mendham, N.J. **Jason Michael Coker**, 20, Mendham, N.J. **Gary Leonard Colasanti**, 20, Melrose, Mass. **Bridget Concannon**, 53, Oxfordshire, England. **Sean Concannon**, 16, Oxfordshire, England. **Thomas Concannon**, 51, Oxfordshire, England. **Tracey Jane Corner**, 17, Sheffield, England. **Scott**

Cory, 20, Old Lyme Court, Conn. **Willis Larry Coursey,** 40, San Antonio, Texas. **Patricia Mary Coyle,** 20, Wallingford, Conn. **John Binning Cummock,** 38, Coral Gables, Fla. **Joseph Patrick Curry,** 31, Fort Devens, Mass. **William Allan Daniels,** 40, Belle Mead, N.J. **Gretchen Joyce Dater,** 20, Ramsay, N.J. **Shannon Davis,** 19, Shelton, Conn. **Gabriel Della-Ripa,** 46, Floral Park, N.Y. **Joyce Christine Dimauro,** 32, New York, N.Y. **Gianfranca Dinardo,** 26, London, England. **Peter Thomas Stanley Dix,** 35, London, England. **Om Dixit,** 54, Fairborn, Ohio. **Shanti Dixit,** 54, Fairborn, Ohio. **David Scott Dornstein,** 25, Philadelphia, Pa. **Michael Joseph Doyle,** 30, Voorhees, N.J. **Edgar Howard Eggleston III,** 24, Glens Falls, N.Y. **Siv Ulla Engstrom,** 51, Berkshire, England. **Turhan Ergin,** 22, West Hartford, Conn. **Charles Thomas Fisher IV,** 34, London, England. **Joanne Flannigan,** 10, Lockerbie, Scotland. **Kathleen Mary Flannigan,** 41, Lockerbie, Scotland. **Thomas Brown Flannigan,** 44, Lockerbie, Scotland. **Clayton Lee Flick,** 25, Coventry, England. **John Patrick Flynn,** 21, Montville, N.J. **Arthur Fondiler,** 33, West Armonk, N.Y. **Robert Gerard Fortune,** 40, Jackson Heights, N.Y. **Stacie Denise Franklin,** 20, San Diego, Calif. **Paul M. S. Freeman,** 25, London, England. **James Ralph Fuller,** 50, Bloomfield Hills, Mich. **Ibolya Robertine Gabor,** 79, Budapest, Hungary. **Amy Beth Gallagher,** 22, Quebec, Canada. **Matthew Kevin Gannon,** 34, Los Angeles, Calif. **Kenneth Raymond Garczynski,** 37, North Brunswick, N.J. **Paul Isaac Garrett,** 41, Napa, Calif. **Kenneth James Gibson,** 20, Romulus, Mich. **William David Giebler,** 29, London, England. **Olive Leonora Gordon,** 25, London, England. **Linda Susan Gordon-Gorgacz,** 39, London, England. **Anne Madelene Gorgacz,** 76, Newcastle, Pa. **Loretta Anne Gorgacz,** 47, Newcastle, Pa. **David J. Gould,** 45, Pittsburgh, Pa. **Andre Nikolai Guevorgian,** 32, Seacliffe, N.Y. **Nicola Jane Hall,** 23, Sandton, South Africa. **Lorraine Frances Halsch,** 31, Fairport, N.Y. **Lynne Carol Hartunian,** 21, Schenectady, N.Y. **Anthony Lacey Hawkins,** 57, Brooklyn, N.Y. **Dora Henrietta Henry,** 56,

Lockerbie, Scotland. **Maurice Peter Henry**, 63, Lockerbie, Scotland. **Pamela Elaine Herbert**, 19, Battle Creek, Mich. **Rodney Peter Hilbert**, 40, Newton, Pa. **Alfred Hill**, 29, Sonthofen, West Germany. **Katherine Augusta Hollister**, 20, Rego Park, N.Y. **Josephine Lisa Hudson**, 22, London, England. **Melina Kristina Hudson**, 16, Albany, N.Y. **Sophie Ailette Miriam Hudson**, 26, Paris, France. **Karen Lee Hunt**, 20, Webster, N.Y. **Roger Elwood Hurst**, 38, Ringwood, N.J. **Elizabeth Sophie Ivell**, 19, East Sussex, England. **Khalid Nazir Jaafar**, 20, Dearborn, Mich. **Robert Van Houten Jeck**, 57, Mountain Lakes, N.J. **Paul Avron Jeffreys**, 36, Surrey, England. **Rachel Jeffreys**, 23, Surrey, England. **Kathleen Mary Jermyn**, 20, Staten Island, N.Y. **Beth Ann Johnson**, 21, Greensburg, Pa. **Mary Alice Lincoln Johnson**, 25, Wayland, Mass. **Timothy Baron Johnson**, 21, Neptune, N.J. **Christopher Andrew Jones**, 20, Claverack, N.Y. **Julianne Frances Kelly**, 20, Dedham, Mass. **Jay Joseph Kingham**, 44, Potomac, Md. **Patricia Ann Klein**, 35, Trenton, N.J. **Gregory Kosmowski**, 40, Milford, Mich. **Elke Etha Kuhne**, 43, Hanover, West Germany. **Minas Christopher Kulukundis**, 38, London, England. **Mary Lancaster**, 81, Lockerbie, Scotland. **Ronald Albert Lariviere**, 33, Alexandria, Va. **Maria Nieves Larracoechea**, 39, Madrid, Spain. **Robert Milton Leckburg**, 30, Piscataway, N.J. **William Chase Leyrer**, 46, Bayshore, N.Y. **Wendy Anne Lincoln**, 23, North Adams, Mass. **Alexander Silas Lowenstein**, 21, Morristown, N.J. **Lloyd David Ludlow**, 41, Macksville, Kan. **Maria Theresia Lurbke**, 25, Balve Beckum, West Germany. **William Edward Mack**, 30, New York, N.Y. **James Bruce Macquarrie**, 55, Kensington, N.H. **Douglas Eugene Malicote**, Army specialist four, 22, Lebanon, Ohio. **Wendy Gay Malicote**, 21, Lebanon, Ohio. **Elizabeth Lillian Marek**, 30, New York, N.Y. **Louis Anthony Marengo**, 33, Rochester, Mich. **Noel George Martin**, 27, Clapton, England. **Diane Marie Maslowski**, 30, New York, N.Y. **William John McAllister**, 26, Middlesex, England. **Lilibeth Tobila McAlolooy**, 27, Kelsterback, West Germany. **Daniel**

Emmet McCarthy, 31, Brooklyn, N.Y. Robert Eugene McCollum, 61, Wayne, Pa. Charles Dennis McKee, 40, Arlington Hall Station, Va. Bernard Joseph McLaughlin, 30, Cranston, R.I. Jane Susan Melber, 27, Middlesex, England. John Merrill, 35, Hertfordshire, England. Suzanne Marie Miazga, 22, Marcy, N.Y. Joseph Kenneth Miller, 56, Woodmere, N.Y. Jewel Courtney Mitchell, 32, Brooklyn, N.Y. Richard Paul Monetti, 20, Cherry Hill, N.J. Jane Ann Morgan, 37, London, England. Eva Ingeborg Morson, 48, New York, N.Y. Helga Rachael Mosey, 19, West Midlands, England. Ingrid Elizabeth Mulroy, 25, Lund, Sweden. John Mulroy, 59, East Northport, N.Y. Sean Kevin Mulroy, 25, Lund, Sweden. Mary Geraldine Murphy, 51, Middlesex, England. Jean Aitken Murray, 82, Lockerbie, Scotland. Karen Elizabeth Noonan, 20, Potomac, Md. Daniel Emmett O'Connor, 31, Dorchester, Mass. Mary Denice O'Neill, 21, Bronx, N.Y. Anne Linidsey Otenasek, 21, Baltimore, Md. Bryony Elise Owen, 18 months, Bristol, England. Gwyneth Y. M. Owen, 29, Bristol, England. Laura Abigail Owens, 8, Cherry Hill, N.J. Martha Owens, 44, Cherry Hill, N.J. Robert Plack Owens, 45, Cherry Hill, N.J. Sarah Rebecca Owens, 14, Cherry Hill, N.J. Robert Italo Pagnucco, 51, South Salem, N.Y. Christos M. Papadopoulos, 45, North Lawrence, N.Y. Peter Raymond Peirce, 40, Perrysburgh, Ohio. Michael Pescatore, 33, Solon, Ohio. Sarah S. B. Phillips, 20, Newtonville, Mass. Frederick Sandford, Phillips, 27, Little Rock, Ark. James Andrew Campbell Pitt, 24, South Hadley, Mass. David Platt, 33, Staten Island, N.Y. Walter Leonard Porter, 35, Brooklyn, N.Y. Pamela Lynn Posen, 20, Harrison, N.Y. William Pugh, 56, Margate, N.J. Crisostomo Estrella Quiguyan, 43, London, England. Rajesh Tarsis Priskel Ramses, 35, Leicester, England. Anmol Rattan, 2, Warren, Mich. Garima Rattan, 29, Warren, Mich. Suruchi Rattan, 3, Warren, Mich. Anita Lynn Reeves, 24, Laurel, Md. Mark Alan Rein, 44, New York, N.Y. Jocelyn Reina, 26, Middlesex, England. Diane Marie Rencevicz, 21, Burlington, N.J. Louise Ann Rogers, 20,

Olney, Md. **Edina Roller**, 5, Hungary. **Janos Gabor Roller**, 29, Hungary. **Zsuzsana Roller**, 27, Hungary. **Hanne Maria Root**, 26, Toronto, Canada. **Saul Mark Rosen**, 35, Morris Plains, N.J. **Andrea Victoria Rosenthal**, 22, New York, N.Y. **Daniel Peter Rosenthal**, 20, Staten Island, N.Y. **Myra Josephine Royal**, 30, London, England. **Arnaud David Rubin**, 28, Waterloo, Belgium. **Elyse Jeanne Saraceni**, 20, East London, England. **Scott Christopher Saunders**, 21, Macungie, Pa. **Theresa E. J. Saunders**, 28, Middlesex, England. **Johannes Otto Schauble**, 41, Kappellenweg, West Germany. **Robert Thomas Schlageter**, 20, Warwick, R.I. **Thomas Britton Schultz**, 20, Ridgefield, Conn. **Sally Elizabeth Scott**, 22, Huntington, N.Y. **Amy Elizabeth Shapiro**, 21, Stamford, Conn. **Mridula Shastri**, 24, Oxford, England. **Joan Sheanshang**, 46, New York, N.Y. **Irving Stanley Sigal**, 35, Pennington, N.J. **Martin B. C. Simpson**, 52, Brooklyn, N.Y. **Irja Syhnove Skabo**, 38, Oslo, Norway. **Cynthia Joan Smith**, 21, Milton, Mass. **Ingrid Anita Smith**, 31, Berkshire, England. **James Alvin Smith**, 55, New York, N.Y. **Mary Edna Smith**, 34, Kalamazoo, Mich. **John Somerville**, 40, Lockerbie, Scotland. **Lyndsey Ann Somerville**, 10, Lockerbie, Scotland. **Paul Somerville**, 13, Lockerbie, Scotland. **Rosaleen Somerville**, 40, Lockerbie, Scotland. **Geraldine Anne Stevenson**, 37, Surrey, England. **Hannah Louise Stevenson**, 10, Surrey, England. **John Charles Stevenson**, 38, Surrey, England. **Rachael Stevenson**, 8, Surrey, England. **Charlotte Ann Stinnett**, 36, Duncanville, Texas. **Michael Gary Stinnett**, 26, Duncanville, Texas. **Stacey Leanne Stinnett**, 9, Duncanville, Texas. **James Ralph Stow**, 49, New York, N.Y. **Elia G. Stratis**, 43, Montvale, N.J. **Anthony Selwyn Swan**, 29, Brooklyn, N.Y. **Flora MacDonald Margaret Swire**, 24, London, England. **Marc Alex Tager**, 22, London, England. **Hidekazu Tanaka**, 26, London, England. **Andrew Alexander Teran**, 20, New Haven, Conn. **Arva Anthony Thomas**, 17, Detroit, Mich. **Jonathan Ryan Thomas**, 2 months, Southfield, Mich. **LaWanda Thomas**, 21, Southfield, Mich. **Mark Lawrence Tobin**, 21, North Hempstead,

N.Y. David William Trimmer-Smith, 51, New York, N.Y. Alexia Kathryn Tsairis, 20, Franklin Lakes, N.J. Barry Joseph Valentino, 28, San Francisco, Calif. Tomas Floro Van-Tienhoven, 45, Buenos Aires, Argentina. Asaad Eidi Vejdany, 46, South Great Neck, N.Y. Milutin Velimirovich, 35, Middlesex, England. Nicholas Andreas Vrenios, 20, Washington, D.C. Peter Vulcu, 21, Alliance, Ohio. Raymond Ronald Wagner, 52, Pennington, N.J. Janina Jozefa Waido, 61, Chicago, Ill. Thomas Edwin Walker, 47, Quincy, Mass. Kesha Weedon, 20, Bronx, N.Y. Jerome lee Weston, 45, Baldwin, N.Y. Jonathan White, 33, North Hollywood, Calif. Bonnie Leigh Williams, 21, Crown Point, N.Y. Eric Jon Williams, 24, Crown Point, N.Y. George Waterson Williams, 24, Joppa, Md. Brittany Leigh Williams, 2 months, Crown Point, N.Y. Stephanie Leigh Williams, 1, Crown Point, N.Y. Miriam Luby Wolfe, 20, Severna Park, Md. Chelsea Marie Woods, 10 months, Willingboro, N.J. Dedera Lynn Woods, 27, Willingboro, N.J. Joe Nathan Woods, 28, Willingboro, N.J. Joe Nathan Woods, Jr., 2, Willingboro, N.J. Andrew C. G. Wright, 24, Surrey, England. Mark James Zwynenburg, 29, West Nyack, N.Y.

* * *

A message arrives, by letter or phone, we cannot now remember. Scottish Lord Advocate Peter Fraser forbids bereaved relatives to see the bodies. A psychiatrist at the Royal Crichton Hospital in Dumfries has advised that Fraser should in no circumstances allow relatives to view the victims. I know from my experience as a doctor that relatives should never be told they ought to see a body, but equally true we must never prevent it. Fraser's unfeeling command will prove to be my first contact with a wall growing higher and wider as the years pass. Finally, with the help of friends and my authority as a practicing doctor, I track down the consultant in charge of the Lockerbie post-mortems. He understands our anguish: 'You may see Flora, one day soon, by arrangement. But keep it to yourself. It's important that you do that.'

And today, 5 January 1989, there is to be a memorial service at Lockerbie's Dryfesdale Parish church. We drive 205 miles up the M5, M6, Manchester, Preston, Lancaster, the Lakes, then the sleepy town with its great scar of death, then through quiet streets to the church.

As the senior of the family I must go where others fear to go. Leaving Jane and the children, I drive to the edge of the town where stands a shabby redbrick ice rink deeply uncertain of its new-found role as Lockerbie's only mass cold storage facility. A policeman stands by the doorway. He glances at me but does not react, presuming I am one of many officials in town for the day.

I let go the double glass doors and they slam behind me. The crash echoes across a silent ice rink laden with humps of white linen resting on wooden pallets. The cold of ice, the echo of ice, burns into my mind. I do not know it yet, but this memory will be my prop, my staff, as I face prime ministers, ambassadors of the United Nations, and a man to be described as the Arch Satan who killed my daughter, Muammar Gaddafi of Libya.

Waiting for me is the kindly pathologist who so secretly has agreed that a man might see his dead child. She is newly laid out away from the ice rink, away from the smell, in a tiny room with flowers all around. Beneath the white sheet she seems at peace.

The pathologist quietly asks, 'Can you tell me of any distinguishing marks?'

I say, 'She has a mole on her right big toe.'

The sheet is rolled back. Toe undamaged, identity confirmed.

'Would you like . . .?' the pathologist hesitates.

The word 'Yes' sticks in my throat. I fear that if I speak I will choke in agony. I silently nod.

The pathologist goes to a side room. I stand alone for a few endless moments beside my daughter. The pathologist returns, in his hand a pair of surgical scissors. He slides back the sheet where the head should be. Fighting my dizziness I suck in the icy air. Flora's lovely face is puffed out by the decompression then flattened by the impact, and a small part of her head is missing, no doubt lying still upon a Scottish hillside.

The pathologist snips away a lock of raven hair, replaces the sheet, and she is again an anonymous shape. Avoiding my eyes he slides it into a plastic bag and places it on my palm. I ease open the bag, curl the hair around my fingers and softly brush it across my cheek. Out of the shadows come memories of her snuggling to me, the scent of her hair, but all I can smell now is formalin. I'd expected rage, but a wave of sadness, an endless flying carpet of sadness, flows over me.

'What the Hell are you doing here? How did you get in?' A new policeman stands in the doorway, blocking my exit.

'Just visiting. Identifying my daughter's body.'

'You're not getting out of here without completing this form. I've got my orders.' Thus, indemnity form completed, I drive unsteadily towards Dryfesdale Parish church, there to meet with God and the American ambassador.

Crammed at the rear of the church among other relatives, what remains of our family peers over the shoulders of the crowd and there, arrayed two rows deep at the front, are the backs of the heads of the Mighty Ones. The American ambassador advances to the lectern and reads the story of Jesus, Martha and the resurrection of Lazarus. I stop my ears with my mind. Lazarus may have arisen but Flora seems forever lost. Jane clings to my arm as inside me, around my heart, wash great black waves of anger.

The service ends. Now we all must walk to the Town Hall, through the granite doorway and up the stairs to the town meeting place. There's a crowd, a low hushed murmur, scattered around the room are confused faces, some in groups, some alone, turning this way and that, hovering by the walls. We talk to some of them. It's easy to relate to these souls, few words yet

deep understanding. Others are walking round the room, standing tall, authoritative, firm not sad, some even smiling, all with
hand extended and offering, seeming commissioned to offer,
consolation; councillors and clergymen and doctors and politicians and people unknown, all wearing consolation. Who are
they, these people? How dare they wear our grief? They seem to
be controlling when and where we meet, how we should mourn.
Is it but a job, a duty, a prerogative?

Now is time for tea and biscuits. As we juggle our cups and
saucers and tiny plates an anonymous official steers us towards
a moving, milling island of people. A second official ushers us
through to shake hands with the prime minister. She seems
busy, impatient, while around and behind her hover a suited
cohort in continuous touch with the world. Mrs Thatcher says
the right things, but still I sense the royal 'We' behind the smile.
Surely I'm wrong, judgemental? Dennis seems warmer, more
genuine. But why within myself do I feel this rage, pushing me
into the darkness, almost uncontrollable? Afraid of what I
might say I back away from the conversation. Surely Mrs
Thatcher, a mother, has mother's feelings? Yet she seems
unmoved by our sadness.

We still possess a personal memoir of that day. We cannot
remember who wrote it. Perhaps a friend?

The service was beautiful in its simplicity and sincerity.
Church and State and townspeople and visitors all gathered together in one small church. Churchmen representing all sects of Christianity and other religions united in
grief, showed solidarity unmatched by previous history.

The Moderator of the Church of Scotland preached a
moving sermon. Do not, he pleaded, let violence be
matched with violence. They all listened. While on the
same day the Americans shot down two Libyan planes. Let
there be a gentler America, said George Bush at his inaugu-
ration. And Britain agreed.

Death is too easy an option for the twisted minds of terrorists. Fanatics crave death. They become posthumous heroes. So bring him here, whoever he may be. Let him live among the people of Lockerbie for the rest of his life. Let him meet the relatives of all the victims and never let him forget what he has done.

* * *

Jane and I cannot face the train, the evasive eyes of passers-by, the rain slashed windows, a sky full of white vapour trails heading north from Heathrow to Scotland and beyond. So we drive to Flora's place in London, a bedsit in William Goodenough House in Mecklenburgh Square, unlock the door, and it swings open to an empty room. On the desk, addressed to Flora, lies a letter from Cambridge University. 'We are pleased to inform you that you have been accepted for a post-graduate course in Medicine.' Jane and I both met at Cambridge. Flora had hinted that she had some exciting news and had kept it secret.

Central TV arrive at Caspidge House. Would we mind help-ing them with a documentary to be screened on Good Friday? The interview will prove to be our first encounter with what will grow to become a painful kind of stardom. Canon Eric James, my former chaplain at Cambridge and Flora's godfather, is to present the programme and, wrapped warm against the March wind, we three stroll the fields and woods. Eric has known us from our teenage years and assisted at our marriage ceremony.

Jane relates the entire story, the night of the crash, the televi-sion images, the numbness. She is quiet and firm in her telling; is this a new beginning, a catharsis? Gently we answer Eric's questions as best we can, seeking a rationale for our tears.

Eric, in the final version, sitting before the altar of St Margaret's Chapel, Westminster Abbey, will read aloud a letter that Jane posted on the day of Lockerbie, eight hours before Flight 103 exploded.

. . . William is sixteen now. He's been delivering post from seven thirty this morning, and he works in McDonalds from eleven to six. He wants to earn enough money to be able to get to America for a holiday. Cathy's reading English. She's in her second year at Oxford now. Flora's doing well. She's completed her Medicine at Nottingham and hopes to get into Cambridge. Hart, her American boyfriend, he's in Boston now, and Flora flies there at six tonight, so she will not be with us at Christmas. You can't really hang on to them . . .

Eric will speak of those who die from earthquakes, disease, poverty, war, a pain that only a crucified God may bear. Already, as I search for something I cannot yet define, in the silence of the morning hours I sense that I am but a tiny fragment of the great cry of anguish, the voice of millions suffering at the hands of the untouchables who manage this sad and confused world. I tell Eric: 'My faith in God is so much stronger since this disaster happened. Certainly my faith in the survival of life, the central meaning of love in people's lives has been rein-forced by our suffering.'

Jane remains deep in despair. Has her faith in God strength-ened after the bombing? 'No, I can't honestly say it is true. I so much hoped and believed when we said "Deliver us from evil" that that would happen, and that God would protect us and be in the centre of our lives. This clearly did not happen. Our daughter was in that plane crash and she died. She had faith when she bought that ticket that it would get her to America, and I had faith in God that he would protect us. In fact, neither of those things happened and this has been quite hard to come to terms with. Like every mother who loses a child I wanted to go to the hills and find her. And her death is a place from where no one returns. I can understand now why some seek spiritual-ists and some suicide.'

Eric asks, 'What keeps you from suicide?'

The whispered reply comes from the heart. 'My family, love for my family, for living. I wouldn't want to cause them any more pain than they've suffered from losing Flora.'

Jane has not seen Flora's body, is still unable to close her heart's sadness. Yet I believe deeply that we have not seen the last of Flora. One day – I know for sure – we will again be joined as a family. It was pure chance that Flora was on the plane. I do not believe that God interferes in his creation. Evil comes from man using his God-given free will in a world where the laws of mathematics and physics operate without hindrance. Flora would agree with me on that. Jane feels deeply the warmth and love shown to them by friends in recent weeks. We have always been just a quiet private couple, and me just an ordinary country doctor. Now we look through the camera's soulless eye into 10 million pairs of eyes, and within me stirs a force new and powerful. Soon I will ask Jane, Cathy and William to be at my side on a journey on which few may venture; a challenge to the governments of three continents and an army of intelligence agents who walk in the shadows.

* * *

Spring 1989 is not a happy time. After three weeks the authorities release Flora's body. With Cathy and William, Jane and I accompany the coffin to Glasgow for a funeral at the city's crematorium. We take Flora's ashes home and Jane places them in pride of place in our main bedroom. She will cling to what remains of Flora through the spring and summer. Her feelings of guilt at not being there to hold Flora's hand in those final moments are like the pain of being burned alive. She will be driven to read all she can about the technology of the disintegration of planes, will research in medical books the expected seconds of human consciousness when a plane explodes at altitude. She will picture over and over in her imagination what Flora saw and heard and felt in that starry sky as a monstrous silver plane split wide apart and the faces of fellow passengers fell into the darkness. Day after day her eyes will focus on the kitchen clock as a thin black second-hand ticks away the fifteen seconds that Flora endured before death claimed her.

Then as autumn touches the tips of the leaves we travel to Loch Caroy on the Isle of Skye, to the graveyard of the ruined chapel of St John the Apostle where lie the bodies of my father and mother. There, ancient basalt walls cling to a hillside flowing with bracken and sycamores gnarled by North Atlantic winds. With my arm wrapped around Jane I force open the protesting iron gates. We struggle down the uneven path to a black granite headstone to lay Flora's ashes into the ground.

* * *

As winter advances, Caspidge remains for me some kind of prison. Yet still the sun melts the frosted fields, the woodpecker in the copse laughs away the intruder. By coincidence I have 1,500 trees ready for planting: ash, beech and wild cherry. They stand neglected, wrapped in sackcloth, freezing away their roots by night, drying in winter sun by day. Soon, caring friends come to help, digging the bundles into the ground just enough to keep them alive.

Summoning what remains of my strength I drag the bundles to a tiny valley to the west of Caspidge. I disentangle the first sapling, hammer downward with the spade, ease wide the wound, drop in the root, squeeze down the soil with my heel, then onward to the next, my mind still flowing with an ocean of rage.

I order 3,000 more ash and wild cherry, and 250 oak, then set aside two careful weeks of measuring and marking out. It will take many months to complete, a mighty task born in the soul of despair, moulded firmer each day by hands stronger with hope. My statement to the world will be special; I desperately want the Americans to see it with their satellites, the width of my linear oak wood matching the wingspan of that fallen

Boeing 747. As the years pass, a kindly forestry expert will offer his own contribution, persuading the Ordnance Survey people to name my labour of love. Amid the surrounding ash, beech and cherry will stand proud an oaken wood in the shape of a great capital 'F' to be known as long as there are maps as 'Flora's Wood'.

Chapter 2

WITHIN DAYS OF the fall of Pan Am 103, widespread searches had begun. Teams of police and volunteers mingled with FBI searchers and other anonymous Americans scouring the Scottish hills as far as the North Sea shore. To the north of the search area are said to be found diplomatic papers; are they the files of Charles McKee, the leader of a CIA team returning from Lebanon? Jassar Arafat[1] has now declared Mossad[2] responsible for the bombing and launched his own inquiry. A calculated diversion from the truth? Who can tell?

The Dumfries and Galloway police force is doing all it can. Senior officers secretly complain that the Americans are giving them limited information, just enough to enable police search teams to be useful to American objectives. Chief Superintendent John Orr tells the media of his force's total cooperation. But when asked about an apparent lack of assistance from his German counterparts in the BKA[3] he seems puzzled. His colleague, Lord Advocate Fraser, reveals that he's requested the Germans to look into the activities of the Popular Front for the Liberation of Palestine General Command, the PFLP-GC. It is an acronym that will haunt my dreams.

British Minister for Transport Paul Channon flies to Canada for discussions. While there, he authoritatively pronounces that the bomb was concealed in a radio-cassette player inserted into a suitcase, then onto Frankfurt Airport flight Pan Am 103A, then into baggage container 14L at Heathrow destined for flight Pan Am 103. Within days, government sources say he's blotted his copy book – reasons not explained – and will shortly resign.

Today we learn of a series of arrests in Germany, in October 1988, of a group of seventeen PFLP-GC terrorists. Their leader, Ahmed Jibril, was in a safe location in Damascus. Using a flat in Neuss they had in their possession several tape-cassette record-ers, some rigged with barometric switches and electronic timers, and packed with Semtex. The group's bomb maker was a Jordanian, Marwan Khreesat. He was proved to have constructed at least five bombs, one of which disappeared from the flat one day before the arrests. Fourteen of Khreesat's colleagues were released without charge, and Khreesat was not charged with conspiring to blow up an aircraft, even though the BKA knew that he had made at least five bombs, that he and his colleagues had discussed an attack on US planes flying from Frankfurt Airport, and that he had in the boot of his car when arrested an IED designed to explode at height, for example in the hold of a plane.

Khreesat is said to be an agent for the Jordanian secret services and a CIA asset. After several days in police custody, on 5 November 1988 – six weeks before the Lockerbie attack – he asked to make a phone call to Amman, Jordan. The BKA placed the call for him. He spoke to someone, talking about the need to expedite legal matters in Germany. Five days later he was released by a German judge with the Orwellian ruling that 'no strong suspicion of a crime can be confirmed'.[4]

Channon has not allowed an inquiry. Why will his successor Cecil Parkinson not allow one? Why was the flight one-third empty three days before Christmas? Why did certain promi-nent people change their travel plans? Why, eight days before the attack, was the following bulletin displayed on the staff notice board in the US Moscow embassy? Why were only government employees advised to use their 'discretion' in a choice of airline? Why not my daughter Flora and everyone flying from Heathrow on that fateful evening?

Post[5] has been notified by the Federal Aviation Administration that on 5th December 1988 an unidentified individual telephoned a US diplomatic facility in Europe and stated that sometime within the next two weeks there would be a bombing attempt against a Pan American airliner flying from Frankfurt to the United States. The FAA reports that the reliability of the information cannot be assessed at this point, but the appropriate police authorities have been notified and are pursuing the matter. Pan Am has also been notified.

In view of the lack of confirmation of this information, post leaves to the discretion of individual travellers any decisions on altering travel plans or changing to another American carrier.

The reactions of police and others to my persistent questioning soon make it clear that I have become a 'person of interest' to the security services, and yet I sense the beginning of relationships with several members of the Thatcher Cabinet. Are they assessing how much I know and reporting all to MI5? Or are they calculating how dangerous I might become? The truth, exposed only in 2018, will prove more sinister. Even as our family's inner torture continued throughout the summer of 1989, the machinery of government and intelligence coldly observed from a safe distance. On 10 August, the Foreign Office wrote to the Scottish Lord Advocate, Lord Fraser of Carmyllie: 'Another aspect which will need careful watching is the activities of relatives of Pan Am 103 victims . . .'[6]

My first Cabinet-level contact is Paul Channon. Our conversations at the Department of Transport quickly turn uneasy. Channon's successor Cecil Parkinson seems friendlier, and his colleague Douglas Hogg has also offered to help with my enquiries.

Another Cabinet member, Foreign Secretary Douglas Hurd, seems to me the archetypal gentleman, well-informed about Lockerbie and apparently sharing the confidence of Prime Minister Thatcher. But I sense the need to be careful; Hurd's advisers include members of MI5 and MI6. There are hints that foreign policy issues are already clouding the investigation. Hurd writes to me claiming there is '. . . no evidence of involvement of states other than Libya'. Why Libya? Until now no one has mentioned Libya. And the story of the Neuss arrests of the Jibril group has – for the time being – vanished from the media.

* * *

AUGUST 1989

It seems but days since our first memorial gathering in Dryfesdale Parish church. Yet today we British and American relatives have begun a campaign, emerging from our initial trauma to become *UK Families Flight 103*. Things have slowly shaped themselves to reveal leaders and followers, with myself, John Mosey and Martin Cadman in the British hot seat, and an American gentleman chairman, Bert Ammerman. An irresistible drive within me – is it my dark rage or something worse? – has already and unexpectedly pushed me forward to national recognition by the British media. Jane is convinced it is my way of responding to grief. I cannot just sit and think about Flora; I know for sure that that will cause me to go mad. And there will be, in the years to come, days when this almost comes to pass.

American Elizabeth Delude-Dix lost her Irish husband Peter Dix in the attack. A while ago, in a televised interview, she called for the Lockerbie bereaved to meet. It's taken a while to fix things, and here we all are in the Hotel Russell,

Bloomsbury. Here also is journalist David Ben Aryeah sitting quietly in a corner studying our every word. A large man, a round, pleasant face, a head crowned by a comfortable cloth cap when out of doors, and a mouth that favours a well-chewed pipe. Most striking is his voice: a soft Edinburgh lilt that tells a good tale.

Last evening I met with our group chairman, Bert Ammerman, and David to consider how to handle what we expect will be an overwhelming media interest in our activities. David will do all he can to assist us, but to protect our confidentiality he will not attend group meetings, and he will pay his own expenses. He emphasises a basic principle: 'Keep it simple – Truth and Justice.'

On the night of the Lockerbie attack David was the first newsman on the scene. After a couple of phone calls to America he was signed-up with CBS. He cut four tapes off the cuff. Then, after a couple of hours of sleep, he began what for an experienced journalist is serious work. He sat on a wall, lit his pipe and watched as the little town grew to a new existence and a place in history.

During the morning of that first day he witnessed some unusual happenings. He'd heard rumours of Americans in the woods, then a squad of them walked down the main street wearing dark blue wind-jackets and baseball hats with large white letters 'FBI'. Overhead was the constant sound of helicopters. One was entirely white, a tiny Stars and Stripes on its tail, launched from the secret US Navy airbase at Machrihanish, and said by eyewitnesses to have a man in the open doorway holding a rifle with a telescopic sight.[7] The helicopter was filmed by local people as it flew over the hills and away to the south.

It was two days before Christmas. Many husbands, wives, sons, daughters, sisters, brothers, fathers, mothers would never be home again. Compassion was the watchword. David's New Year message to America, spoken without notes, would make broadcasting history. Then came a unique prize, the Ben Grauer Award, granted by the Overseas Press Club of America. David flew to New York to a gathering of 2,000 journalists, among them heroes of the American media. He caused a sensation, striding into the hall wearing full Scottish clan tartan.

Among our first gatherings moves a Linda Mack, who claims she lost a Cambridge friend in the attack. We spot a tiny microphone jutting from a fold in her coat. Is she a journalist, or worse? We ask her to leave and she does. She will later work as junior researcher in the office of Pierre Salinger, former press secretary to Presidents John F. Kennedy and Lyndon B. Johnson. Much later, Salinger will confess to David that only after Linda Mack left his employ did he get the clear impression she'd been working for British MI5.[8]

From Britain and America, we are united by our loss of loved ones. Occasionally some of the Americans hint at revenge. We all feel let down by our governments. As our discussions proceed I suddenly find myself appointed British spokesman/dogsbody/do-it-all who'll be in charge when things fall apart.

Our campaign gets off to a tricky start. We cannot understand why only a couple of agency reporters and photographers have turned up for our first official press conference. Then we discover that overnight a River Thames pleasure cruiser, *The Marchioness*, has sunk with a party of revellers on board with many drowned or missing. The world's media has flocked to the scene.

Elizabeth Delude-Dix has obtained a copy of a US Federal Aviation Authority security bulletin concerning a telephoned warning to the US Helsinki embassy of an impending attack against US passenger planes. It lists terrorist names, their membership of the Abu Nidal Group and how they intend to insert a bomb onto a plane. The British government does not know that we relatives have the bulletin. Responsible ministers pronounce in the House of Commons that the Helsinki warning was one of many received each year: 'If everything has to stop for each warning, planes will never fly.' They do not reveal that in 1988 eighteen such warnings were received.

* * *

Fate has marked Jane and me for deep friendship with a soft-spoken couple from the West Midlands, John and Lisa Mosey, who also lost their daughter on Pan Am 103. John is a pastor at a Pentecostal church: quiet and thoughtful, a steady gaze, a careful manner of speech. Their daughter, Helga, together with Flora and Catherine, attended King Edward's High School for Girls in Birmingham.

'Were you at the Lockerbie memorial service?' asks Jane.

'Yes,' confides John. 'We had a letter or a phone call; it's so difficult to remember now. While we were driving to Lockerbie, as we went past Gretna Green there was a great rainbow in the sky. We prayed as we drove. Before the service we went to the police station to see if they had any news about our daughter Helga. But they had no information at all. They sent us to the incident centre. The word "incident" stayed with me, even made me angry for a moment. This was no "incidental" matter; it was the main event. When Mrs Thatcher was talking to the other relatives, we sat next to one of the Pan Am stewardesses, a French lady. They gave us tea and sandwiches.'

Born in Coventry during the Second World War, at the age of twenty-four John left a successful career as a technical illustrator and graphic designer to train as a minister. He pastored churches in Yorkshire, Devon, Derbyshire and the West Midlands. For eight years he served his church as director of missions for Asia/ Pacific, the Middle East and the Americas. He remains to this day an active teacher and aid facilitator to some of the world's neediest people from Afghanistan to the Philippines.

The loss of Helga was widely broadcast, and soon the phone and postman were busy. Questions like 'How can you forgive the animals who did this?' were deflected by affirmation of a deep faith in God and His redemption of every sin, however terrible. A number of John's interviews have been broadcast around the world. People will long remember being moved and helped by a father's forgiveness of a great and evil deed. Throughout the campaign he will be at my shoulder and the calm centre of occasional storms.

Today we plan; tomorrow we will speak to the world. How did I become spokesman? Perhaps because I am tall, white haired and try always to speak nicely. A local journalist features a full-page spread: 'Jim Swire has aged visibly: a gaunt, intense man investing every minute of his spare time in the pursuit of justice.'

* * *

Our group has been busy. We've already discovered serious deficiencies in UK air security, and there's a rumour in the media of a German secret service brochure about a bomb in a tape-cassette recorder, with instructions issued by Heathrow security chiefs concerning 'suspicious devices'. We resolve to go public in our campaign, be afraid of no one, face up to the highest in the land.

Dear Prime Minister,

We remember that you made time to visit Lockerbie, and spoke to some of us and some of the American relatives on the day of the memorial service. During the week of 21st August 1989 some of those American relatives, including their president, Mr Ammerman, will be in this country, and we will be discussing our common aims with them. They have requested, but have not been granted, a meeting with you during their time here. Instead, they were promised a meeting with an official in the Department of Transport.

For two hundred and seventy families strung across the world, the hurt of Lockerbie remains unbearable. The American relatives have just achieved one objective and persuaded President Bush to order an inquiry into events leading up to Lockerbie.

In this country we have watched an inquiry carried through into those responsible for public safety at Hillsborough, whilst no such inquiry has been promised into the conduct of those responsible for the safety of those vibrant young people who plunged to their deaths at Lockerbie, from a plane that had been under the security protection of the Department of Transport at Heathrow.

While the eyes of the world are upon us as we hold a joint press conference on Sunday 20th August 1989 we should feel that our country was offering more appropriate support if we could at least announce that you were able to find the time to meet a joint delegation from the UK and the USA relatives' groups.

We do hope that you will reconsider your decision, particularly now that you know that the British relatives are involved as well as the Americans.

Yours sincerely,

Jim Swire

But Mrs Thatcher will never be for turning. The response is predictable, unhelpful and cruel:

Dear Dr Swire,

Thank you for your letter of 10th August to the Prime Minister. You subsequently spoke to Roy Griffins in Cecil Parkinson's office. You will by now have seen his letter of 14th August. I hope you will accept that as a response to your main point. Naturally the Prime Minister will be interested to learn from Mr Parkinson of any points which emerge from the meeting fixed with him for the 19th September.

Yours,

Dominic Morris,

Private Secretary to the Prime Minister

We have asked for a meeting with the boss. Our letter has bounced between four Whitehall offices; a single straw dancing in the winds of resistance that we face as the years pass. Nevertheless, we meet Cecil Parkinson[9] as arranged and assail his ears with questions. Kindly he agrees to again take the issue to the prime minister to seek some form of inquiry. Because the security services are involved there will inevitably be some suspicion if certain information cannot be made public. So he wonders if he might ask a High Court judge to look privately into the security aspects and report to him.

He advises, 'When you get into the Lockerbie business – how did we find out certain information, how did we know this, how did we know that? – we'll have to question not only our own intelligence people and sources but also our overseas people. That's when it gets dangerous for them. So, it has to be a closed area. But I will put it to the Prime Minister and recommend that we go as far as we can without damaging our security arrangements.'

So truth must wait patiently at the door while a government secretly debates the fate of the dead and the living? Or is it that British security systems are so weak and ineffective that fear is the spur to secrecy? Will only time and history reveal the ultimate truth? Around the altar of America's Neo-Conservative ambitions for the planet, with special focus on the Middle East and Libya, is Britain but an acolyte? As for Parkinson, within days he's back with a resounding 'No'. He's been handbagged.

Chapter 3

A FRIEND FAXES to me an article from the *Washington Post* by American columnist Jack Anderson. According to Anderson, George Bush and Margaret Thatcher secretly agreed in spring 1989 to play down the truth about who blew up Pan Am Flight 103. 'Both had received intelligence reports pointing the finger at the PFLP-GC group paid by Ayatollah Khomeini of Iran. They agreed that neither could stand the political heat of making the evidence public because both were impotent to retaliate against Iran.' Top officials con-ducting the Pan Am investigation were under instruction not to discuss in public the role of Ahmed Jibril or Iran. Journalists have asked for a comment from Downing Street and receive only denials.

My filing cabinet is filling rapidly; I will soon cast around for a second one. Apart from the reams of information extracted from sources public and secret by David Ben Aryeah, faxes arrive daily from around the world, but mainly from America. The American relatives are extremely busy, and the relative ease of available information about US government activities is a boon and a burden.

Among the documents pumping out of my machine are the minutes of two Congressional inquiries. In contrast with the sluggish complacency exhibited by British authorities, the first is *The President's Commission on Aviation Security*.[1] The terms of reference include:

To study and evaluate existing US aviation policies and practices regarding terrorist threats.

To investigate options of informing US aviation customers of possible terrorist threats.

To review US laws, policies, and practices dealing with the families of terrorists' victims.

To carry out these provisions with particular attention to the destruction of Pan Am Flight 103, but without jeopardizing on-going intelligence and criminal operations.

The Executive Order enabling the Commission requires its final report to be screened for classified information. Only a declassified text will be released to the general public. The Commission's final report will contain sixty-four recommendations examining security matters, but few of its conclusions will have a major impact. The CIA have briefed the Commission in advance of its hearing. Included in their brief are four denials that will prove central to the Scottish police investigation.

1. It has been alleged by some in the media and several intelligence investigators that there was a CIA operation named 'Corea' to smuggle drugs through Pan Am's Frankfurt terminal as part of a larger drugs-for-hostages operation. This operation purportedly used Monzer al-Kassar, a Syrian drug dealer with well-known terrorist links.

2. PFLP-GC leader Ahmed Jibril knew of the drug operation and used it to place a bomb aboard Pan Am Flight 103.

3. The Israelis warned the Germans and the CIA of the threat, but the CIA failed to act on it in order to protect the said CIA drug operation.

4. The CIA received no warning in advance of the Lockerbie attack. The so-called 'Helsinki warning' was supplied by a proven 'fabricator'.[2]

Even as their inquiry is on-going, in February 1990 members of the Commission travel to the US embassy in London and meet with our British relatives' group. They assure us that the Federal Aviation Authority will introduce wide-ranging improvements.

Our meeting ends, we walk towards the exit. An elderly congressman invites one of us, Martin Cadman, to one side. The two converse in low tones.

Outside the embassy, as we walk across the square, I move to Martin's side. 'What did he tell you?'

'He said: "Your government and ours know exactly what happened, but they're never going to tell".'[3]

* * *

In 1993 Steven Donahue, a former criminal and later an asset for the US Drug Enforcement Agency, will give a filmed interview for the documentary *The Maltese Double Cross*. Donahue will talk of his activities over several years, including 1988, the year of the Lockerbie bombing: 'I came to be involved with the DEA. I got involved in trafficking in cannabis products, and eventually was arrested, and struck a secret plea agreement with the government whereby they eventually decided to send me to Lebanon, not for cannabis products, but, basically to bust the largest heroin producers on the planet.'

Donahue's statement will be confirmed, again in 1993, and again in a filmed interview, by Lester Coleman, a former member of the US Defense Intelligence Agency.[4] Coleman will add that the DEA could not eradicate the drugs in Lebanon, so they could only do two things: firstly, monitor what was being produced, and how it was being shipped out; secondly, use DEA informants in Lebanon, in drug sting operations in the

United States, to set up drug buys and to catch buyers in America. 'The DEA informants would fly into Los Angeles, for example, or Detroit, and they would be loaned out to the local DEA office and used in a drug sting operation. Many times they would haul in heroin in a controlled delivery. Sometimes they would take in cash, and act as a buyer ... A controlled delivery is a delivery where a courier carries a pre-determined amount of heroin through security checkpoints with the knowledge and consent of the local law enforcement people. For example, the Germans in Frankfurt or the British Customs and Excise service in London.'

There will then emerge a name new to me. In the 1980s, Monzer al-Kassar was probably the most notorious weapons and drug supplier in the Middle East. Coleman will continue: 'Nothing went down in the Bekaa Valley relating to narcotics, for example, without the explicit approval of Rifaat Assad[5] and Monzer al-Kassar. Not the hostages, not the opium trade, not the heroin laboratories, not the cocaine producing laboratories. None of that could have happened without the express consent and involvement of Rifaat Assad, and his partner Monzer al-Kassar.'

Chapter 4

A LARGE ENVELOPE arrives from David Ben Aryeah. Inside is a classified government telex. I speed read it and feel I've been struck by lightning. I push it across the breakfast table to Jane: 'Tell me it's not a dream.'

It is dated 22 November 1988 – one month before the Lockerbie attack – and sent to all British Airline security managers. It recounts the October 1988 arrest of Jibril and Khreesat, and fifteen other conspirators in an operation known as 'Autumn Leaves'. It speaks of the telephoned warning of an attack on aircraft flying to the United States. Copies are forwarded to all embassies. There's no advice to members of the public. It is signed by James Jack of the British Department of Transport.

Another week has passed. Today David has sent a copy of a second classified telex issued by the British Department of Transport. It's dated 19 December 1988 – two days before the bombing.

Here is a photo of a radio-cassette player with the rear cover removed. Additional batteries, an 'ice-cube' timer, detonator and Semtex are in place. It's small enough to avoid detection, yet large enough to split open an aircraft. More devices may have been constructed.

I wonder what a member of staff should do if a suspicious device is discovered during check-in. The writer of the telex, James Jack, provides the answer: 'Any item about which a searcher is unable to satisfy himself/herself must, if it is to be carried in the aircraft, be consigned to the aircraft hold.' Exactly where the Lockerbie bomb did explode.

The man seems conditioned by Whitehall thinking. He believes that a bomber will be thwarted simply by separating him from his weapon. And in the week preceding the Lockerbie attack the travelling public knew nothing of it.

And there is more to come: a rumour of a detailed warning by the German police, based on information obtained prior to and following the arrests of the seventeen PFLP-GC terrorists. But until now nothing has appeared in the media in Europe, America or Britain.

* * *

I'm waiting in the foyer of London's Churchill Hotel. A man is sitting at the rear of a group of armchairs, occasionally glancing my way. Suddenly he stands and walks over: 'Hello Dr Swire, I am Bernard Adamczewski.'

People say if you're really angry about something, write to *The Times*. I did, I didn't keep a copy, can't remember what I wrote, but it was all about Lockerbie. Four days later came a letter of reply from a Bernard Adamczewski. The world was informed that a Dr Swire from Bromsgrove hadn't a clue what he was talking about. So I wrote a second letter, asking *The Times* to pass it to Adamczewski, explaining why he was wrong and telling him of our loss of Flora. Bernard's reply contained profuse apologies and a request for a meeting.

He invites me to sit with him. We talk and check each other out. I ask about that rumour by the German authorities of a prior warning of a bomb or bombs. 'Might I see it?' I ask.

Bernard reflects for a few moments. 'I'll think about it and let you know.'

* * *

Eight days have passed. Today is a beautiful spring day. At Euston Station we meet as friends and cruise to Bernard's apartment in Maida Vale. In his sitting room he walks to a corner desk, opens it and turns around. In his hand is a colour brochure of some twenty pages. 'This is classified. It was put together by the BKA when they arrested Jibril and his people. I've got it for two hours. You can have it for five minutes.'[1]

Behind a huge avocado tree standing in a pot is a French window leading to a fire escape. Beyond the window is bright sunlight. I'm shaking with excitement. I slide my camera from its case and raise a questioning eyebrow. Bernard smiles and looks away.

Within minutes I've photographed every page, the brochure is back where it came from, and I'm huddled on the afternoon train to Birmingham gripping my camera so hard that the leather's creaking.

Next morning the photos come out fine. The brochure is in German: a warning by the BKA to Interpol, to every government. In my rush to take the photos my camera strap caused a shadow across the front cover, but the inside pages are clear. I have a friend at the Press Association. I pick up the phone.

How far will the story go? A week later the friend sends me a faxed copy of the *South China News*. In flagrante, my full-colour picture of a Toshiba 453 radio-cassette player bulging with a barometric switch, a detonator and a block of Semtex high explosive. My photo was of a mock-up 'bomb' constructed by BKA technicians. We will later discover, in evidence given by BKA explosives expert Rainer Gobel during the eventual trial of two Libyans, that central to the murderous assembly of the real PFLP-GC bombs lay 'ice-cube' timers. These had the appearance of cubes of ice, and were designed to trigger explosions approximately thirty minutes after initiation by a drop in air pressure similar to that of an aircraft ascending after take-off.

* * *

FRIDAY 18 MAY 1990

Suitcase in hand, shaking with fear, I'm standing in Heathrow Airport's check-in lounge. I have a plan and Jane won't like it. It's so easy to spot I'll be amazed if they don't find it. I bought a tape recorder, some electronic components from a local store in Redditch, assembled a timing circuit and a pressure switch, and fitted them all together. It's a black tape recorder, quite like the one in the BKA brochure: single speaker with 400g of marzipan instead of Semtex. Stuck on the rear with Sellotape is a bright-red socket, and if it were a real bomb, to prime it you would just plug in the connector.

I'm taking an overnight flight to America to join the bereaved relatives doing the rounds of the US authorities. I want to find out what is happening in Washington. In my suitcase is a present for the man who could not say 'Yes', Cecil Parkinson. Fourteen months ago, Parkinson's predecessor, Paul Channon, assured me that British aviation security is the best: 'You should leave this kind of thing to the experts.' And I am about to offer him a special kind of reply.

America's Federal Aviation Authority has already started to investigate Pan Am. Only one day after the bombing they commenced a thorough inspection of Pan Am systems at Frankfurt and Heathrow airports. They discovered major breaches of security and fined the airline $630,000. To boot, President Bush Sr has focused a criminal investigation, led by the CIA and FBI, into Pan American Airways and the management of Frankfurt Airport. The British government, however, refuses any kind of inquiry: 'There is a criminal investigation in progress.' Fourteen months have elapsed since the BKA brochure; fourteen months to review and improve security systems; fourteen months to install better scanners and X-ray machines.

Strangely, my flight has been selected for special security and they're searching everyone's bags. My luggage is spread across the desk. A young security guard is looking intently at the tape recorder. She's puzzled. She picks it up, turns it over. Inside, a loose component rattles. Through the louvre at the back I can see the yellow marzipan, and proud as punch is the scarlet priming socket with the plug already stuck in the hole.

She's holding it out towards me. Here it comes: *Bromsgrove doctor arrested*.

She says, 'Safety rules, sir. Have you taken the batteries out?'

'Batteries? Oh . . . Yes. Batteries? Of course!'

She stows it neatly into the suitcase.

It's not a Pan Am plane, but it is a Boeing 747 just like the Lockerbie flight. I look for the seat that Flora occupied – 39D, middle of the plane, centre seats, right-hand side as you look towards the rear. A middle-aged American lady is settling herself down. I ask politely, would she mind if we swap places? She's not amused, and she does mind.

The silver bird soars to a purple sky. Stewardesses move quietly along the aisles preparing for dinner. An hour later, at the cruising altitude of 31,000 feet I pass through the space where my child's plane exploded.

Now I'm in John F. Kennedy Airport walking unchallenged through customs onto an internal flight. Another bereaved relative, Barry Flick, has flown with me but knew nothing about the bomb until the Heathrow security girl innocently drew his attention to a strangley modified black recorder. Barry's face was a picture.

We stay overnight at the Marriott in Andover, Massachusetts, then travel onward for a series of meetings. First, with Glenn Johnson and his lovely wife, Carol, at their home, then next day to Washington, DC, to meet State Department counter-terrorism officials.

We eventually meet with several American relatives led by Bert Ammerman. The Americans solemnly boast of how the FAA is tightening things up. Meanwhile, standing to attention beside my chair is a suitcase containing a 'bomb'.

Suddenly, I tell them. The meeting becomes somewhat lively. They say: 'You stupid fool! You might have caused a panic!' To

calm them I take out the bomb, open it up, remove the marzipan, break off a piece and eat it.

As their gasps subside, an understanding begins. Can we
turn this foolish prank to advantage? Still, if all is revealed too
soon it might derail the security reforms under way in the US,
so I agree to leave the bomb in their safe-keeping, go back to
England and wait for six weeks. Then we all will decide how to
release the story.

* * *

30 JUNE 1990

In the graveyard of Tundergarth church, near Lockerbie, stands
a tiny hut – a *bothy* – with a slate roof and walls of Dumfries
sandstone. Here, on an unusually chilly and wet day, we relatives dedicate a shrine to the deceased of Pan Am 103.

Where once stood the gardener's equipment a memorial
altar has been constructed on which rests a beautiful calli-
graphic roll of honour prepared by local members of the
congregation. It lists the 270 victims. Beside that lies a hard-
covered volume prepared by the American relatives' group –
On Eagles' Wings – containing, for most of the dead, a short
biography and photograph. Some forty have neither biography nor photograph. They are the true lost ones of Lockerbie.
Members of the Tundergarth congregation will ensure that
each day a new page will turn and every victim of Pan Am
103 be honoured in sequence. Across the wall behind the
altar is carved a statement by St Paul: 'There are three things
that last: Faith, Hope and Love. And the greatest of these is
Love.'

Meanwhile my trust in Labour's shadow transport spokesman, John Prescott, has proved misplaced. I advised John: 'I
don't think we should go public on the bomb thing. We should
wait a while.' But as I thunder homeward down the M6 he
comes on the radio and reveals all.

My mobile goes crazy, and on arrival I discover the driveway to be totally blocked by media crews. After some negotiation I persuade them to follow me up to the house and we set up a crowded press conference in the garage. I lay a couple of old doors on trestles to serve as tables, bring in a few chairs, the technicians plug in their lights to add to an already huge electricity bill, and the BBC, CNN, ABC, Press Association, Reuters – and a few more I can't identify – get to it.

My relationship with the American bereaved will never be the same, but one of them, Helen Tobin,[2] will later praise me for initiative: 'Full marks for Dr Swire. I'm beginning to think that more of us should do something similar to test security.' Her hopes will never be honoured. America's slack domestic flight security systems will continue until the destruction of the World Trade Center, New York's Twin Towers, on 11 September 2001.

Even as our Caspidge press conference proceeds, those American relatives still in Lockerbie are caught off-guard. Has my marzipan bomb totally backfired? They're worried sick that Bush might hold up reforms until the FAA looks into how an eccentric Scotsman took what appeared to be a real bomb onto an inland flight from JFK to Boston.

Next day, midway through an evening surgery, the phone rings. An official from the Department of Transport demands: 'Dr Swire, Cecil Parkinson would like you to come to his London office for a chat. You and Barry Flick. Now.'

The dovecotes of Whitehall are a-fluttering and I am shaking like a leaf. I try to sound calm. 'I'm busy with some patients at the moment. Ask Mr Parkinson if he'd be kind enough to wait until I've finished my surgery.'

With Barry Flick I catch a late train to London, wondering what we're in for. The train slides into Euston to a welcome by a scrum of reporters and a TV crew. I try to organise an interview on the platform, but the reporters surround me in a confused mob. They clap me on the shoulders: 'Great job! You show 'em!' Suddenly, we British relatives have become celebrities. A year and a half now since Flora died, and Pan Am 103 is still headline news on both sides of the Atlantic.

At 11 p.m. we are ushered into the Department's head office in Marsham Street. A silver-haired Cecil Parkinson welcomes us, around him a defensive phalanx of officials. Meanwhile I've created a new weapon. Stuck to the side of my briefcase is a large photo of a smiling Flora, her raven hair flowing to her shoulders. Beneath are words that can be read even across a Whitehall office: 'Why, oh why, Flora?' I place it strategically on the table. Across the polished surface official eyes open wide.

I explain into the early hours all that I've done. On either side of Parkinson sit security and transport experts. He's most courteous: 'Is it true that . . . Tell us all about it, etc.' Almost opposite me sits James Jack. He doesn't say a word. By now I'm feeling sorry for that poor security girl at Heathrow.

Parkinson will later offer an explanation to the media. He will tell assembled reporters that an investigation will be conducted into how Jim Swire did it: 'I cannot stress strongly enough the government's determination to enforce the highest standards in aviation security. When our new aviation and maritime security bill becomes law, I will have the powers to ground airlines and close airports that fail to meet those standards. I will not hesitate to use them.' As time passes, several British airports will fail, yet as I write these lines I've not yet discovered a single instant when closure has even been threatened.

Later, the Heathrow security staff will claim that they knew what I was up to; that they allowed me to break the law; that they watched as a grieving father carried on board what might be a real bomb to join his daughter in the skies over Lockerbie.

Meanwhile, Parkinson's people demand that I attend next day at Heathrow police station. There, I set down a statement listing all that I've done. The sergeant asks me to wait on a bench in the front reception. After a few minutes another sergeant comes to the desk. In his hand is my statement. He looks at me sternly: 'Dr Swire, in view of what you've told us, it would appear that an offence has been committed.'

'Oh?'

'Yes, sir, under British law it is an offence to bring an imitation explosive into an airport.'

'I'm aware of that.'

'Hmm. I shall have to talk to my superiors about this.'

He goes out. A few minutes later he returns. 'We must warn you that should this happen again, your actions will be viewed with the greatest seriousness.'

I say, 'Thank you, goodbye.'

Outside the station lurks an assembly of pressmen. They've picked up on last night's meeting with Parkinson and pursued me throughout the day. By my side is a lawyer from the Lockerbie Air Disaster Group. I need to say something but I'm so dog-tired that I let the man speak on my behalf. Big mistake. The man is all apologetic, 'Won't do it again, Sir.' I wish so much that he'd just shut up. Still, the message about weak British airline security is running around the world, and inside me boils a mixture of fury and relief; we've shown them up for what they are.

Chapter 5

ON THIS DAY begins a Fatal Accident Inquiry (FAI) into the bombing of Pan Am 103 and the murder of 270 people.[1] It's proving an unusual affair. Sheriff Principal John S. Mowat QC has decided that none of the courthouses in his sheriffdom are large enough, so he has persuaded Dumfries and Galloway Health Board to make available Easterbrook Hall.

Bereaved relatives have been invited to make submissions, and for this inquiry we will be assisted by a group of solicitors, the Lockerbie Air Disaster Group (LADG). We do not know who is funding the LADG. Is it the government? Can we trust these solicitors to faithfully advise the QCs who will address the inquiry? We are all somewhat suspicious, but – with one exception, Marina Larracoechea – we sign the necessary contract.

Soon, however, it becomes clear that the LADG are refusing to call witnesses whom some of us regard as highly relevant. Nor will they ask questions which some of us believe will delve into the truth.

John Mosey has experienced a sinister pattern of events.[2] Two police witnesses recently maintained that there were no major drug finds at the Lockerbie site. John believes otherwise. The day after the crash, Farmer Jim Wilson of Tundergarth Mains farm discovered a suitcase in the hedgerow of one of his fields. It had been missed by the searchers. The top of the case had sprung open on impact. Wilson described to John how he removed some clothes to look inside. There he saw a long plastic bag divided into compartments and folded in zig-zag fashion. Wilson used his hands to illustrate the shape, saying that it seemed to him to be some kind of belt. Each compartment contained a measure of white powder.

Fearing that his cattle might get their noses into the powder he took the suitcase back to his farmhouse and telephoned the police.

Within minutes a policeman arrived accompanied by an American whom Wilson described as 'extremely angry about something'. The suitcase was handcuffed to the wrist of the policeman and the two departed.

John went to see Brian Gill QC of the LADG and asked him to again raise the matter of drugs finds at the Lockerbie site. Gill listened to John's request but gave no commitment that he would accede to it, and in the event took no action.

John asked Gill again. Gill openly refused. John repeated his request through Peter Watson, the newly appointed secretary of the LADG. As coordinator for the group, Watson had authority to ensure that a reasonable request from one of the relatives would be honoured. Yet Gill refused for a third time. Indeed, he angrily told John that if he persisted with the matter, he would no longer represent him.

And now to John it all seems to be some form of distasteful blackmail. He faces a serious paradox. His conscience tells him that Wilson's account is accurate. Yet here is a Queen's Counsel, supposedly representing a bereaved relative, refusing to assist him. He puts his concerns in writing. Reminding Gill of his responsibilities towards the relatives: 'Having spoken to you, my legal representative at this Inquiry, on two occasions and now having committed myself to paper, I feel that my conscience is clear. The moral responsibility for this information is now yours.' John hands the letter to Colin Campbell QC and copies it to Gill and to his own solicitor in Birmingham.

Eventually the letter reaches the Lord Advocate, Peter Fraser, and then Chief Superintendent John Orr. They invite John to meet them. They claim that Farmer Wilson has been re-interviewed and has nothing to say about the suitcase – a complete contradiction of what John believes to be true. He demands that Wilson be interviewed again and a specific question regarding the suitcase be put to him. Orr promises a further interview by a senior police officer. In the event, Gill will not raise the matter in the FAI and John never will discover if a re-interview of farmer Wilson has occurred.

John confesses to me his deep sadness. So soon after the destruction of Pan Am 103 we find ourselves still in shock and confused, surrounded by a complex organisation we do not understand, and by people who say they are here to help. It's a matter of trust, and betrayal of trust.

Is the drugs find connected to the bombing? The suitcase has disappeared. To remove evidence from a crime scene is a criminal offence. But on this matter Sheriff Principal Mowat remains silent.

Daily my inner fury grows. If I were to even speak to one of these paid-for people I cannot be sure to contain my anger. 'Ensure that it goes into the hold of the plane.' Now, standing before me are representatives of the rulers of my country, a nation of which I have throughout my life so far been deeply proud, denying it all. Only John Mosey seems to be at peace with his emotions. Suddenly I am resolved; I will represent myself; I will follow the example of Marina Larracoechea and from the floor challenge them all.

Addressing Sheriff Principal Mowat I request that former Prime Minister Thatcher and her former transport secretary come to Scotland to give evidence and be cross-examined. I intend to compel them under pain of a fine not exceeding £250. The reply is immediate: 'Unable to attend due to pressing business in the House.'

I widen my challenge; the inquiry members listen politely but their eyes betray disdain. Wherever I choose to turn I am rebuffed: 'This matter has already been dealt with by Crown Counsel.'

I do, however, manage to insert one important statement through the bars of their portcullis and into the record. Had the British government given more support to the development of airline security technology, the Lockerbie disaster might have been prevented. I quote expert evidence by Professor Paul Wilkinson, Professor of International Relations at the University of St Andrews, regarding the inadequacies of British and foreign airport security; I remind the inquiry members of those disastrous Department of Transport delays in issuing colour photographs of the PFLP-GC bomb; I add that if an X-ray picture had been included with the circular of 22 November 1988 issued by James Jack, airport baggage screeners would have better known what to look for.

Rattling around my brain is the knowledge that the LADG solicitors not only are commissioned by the UK's Department of Transport; some of them represent American relatives suing Pan American Airways with a massive compensation claim. Until now, however, not a single conflict of interest has been recorded.

Sheriff Principal Mowat will not allow me to raise any matter that might interfere with the criminal investigation currently under way. I may not mention the Lockerbie bomb, ask who was responsible for its construction and use, nor explore anything to do with the attack and its aftermath.

Furthermore, a Mr McEachrean, for the Department of Transport, has today maintained that any discussion of the involvement of the intelligence agencies of the United Kingdom is 'contrary to the national interest'. I fail to understand how, if intelligence services received warnings of bombs on airliners and did not inform potential passengers, they can be excused attendance at this inquiry.

As the hearings continue the government persists with its own agenda. Five public interest immunity certificates close down all discussion of the size and shape of the Lockerbie bomb, the amount of Semtex used and the contents of communications with 'other governments'. In addition, the home secretary signs a gagging certificate concerning national security, the contents of which we relatives will never discover.

We may continue to attend, but must restrain ourselves as Sheriff Principal Mowat allows key evidential issues to be presented by advocates of the British government. Advocate Depute Andrew Hardie QC claims that Pan Am 103 was under continuous guard during its time on the tarmac at Heathrow Airport. There was no opportunity to plant a bomb. This ignores completely evidence given in police statements by a man who was on the tarmac by the Pan Am gate at the time. Baggage handler John Bedford was one of the team responsible for loading the luggage container in which the bomb was placed. He firmly maintains that he returned from a thirty-minute break to discover that an unknown person had placed two Samsonite-type suitcases in front of several cases already loaded. From Bedford's evidence it is clear that the baggage container was in half-darkness and unsupervised for forty-five minutes before the arrival of Pan Am 103A from Frankfurt.

Bedford is not a witness at the FAI. His statements appear to have been ignored by both Crown and police representatives. In addition, Pan Am 103 is claimed to have been under some kind of guard – of what form is never made clear – but not the luggage container that will be placed in the hold six feet below the passengers.

Hardie continues with his proclamation of British government innocence. No reconciliation was carried out between those bags transferred from Pan Am 103A and the list of passengers booked to fly onward to New York. Had Pan Am reconciled all bags with passengers, the bombing would have been prevented. The Crown, maintains Hardie, makes no submission that the bag containing the device came to Frankfurt as an interline[3] bag. He will not, however, 'seek to discourage' such a finding.

The inquiry then hears from a Mr Baird, representing the widow of a known drug courier for the DEA and a passenger on Pan Am 103, Khaled Jafaar. He states – without challenge or question – that the suitcase containing the bomb was 'positioned on the second layer at the front of the said container . . .' and arrived from Frankfurt on Flight 103A. The allowance by Sheriff Principal Mowat of this statement as if it were a proven fact contradicts his restriction placed upon us of discussion of any matters that might impinge upon the criminal inquiry at that time under way by the Scottish police.

Similarly, a Mr Anderson, representing Pan Am and aircraft security firm Alert, maintains that 'the device which caused the disaster . . . was not of the type contained in the Toshiba warning and there was no evidence that it had a barometric trigger'. This matter is central to the issue of source of the bomb and identity of the culprits. It is also central to the criminal investigation. Yet no challenge or questioning takes place and the claim is skated over as if it is a proven fact.

So, what, in the end, is the inquiry's conclusion?

That 270 persons were murdered by a bomb, and no one in the British government or airline security service can be held responsible for anything that occurred.

We can now see it all: they who look down upon the bereaved relatives are from a different world. Their employers follow an agenda unknown to the common man. It's been a lonely experience for us all, leaving us at times vulnerable and deeply disillusioned. Only through the brave example of Marina Larracoechea have I found the courage to take them on. But where is the investigation now? If the PFLP-GC group are suspects, why are they not being arrested? The intelligence services of three nations surely know how to capture them.

Two 'Guilty' Men?

Chapter 6

DEEP IN FLORA'S Wood there's some tidying to be done, keeping the young trees clear of weeds and meadow grass, and by a tiny lake I'm building a summer house. Will it survive the surrounding attrition of so many trees? It's a risk, but I'll take it.

My mobile rings. It's Jane. 'Jim, come quick. The TV, an announcement.'

On a podium stands the solid figure of US Attorney General William Barr: 'For three years the United States and Scotland have been conducting one of the most exhaustive and complex investigations in history. Today we are announcing an indictment in the case. We charge that two Libyan officials, Abdelbaset al-Megrahi and Khalifa Fhimah, acting as operatives of the Libyan intelligence service, along with other co-conspirators, planted and detonated the bomb that destroyed Pan Am 103.'

Through 1989 to early 1991 all we British relatives could know was that Iran and the PFLP-GC group were the targets of an investigation. As late as 22 December 1989 the US Defense Intelligence Agency (DIA) told journalists, 'a compelling body of evidence indicates that the PFLP-GC placed a sophisticated altimeter-fused, radio-encased bomb aboard Pan Am Flight 103'.[1] In September 1990, following a meeting with the Syrian foreign minister, US Secretary of State James Baker declared, 'although the US has provided evidence of PFLP-GC complicity, the Syrian government has dismissed it as insufficient'.[2] In February 1991, the DIA described Iran's Interior Minister Ali Akbar Mohtashemi's payment of $10 million to the PFLP-GC as proof of Iran's involvement.[3]

There were hints from various sources of surprises to come, but nothing has prepared me for this. Today Iran is forgotten; it's all about Libya.

The US has issued briefing sheets listing the evidence. Scottish Lord Advocate Peter Fraser confirms it: 'We have witnesses who will prove the case beyond reasonable doubt.' A Libyan agent bought clothes from a shop in Malta. He is identified in several statements by the shop owner. Fragments of the clothing were at the crash site. A reliable witness spotted the Libyan agent with another agent at Malta's Luqa Airport on the day of the bombing. They carried a suitcase of which fragments were found at the crash site. A fragment of a digital timer triggering the bomb has been found at the crash site. It is from a batch of twenty timers delivered to Libya in 1985.

* * *

6 DECEMBER 1991

There goes the phone again. A voice crackles down a bad line. 'Dr Swire, I'm Nabil Nagameldin, from the *Al Ahram* newspaper in Cairo. May I talk to you about the indictments against al-Megrahi and Fhimah?'[4]

Next evening he's on the doorstep at Caspidge. The man is Nubian by birth, of slender build, a square face and firm jaw, hair neatly brushed back, a tidy jacket, shirt and tie. In the glow of the fire his eyes gleam from behind large spectacles. We talk. Can Bush be trusted? Thatcher won't help. What evidence have the Americans got? Where's Jibril gone to? What *are* the CIA doing? And after an hour of unproductive meandering, we're stuck. How to move it along, get the suspects to a Scottish court where the full story can emerge? Would it help if I write a letter to Gaddafi?

Nabil leans back in his chair. 'Go and see him. Persuade him to hand over al-Megrahi and Fhimah.'

'*Me*, persuade *him*?'

Nabil looks deep into the fire. 'You've lost a daughter, so has he; his stepdaughter Hanna was killed during the American bombing in 1986. You have something in common. Just go, Jim. We'll arrange the flights and hotel. You make sure your people don't know. They'll go nuts if they find out. And give me the story when it's over.'

Next day I phone the one man I can trust for such a venture, David Ben Aryeah. I try to sound casual. 'I'm flying to Geneva and Tripoli.'

There's a short silence. 'Hmm. That'll be nice. Cuckoo clocks and chocolate. Hope you understand what you're doing. The Colonel's not top of the pops.'

Suddenly I realise the enormity of it all and I'm terrified. 'Can you speak to your friends? Tell me what to do and say?'

Another silence, then: 'Intelligence will listen to every call you make. Every fax. They'll read it before you do.'

We design an emergency code. 'Tell Jane and the family everything is alright' means what it says. 'Tell Jane that everything's alright' means things are fine, but not a bundle of laughs. 'Tell everyone everything's alright' means 'Help! Get me out!' I rehearse the words over and over, hoping I can remember them all.

Two weeks later Nabil and I meet at a London hotel then take a taxi to Heathrow and a flight to Geneva. I've booked a forward seat, Nabil is at the rear. I'm keeping my head well down. If a journalist spots me I haven't a clue what to do.

Onward to Tripoli. The door swings open to a searing day. We wait until every other passenger is off the plane, then emerge. Straight ahead on a spectator balcony is a milling, curious group of reporters and cameramen. I'm not having it. I grab Nabil's arm and pull him back inside. 'It's a bloody circus. Get rid of them.'

Nabil steps outside and talks in Arabic to a shortish man who seems to be some kind of minder. The man stands at the top of the aircraft steps, shouts a few words in Arabic, and within seconds they're all gone apart from half a dozen nervous officials standing at the foot of the steps.

'What did you say to him?'

Downcast, Nabil mutters, 'Exactly what you said.'

On the tarmac the minder takes us through the introductions, and we three get into a big black Mercedes. It's looking good; I'm chaperoned by a man who can put the wind up even Libyan journalists, and soon our Mercedes purrs to a halt before the magnificent Al Mahari Hotel.

Nabil whispers, 'Jim, a Mahari is a pedigree racing camel. Sort of turbo-charged. Gaddafi owns a herd of them. He never loses.'

A hotel official steers me up to a room that is ultimate luxury with an amazing bathroom. I'm beginning to wish now that I'd brought Jane. Opening the floor-to-ceiling windows I stroll along the balcony and survey my temporary palace, then onward to the deep carpeted corridors of the main hotel. I solemnly tell all who greet me: 'I wish to meet your leader. I seek the truth about Lockerbie.'

Within an hour a group of doctors proudly show me round one of Tripoli's elegant hospitals, inviting an inspection of medical records. The documents are immaculate. Are they specially prepared for the visitor?

I ask to meet relatives of those killed in the July 1986 US bombings. The minder introduces me to an architect who lost five members of his family. The architect's friend is an engineer whose wife was paralysed by an American missile. They are ordinary Libyan citizens. None lived near Gaddafi's home. Their bitterness against America and Britain is striking.

Next, a visit to the Foreign Ministry. The minder asks Nabil to wait in the library and guides me down a corridor into a large office. Just as I settle into my chair a stranger walks in, sits and faces me. He is strikingly handsome, tall, square-shouldered and tanned, his face reminiscent of the film star Lee Marvin. He smiles. His voice is deep with undertones. 'Good afternoon Dr Swire. I am Moussa Koussa.'

After asking a few simple questions about Libya I begin to sense menace. Koussa's face is calm but his body restless. He does not reveal what he does for Libya. He seems a military man, an action man. Was he part of the bombing of Flora's plane? If I mention Flora will he react badly? Is he one of the Colonel's right-hand men, testing, checking? I want him on my side, to tell Gaddafi that all is 'safe'. Does Gaddafi trust him? Perhaps he's got to be right or he's dead. Suddenly, halfway through one of my questions, he stands and ends our meeting with a polite and firm handshake.

As we walk to the car Nabil quietly explains: 'In '89 Koussa was accused by the French of bombing a Transport Aerienne airliner. He was never prosecuted.'

Another Mercedes joins in. We speed in convoy to meet His Excellency Judge M'hammud Aljadi, chairman of the Libyan Supreme Court. His office matches his name and title. Here is a man of learning, to all appearances a good man. The translator, Khalifa, seems at ease, mediating a complex discussion with style.

We review the indictments against al-Megrahi and Fhimah. Aljadi asks for my views as if from an expert in international law. While he weaves through a forest of legal issues my mind turns homeward. Jane will be at the shops. She must be worried sick. I simply told our practice assistant I'd be away for a few days and I didn't say where. Then I disappeared, leaving a sealed letter with my solicitor to be opened if something unusual were to happen. I gave the man no hint of what 'unusual' might signify. Nobody knows where I am; apart from Jane, David Ben Aryeah, MI6, the CIA, the Foreign Office and a major Arab newspaper.

Before our meeting ends, I hand to Aljadi a photograph of Flora. With the help of Nabil I've written on the back in awful Arabic: 'In memory of Hanna, Colonel Gaddafi's daughter. Killed in the 1986 American raid.' Below it in English: 'The consequence of the use of violence is the death of innocent people.' Would Aljadi be so good as to seek permission for it to be displayed in Hanna's room?[5]

Our convoy sweeps back to the hotel. It's been a whirlwind of a day; I'm finding it difficult to make sense of all I've seen and heard. Foremost in my mind hovers the inscrutable face of Moussa Koussa. And Aljadi seemed kind, suspiciously kind.

* * *

It's been a long morning. In the shade of the hotel balcony Nabil and I sit and talk, and wait.

A hotel official approaches, stops and stands before us: 'Dr Swire, there's a gentleman to see you.'

We go downstairs. Enveloped in a chair beside a white marble fountain is a swarthy Libyan wearing a full-length black leather coat. On his head perches a deer stalker hat gripping an untidy mane of shiny black hair. He stands and walks towards us, limping heavily, protecting his left leg from the knee down.

'Good afternoon, Dr Swire. I am here for to guide you.' The words come with an odour of malt whisky.

We exchange pleasantries, he in broken English through translator Nabil, who speaks English, Nubian and Egyptian. He says his name is Saleh. For me he is from this moment *Deerstalker*.

Deerstalker invites, 'Please, Dr Swire, I would like for to show you my office.' He limps ahead. We follow the scent of Scotland. He walks to a large Mercedes with tinted windows, opens the front and rear passenger doors with a flourish and ushers us in. I get into the front, Nabil into the rear. As Deerstalker walks round the car to get to the driver's seat I find that I'm staring at a needle of sunlight forming a tiny bright oval on the black leather sill. In the bottom corner of the wind-screen, encircled by a web of silvery cracks, is a bullet hole.

Deerstalker slams the car into gear and it roars into the noonday traffic. Suddenly cutting sharp left, he weaves through a maze of backstreets filthy with litter and slides to a halt beside a nondescript office block. By the main door leans a group of unkempt men. Deerstalker steps from the car while shouting a command in Arabic. One of the men runs forward and jumps behind the wheel. Nabil and I get out and the car cruises slowly away.

Deerstalker smiles, 'It is safer.'

He goes ahead through a hallway stinking of faeces towards a lift with no glass in the door. As it whines upward to the first level, an aroma of urine belies a still working technology. The lift opens onto a corridor and then to what seems an office. In the centre of the room stands a huge desk with three telephones and a fax machine with a crack down its casing. The wires are unconnected. Stacks of letters and files litter every available space. Empty glasses and tins lie across the carpet. In the corner is a bed, half-made, sheets grey with use.

We all sit down and look at each other. Deerstalker is behind the desk, Nabil to his left. I'm in the far corner on Deerstalker's right. Deerstalker smiles, 'Would you like whisky?' This is a man you do not cross.

'Yes – please – that would be wonderful. A real Scottish treat.' I'm unsure how Nabil will translate that one.

Behind Deerstalker is a big oaken cupboard extending floor to ceiling. He stands, turns around and opens the doors. In serried ranks a dozen rows deep are bottles of Ballantyne's best. He clonks a couple of tumblers onto the desk, uncorks a bottle, pours two triples and slides one towards me. He doesn't look at Nabil, the true believer, who will sit and watch as two decadents get to it.

Deerstalker asks, 'What do you think of Tripoli?', gulps down half a glassful, and, without taking breath, 'Why do you wish to see the Leader?'

This could be tricky. I glance downward. A large empty fruit tin with the word *Fanta* printed across it lies on its side. I nonchalantly lift it upright with the side of my shoe. Glass on knee I lean back in my chair, and while Deerstalker is looking at Nabil for a translation of my latest Scottish tale, pour the whisky away.

As we chat, Deerstalker notices that my glass is empty. He leans over and refills it with a smile. We both smile and say 'Cheers!'

Now we're into our fourth glass. The Fanta tin is half full. Deerstalker rambles on about how he is a senior official with authority. Then he says something in Arabic that I cannot make out. I turn to Nabil for a translation. The man is pale beneath his ebony skin, a bead of sweat on his forehead.

I glance back at Deerstalker. From a holster under his left arm the Libyan has slid an automatic pistol on to his thigh. The barrel points directly at Nabil. Deerstalker is polishing it with the pad of his forefinger, looking straight at Nabil. In a mixture of pidgin English and Arabic he seems to be talking about Scottish islands. Nabil doesn't say a word.

An hour later a second bottle is empty, Fanta is overflowing, and Deerstalker's automatic is back in its holster. Whatever agenda he had in mind has drifted away in a golden mist. The conversation tails away into exhaustion, he tries to stand. 'Now you come . . . I take you back hotel . . .' He sits down again heavily.

We each take an arm, walk him to the lift and down to the pavement. The Mercedes is back by the kerb, engine ticking, a scruffy attendant holding open the door. By now my nerve has cracked. Unhinging myself from Deerstalker I open the rear door and jump in. Nabil, stranded and confused, lets Deerstalker fall heavily onto the driver seat and trots around the car to the rear.

Softly humming some Arabic tune, Deerstalker flips the window down and slaps a wailing green light onto the roof.

The car roars through the back streets, turns a corner and weaves down the centre of a wide road busy with homeward traffic. Seemingly within seconds we are before Hotel Al Mahari.

As we exit the car, Deerstalker mumbles an incoherent something. He pulls away, the still-open door slamming with the acceleration, and the Mercedes disappears into the traffic.

* * *

Today we visit Justice Ahmed Tahev Zawi. He is investigating the two suspects under the terms of the 1971 Montreal Convention. Under its rules, should an international trial prove impossible, citizens accused of an international offence can be tried by their own nation. The suspects are in protective custody. Zawi has asked the Scottish government for the evidence supporting the indictments but the Scottish Crown office refuses to answer. Zawi asks: 'Dr Swire, might you, perhaps, be in a position to obtain the information on our behalf?'

I explain: 'I am not the Lord Advocate's representative. I am the father of a murdered girl.'

Following the shooting of PC Yvonne Fletcher in London by members of the Libyan embassy, direct contact with British officials is embargoed and all communications are routed via the Italian authorities. So I suggest that I take with me to Britain a sealed package from Zawi and hand it to Lord Fraser. Zawi agrees; it will be arranged.

Next morning I'm sitting on a balcony exchanging pleasantries on the phone with Judge Aljadi, Chairman of the Supreme Court of Libya. Nabil is downstairs finishing a late breakfast. Suddenly from the hotel foyer comes a familiar voice: I glance down the stairwell; it's Kate Adie and a production crew.[6]

Shortly after, I head quietly down fire-escape stairs to a rear door. A Mercedes with side window curtains purrs to a halt. I clamber in. No time to tell Nabil; he's on his own for a while.

With curtains drawn we sweep anonymously round the hotel towards the main road, brushing past Kate and her crew.

We glide along the sea front, past elaborate fountains, then some sort of castle, then a museum. The Terry Waite kidnap comes to mind. Four years ago, as the great innocent, he entered Beirut on the invitation of Islamic Jihad to comfort hostages Terry Anderson and Tom Sutherland. He was himself taken as a hostage and released, emaciated, when the indictments were issued.[7]

Gaddafi too had his moments. Seven years ago, four British overseas workers were taken by the Libyans and confirmed as political hostages in exchange for Libyans arrested following the murder of PC Yvonne Fletcher. Only after nine months of strenuous negotiations, including visits and pleas by Terry Waite, were they released.

Today two Libyan officials are at risk of kidnap and rendition for interrogation, or even assassination.[8] Will Libya again seek an exchangeable international currency – Jim Swire? My heart is thundering within me, I take deep breaths to keep calm. On both sides are high walls with dragon's-teeth fencing. We weave past lines of concrete tank-stoppers and intermittent palm trees. In the shade of each tree lolls a soldier with a submachine gun and a two-way radio into which he talks furiously as we pass. Ahead is a high concrete wall. The car slows and heads for the wall. Suddenly a section lifts like a draw-bridge and we ease through a gap just wide enough for the limousine. I glance upward to a row of hydraulic steel teeth capable of crushing the car. We emerge into sunlight and a garden of palm trees and green lawns. My skin turns cold. I'm staring into the muzzle of a Russian tank.

Out of the car is blinding sunlight. A guard opens a steel anti-blast door opening to another garden and what I take to be Gaddafi's former home, now derelict. The walls and paths are festooned with barbed wire and beds of spikes where flowers should be. The rear of the house has broken windows and ominous cracks in the walls. The front has been hit square on by a missile and a hole some fifteen feet across gapes with bent metal bars of reinforced concrete.

At the front of the house stands a giant bronze hand crushing a model of an American F1-11. As we walk through the gap where once stood a front porch, a flock of pigeons flash past us up into the blue, wings whipping the air. Inside is a concourse with an entire wall painted with a lurid mural, *The Night of the Bombing*. The sky is filled with vividly painted aircraft, missiles and explosions. The wall opposite is coated with Arabic graffiti. In the centre of the room, on trestles, are fragments from the carcass of an aircraft. Below it, flat on the floor, is a jet fighter wheel inscribed with 'F1-11'. Lined up like skulls are two American pilot's helmets, each with a dead pilot's name inscribed on the back, just above the neckline. Not bothering to ask permission I carry them outside, arrange them on a wall and take a photograph. I've a vague notion of sending the photo to an American friend for him to pass to the relatives of the dead. As I press the shutter the words 'Greater love hath no man' come to mind.

The minder directs me back into the house and a small room with shrapnel holes in the walls and ceiling, and sections of plaster hanging down. On a tiny table arranged like an altar stand photographs of a child, aged perhaps a year and a half. This is the bedroom of Hanna, the Leader's adopted baby daughter, plucked from obscurity to riches, and said to have been killed in the 1986 American attack on Tripoli.

Now we're in an even more luxurious garden. Two attendants lead me and the minder into a waiting room with thick carpets, ornate Louis XIV-style furniture and plaster carvings burnished with gold. We wait. The minder's getting nervous, on the edge of shaky, lighting one cigarette with another, so I chat to him, and, as a doctor, tell him laughingly of the health risks of smoking. The man cheers up a little. He speaks good English, will be the interpreter, but he's scared. Of what or whom I'm not sure.

He glances at his watch, invites me to stand, and we walk along a white flagstone path. Now there's something odd. A sturdy rope is tied around a great iron peg hammered into the ground; the rope leads off across the lawn not to a canvas, but loops around a reinforced concrete lintel stretching over the entrance to wherever we're going. Then I understand. It's a huge desert tent set into a reinforced concrete underground bunker topped by a grassy mound.

We go through the folds of the door and there, in a flowing green robe, his dark hair glinting from a lamp hanging from the peak of the tent, stands the one the Americans call The Mad Dog. He turns towards us, smiling. A careworn face etched with the burden of office, intelligent, tense, even stressed, but a certain graciousness. His left hand crosses his heart in a gesture of peace. He extends a strong, not overwhelming handshake.

He motions me to a low armchair. Our interpreter hovers in the background. I glance around quickly and nervously. The tent is garishly coloured, in parts green and white stripes, in others Arabic designs and motifs. On two sides, in the shadows, are four or five bodyguards. There too is the glint of submachine guns. Above the guns are gleaming, steady eyes. The bodyguards are women.

Gaddafi asks, 'Dr Swire, I hope that your stay in Tripoli has been comfortable, yes?'

I'm shaking, my hands tremble, my words tumble out: 'Sir, I'm certainly scared of meeting you, but then again, you may be scared of meeting me.'

You fool – what have you said? Here's the man whose people are alleged to have killed your daughter. You're asking him to hand over his citizens for trial. The man must have his doubts: Why has this English doctor come to see me?

Now Gaddafi's smiling at me. Some sort of assurance? Is it that he too is a father who has lost a daughter?

He wishes to discuss the matter of the indictments. So far the word 'trial' has not been mentioned. He commits to nothing, reveals nothing, this long-time swimmer in a sea of sharks. He listens carefully to my explanations then turns to an attendant who whispers something in his ear. He stays motionless for a few seconds, looks heavenward with a distinctive toss of the head. He knows nothing of the cause of Lockerbie. Perhaps freak hailstones, a falling satellite, a collision with another plane. Even if he knows, he won't say. The Lockerbie attack was war by proxy. Place your bomb, retreat to the shadows, watch your enemy squirm.

Gripping my courage hard I look him straight in the eye. 'A trial in a Scottish court is the only way.'

The interpreter ends his version of my challenge. A sharp intake of breath echoes across the tent. Gaddafi shifts in his chair, turns to the interpreter for confirmation, then looks back at me, his eyes mere slits, his voice deep and certain: 'You speak of the Montreal Treaty. Would it not be better for the Libyan people to seek a decision of the International Court of Justice concerning our sovereign rights under that Treaty?'

My tongue sticks to the roof of my mouth. I nod, twice.

An embarrassing silence is broken by two assistants bringing in trays of tea. Luckily, I've heard somewhere that Gaddafi is interested in islands, so I start to tell him about the Hebrides. I offer him a gift: 'Sir, here are two books written by my mother; one about the Isle of Skye, the second about the Outer Hebrides. With these is a folder containing photographs of my daughter, Flora.'

Gaddafi accepts and nods. He flicks through the pages, intensely interested in the photos. His eyes start to smile. He motions to an attendant, who steps forward with a green, hardcover book, with titles and text across the front in gold. Gaddafi studies the first page and looks up: 'This is my philosophy.' He hands it to me, then motions to a second attendant who brings a deep green Koran with gold text and elaborate decoration.

'I wish you to accept the Koran. And I will place one of these photographs of Flora beside that of my daughter Hanna. I have kept her bedroom as it was on that terrible night in 1986.'[9]

We've been talking for an hour. Gaddafi motions with his hands, and we stand. Relief floods into my body and a crazy idea into my head. I reach into my briefcase for a metal badge and, holding it out before me, step towards Gaddafi.

He stands erect and tense. Here I am, twelve inches from, and face-to-face with, the man the world believes to be the murderer of my daughter. I'm looking into his deep brown eyes which once again have become mere slits. Around and behind me submachine guns click to readiness. He does not move, stands solid as stone.

'Sir, this says why I've come to see you.' I fold back the hem of his robe and pin on the badge. The message sparkles bright blue: 'Pan Am 103 – the truth must be known.' I step backward to again a respectful distance; around the tent the sound of deep exhalations of breath.

Farewells are exchanged, Gaddafi and entourage sweep into the shadows. With the minder timidly following, I stroll back to the limousine, adrenaline still pumping, soon back at the Al Mahari drinking strong coffee with a curious Nabil.

Chapter 7

TWO DAYS LATER I'm home again. The word Libya has leaked into the media. For the tenth time this morning the study phone is ringing. I hear Jane have a brief, concerned exchange. Worried by the stress and anxiety of the last few days, she comes out to meet me. 'Your partners at the surgery want to come and see you this evening,' she says.

'Sorry, Jim, you're spending too much time campaigning. This Libyan thing is the last straw. We've had a meeting and we're all agreed. We would like you to resign from the practice so that we can appoint a new man to take your place.'

This devastating news is followed by explanations about the stress of fundholding and the need for a younger man to share the workload. There is an offer by the senior partner of locum work when possible.

The next few weeks are spent in a state of grey, blank shock with emotions further shredded by financial worries. Yet even here there are shafts of sunlight: cards, letters, flowers and poems arrive at the house from friends and patients. People stop me in the street and offer to help. From these messages of concern come comfort, strength and support. Kind and compassionate people who walk beside us for a while quite simply do us good. Our journey becomes less lonely and our burden of sadness less heavy.

I find that I will lose pension rights and suffer a drop in income, but the locum work gives me a job and I can keep my patients. The practice support staff are amazing: today I watch Brenda juggling my diary, bereaved relatives, political and legal enquiries, and a computerised appointment system serving fifteen hundred patients.

The Libya visit has changed me. We have been through so much already: we've been through Lockerbie, we've faced Gaddafi and his henchmen, and now my job is under threat. Like my friend John Mosey, we agree we must try to bring something good out of this terrible tragedy.

One BBC radio interview offers me enormous encouragement. On the phone is Sir Anthony Parsons, former British representative to the United Nations, and an honorary fellow of Balliol College, Oxford. I ask, does he think the Tripoli visit was a sensible thing to do?

Sir Anthony agrees, 'Most sensible.'

I promised Justice Zawi that I would hand-deliver to Peter Fraser, Lord Advocate of Scotland, a sealed letter addressed to the Foreign and Commonwealth Office. I travel to the Scottish Crown office in Edinburgh, give it to Fraser and explain Zawi's responsibility and his problem.

Fraser remains unmoved. The prime minister has reliable information that the two accused Libyans are guilty. Not a shred of evidence will be revealed to Libya. There will be a trial in Scotland or America.

Several American bereaved relatives have written to express puzzlement about my Libya visit. Some are willing to give me a chance to explain. Others are caustic: 'Left his brain behind . . .', 'Gaddafi's dupe . . .', 'Meeting with the Devil.' I well understand their anger, but I'm hurting too. Will they ever understand that I did it as much for them as for my own family? There will never be a trial unless Libya releases the two suspects; and without a trial the truth will never come out.

These things I can say to them. But not this: Gaddafi leads a nation lying on the northern edge of Africa. He is surrounded by supportive governments, including one led by a friend who once enjoyed a long and reflective sojourn on Robben Island – Nelson Mandela.

* * *

July 1992

Six months have flown by. I write to Foreign Secretary Douglas Hurd explaining that a bomb killed 270 people because at Heathrow suitcases were not checked against passenger names. Meanwhile, American bereaved relatives have successfully sued Pan Am for failing to undertake such checks. Hurd thanks me politely and gives no reaction.

The Earl of Caithness now represents the Department of Transport. More in hope than anger I send him a similar broadside. The Earl replies in Whitehall-speak of airline security, bar-coding, the limitations of X-rays, types of lethal materials used by terrorists and the complexities of searching unaccompanied baggage. He offers an assurance: 'My real hope is that the introduction of our new requirements will lead to a considerable reduction in the number of unaccompanied bags handled in the UK thus greatly reducing the potential for such bags to be used by terrorists to attack an aircraft.'

I mentally cross out the words 'hope', 'lead to', 'considerable', 'greatly reducing' and 'potential', and wonder what is left. Should I take comfort that thousands of travellers might have, when new measures are introduced at some undefined point in the future, a reduced probability of oblivion?

In an angry fit of curiosity I pace out the yards between the Department of Transport and the gates of the Palace of Westminster, earning some curious looks from sentry policemen as I stride mechanically past them. It's pretty close to 540 yards – equal to 270 coffins laid end to end. So I work out a plan to have the coffins constructed in black cardboard, folding them up in the back of a van, sneaking in with some helpers shortly before dawn and laying them out so that ministers must walk or drive past them on their way to the House.

That's it! Catch the politicians on camera with coffins and Houses of Parliament in the background.

My friends persuade me otherwise: 'Not the British way . . .'

Well, let's try another. Let's buy some miniature lights, fix them on to 270 tiny boats and float them down the river as Parliament is in evening session.

My friends say that that too will not work.

Right. How about 270 white pigeons with lamps on their legs? Let 'em loose at midnight on 21 December over the Houses of Parliament?

Again my friends caution against.

For the rest of my life I will wish I'd done them all: coffins, boats, pigeons, the lot. Flora would have laughed, indeed she would.

* * *

15 JANUARY 1993

We're on TV again: *The Late Late Show*, compered in Dublin by Irish chat-show host Gay Byrne. Crooner Val Doonican opens the evening with songs and anecdotes. Then comes my turn with my famous photograph of Flora and our cry for 'Truth'. I'm straight from a Dublin seminar on post-disaster care and the adrenaline still flows. Seizing the moment, I explain to what might be an unknowing or unbelieving audience what befell my family and so many at Lockerbie.

I tell of powerful governments refusing even to discuss Lockerbie; of a Fatal Accident Inquiry where a father of two sons, for six weeks not allowed to see their bodies, addressed a silent courtroom, 'Sir, I would remind you that they are my sons, not yours.' I warn that four years after Lockerbie as many as five unaccompanied suitcases are in the hold of every transatlantic airliner that flies over Ireland. Security is important, but what does our government do about it? British Airways is farming out its security to the lowest bidder. Even after five years, full baggage reconciliation has not been introduced. No bag should travel without its owner. They must be forced to act. They will never do it voluntarily.

I speak of those bereaved of Pan Am 103 who secretly and silently twist upon a hook of grief, consumed in mind and body, sometimes unto death. How, by forming groups here and in the USA, and some of the other nineteen nations who lost loved ones, relatives find solace in each other.

I tell of evidence kept secret by MI5, MI6, the FBI; of a meeting at the American embassy in London with a whispering American commissioner who claimed that the truth will never be revealed. I remind them that President Bush, before he became president, was head of the CIA, and that a former working colleague of Colonel Oliver North throughout the entire Iran-Contra scandal is now in charge of the CIA's Lockerbie investigation.

Newly installed President Clinton offers some hope: 'He told us – "Yes, I'll see that it is looked into." ' Yet even as I speak I wonder if Clinton will ever be true to his promise. Or will he, like so many before him, once astride the juggernaut of power, succumb to whispered advice from those who walk in the shadows?

Salman Rushdie, author of *The Satanic Verses*, waits backstage surrounded by security people. The music plays and on he strolls, looking remarkably fit in spite of the millions of dollars promised by Iran to the first believer who will kill him. He tells of government approved death squads, of a crane driver forced to turn his machine over to the authorities so they could hang some rebel and drive the crane around town with the body swinging high above a jubilant crowd. He tells too of a new form of anarchy, where powerful clerics promise a million dollars, point a finger across the world towards a dissident and say to the believer assassin, 'Kill him.'

I feel privileged to meet this hero, freethinker and author. Yet even as we converse, far across the Irish Sea and deep into the night a man born of Lockerbie, Professor Bob Black, is forging a key to the legal impasse. It will offer Libya, the Americans and the British the exit strategy they seek. It will change the legal history of the world.

* * *

MARCH 1993

Michael Kretzmer of BBC Birmingham comes to Caspidge with camera crew and notebook. Jane and I explain that the bombing of Pan Am 103 was not just a terrorist thing; it was an international political event, seemingly the greatest terrorist outrage ever. One part of it was the murder of a lovely daughter, deeply missed.

Kretzmer also interviews John Mosey: 'We're very glad as a group to have someone like Jim. Every group needs someone who is as active and committed and dedicated as he is. He's prepared to go up front and be high profile. We're very glad and are grateful for that, although it has – and will – cost him a great deal.'

The campaign dominates my life. I've composed hundreds of letters to newspapers, prime ministers and presidents, to lawyers and judges, to spies and policemen, to political scientists and computer experts. Some, wrongly, see me as a guru on aviation security, international politics, even explosives.

Yet to Professor Paul Wilkinson, international expert on terrorism and airline security, I am a man misled: 'It is slightly naïve to regard Colonel Gaddafi as just another father. He's been the sugar daddy of international terrorism for several decades. He's responsible, directly or indirectly, for the deaths of many innocent people. The idea that one could have a man-to-man discussion with someone responsible for such things seems to me very disingenuous.'

The BBC track down and interview Nabil Nagameldin who explains: 'We Arabs know the West more than the West knows the Arabs. The trip of Dr Swire was a step in that direction, to lay a bridge of understanding between peoples.'

Well, perhaps I am at times irrational, gullible and obsessed. Still, I prove to Kretzmer how easy it is, even five years after the Lockerbie attack, to smuggle an unaccompanied bag on to a plane. Yet when Kretzmer takes his camera to Whitehall, the Earl of Caithness assures him that by the end of 1993 Britain *may* have an aviation security service that will be the envy of the world.

* * *

On Thursday 22 December 1988 – one day after the Lockerbie explosion – Prime Minister Margaret Thatcher walked upon the field where lay the crushed cockpit of *Maid of the Seas*, and by the church of Tundergarth Mains she stood wrapped against the Scottish cold. Around her, across the hills and streets and gardens, lay 270 bodies and bits of bodies, and a broken town. Surrounded by officials and the American ambassador she moved through the debris. She said to journalists: 'One has never seen or ever thought to have seen anything like it. I went to the other site where the petrol contained in the wing exploded. Many houses were damaged. It looks very much worse in daylight.'[1]

We now move forward to November 1993. Today is published the first of her memoirs, *The Downing Street Years*.[2] The book's promo says it encompasses the whole of her time as prime minister, from May 1979 to November 1990.

She writes that while at the Rhodes European Council[3] of the 2nd and 3rd of December 1988, she was invited by German Federal Chancellor Helmut Kohl to meet him at his home in the charming village of Deidesheim. During her next visit, she recalls, 'lunch was potato soup, pig's stomach (which the German Chancellor clearly enjoyed), sausage, liver dumplings and sauerkraut'. The two drove together to the great cathedral at Speyer, in whose crypt was to be found the tombs of at least four Holy Roman emperors. As they entered the cathedral the organ struck up a Bach fugue.

In July 1989, on a visit to the USA, she stood in the heat of Houston, Texas, untroubled in the hot sun.[4] The Americans had fitted underground air conditioning and blew cool air from below so that the assembled dignitaries would feel comfortable.

After the invasion of Kuwait by Iraq, she and President Bush assembled their potential allies. Turkey and Syria were on her list. Of Libya and Colonel Gaddafi, she enthuses about the July 1986 night-time bombing of Tripoli and Benghazi, seeing the slaughter of innocent Libyan citizens as a blow for freedom against terrorism. After such a rebuff, she claims, the much-vaunted Libyan counter-attack did not, and could not, take place. 'There was a marked decline in Libyan sponsored terrorism in succeeding years.'[5]

In September 1989, on a stopover from Tokyo, her plane refuelled at the frozen town of Bratsk. In a chilly barn-like building she met local Communist Party leaders and became engrossed in the intricacies of growing beetroot in a Russian climate. As she departed came a request by Oleg, the KGB guard, who asked for a signed photograph. This she immediately provided, and then – equally quickly observed – a general request for more signed photographs.[6] All remembered and recorded, history in the making.

And yet, a Scottish town strewn with the remains of the dead; a traumatic memorial service in Dryfesdale Parish church; repeated pleas by relatives for a hearing in Downing Street; international terrorism on a massive scale; German, Iranian, Syrian and Palestinian reputations questioned; the most severe attack on Britain since the Second World War;[7] of these there is nothing. Apart from, that is, four words in the chronology: 'December 21 – Lockerbie bombing'.

Such an event demands a chapter of its own. Can it be that the Lady wishes to erase Lockerbie from British and world memory? I agree with the other relatives that a respectful letter be sent: 'Why does your memoir of 1988 not mention Lockerbie?'

From the comfort of her Chester Square home comes the regal reply: 'We wish to add nothing to the text.'

In 2002, Thatcher will finally deign to mention Lockerbie. In her further memoir, a 'lecture' to the planet, *Statecraft: Strategies for a Changing World*, she will claim: 'Libya was clearly behind the bombing of Pan Am 103 . . . [al-Megrahi] was a Libyan intelligence agent, and it exceeds the bounds of credibility to imagine that he was not doing the Libyan leader's bidding.'[8] Thus her entire arsenal of proof that al-Megrahi was guilty of the attack.

It will take a further seven years for a fuller story to emerge. In August 2009 the retired Member of Parliament for Linlithgow Tam Dalyell will reveal that in 2002, in a conversation with Thatcher, she claimed that she had not written about Lockerbie because she 'knew nothing' of Lockerbie.[9]

Dalyell will explain it thus:

I was the chairman of the all-party House of Commons group on Latin America. I'd hosted Dr Alvaro Uribe, the president of Colombia, between the time that he won the election and formally took control in Bogota.

The Colombian ambassador, Victor Ricardo, invited me to dinner at his residence as Dr Uribe wanted to continue the conversations with me.

South Americans are very polite. A woman, even a widow, never goes alone into a formal dinner. And so, to make up numbers, Ricardo invited me to accompany his neighbour Margaret Thatcher. I had not spoken to her, nor her to me, for seventeen years. As we were sitting down to dinner, I tried to break the ice with a joke about a recent vandal attack on her statue in the Guildhall. I said I was sorry about the damage.

She replied pleasantly: 'Tam, I'm not sorry for myself, but I am sorry for the sculptor.'

Raising the soup spoon I ventured: 'Margaret, tell me one thing – why in eight hundred pages . . .'

She purred with obvious pleasure, 'Have you read my autobiography?'

'Yes, I have read it; very carefully. Why in eight hundred pages did you not mention Lockerbie?'

She replied: 'Because I didn't know what happened and I don't write about things that I don't know about.'

My jaw dropped: 'You don't know? But, quite properly as Prime Minister, you went to Lockerbie. You witnessed it first-hand.'

She insisted: 'Yes, but I don't know about it and I don't write in my autobiography things I don't know about.'[10]

Dalyell concludes: 'I'd always taken Lady Thatcher at face value; but to this day my suspicion remains that she had been instructed by the White House not to be too inquisitive about Lockerbie.'

Chapter 8

AMERICAN FILM PRODUCER Allan Francovich[1] is not on his president's Christmas card list. Still, such fripperies are of little interest to a man intent on exposing the nastier side of his nation's foreign policy. With eleven documentaries in an outstanding career, including a 1980 exposé of CIA activities, *On Company Business*,[2] and a powerful three-part documentary studying CIA involvement in Guatemala, El Salvador and Nicaragua, *The Houses are Full of Smoke*,[3] he is the focus of vicious character assassination by US and British authorities. Having watched US Department of Justice worldwide listings of 'facts' proving how the two Libyan suspects are guilty, it deeply angers him to be accused of interfering with 'an ongoing police investigation' with the production of his latest documentary, *The Maltese Double Cross*.[4]

I am in a studio at Channel 4 to watch a cut-down ninety-minute version of the film. The BBC had planned to show it in 1994, but on the eve of the showing the British and Scottish governments issued a deluge of attacks against the film, its backers and contributors. The BBC, in keeping with its courageous tradition of truth, objectivity and free speech, cancelled the screening. The film is banned in the US[5] and on all BBC channels.[6]

Francovich talked to Channel 4's editor for documentaries, Peter Moore. Peter was willing to show the two-and-a-half-hour film in a cut-down ninety-minute version. The reduced length was on the advice of solicitors, and the most contentious sections have been omitted. Against severe pressure from the British and American governments Channel 4 has held its ground with a peak-time viewing slot followed by an invited panel discussion.

The film claims that the Lockerbie bomb was planted by the PFLP-GC team led by Ahmed Jibril. On the fringes of the plot stalked Iran and Syria. The American Drug Enforcement Agency regularly shipped consignments of drugs from the Bekaa Valley to airports in the USA. They were known in the trade as 'controlled deliveries'. Khaled Jafaar worked for the DEA, and on the night of the attack was the courier of a suitcase containing drugs. The PFLP-GC arranged for his suitcase to be switched with an identical suitcase containing the bomb.

CIA Major Charles McKee and his six-man team were passengers on the plane, and Francovich has raised the suspicion that McKee was returning to CIA headquarters to expose an American hostages-for-drugs plot involving the DEA and Colonel Oliver North.

Much of the film's content is evidence spoken into camera by witnesses. Some characters provide suspect contributions – one scene featuring a staged telephone call to former CIA agent Oliver Winter proves farcical.

Several contributors appear to be telling the truth: notably a former Bekaa-based DEA asset Steven Donahue and senior members of Khaled Jafaar's family.[7]

Beside me to watch the film sit Sir Teddy Taylor, MP for Southend, and Allan Francovich. Behind us is Frank Duggan, adviser to the US Presidential Commission on Aviation Security and Terrorism and lawyer for several American bereaved relatives. Beside him are Sharham Chubim of the Graduate School of International Studies, and David Leppard, a *Sunday Times* journalist and author of a series of newspaper articles that in 1989 promoted the PFLP-GC/Jibril theory. Two years later Leppard published a book claiming the exact opposite, namely that Libya and Gaddafi were responsible.

A huge TV monitor dominates the centre of the studio, featuring the head and shoulders of Oliver 'Buck' Revell, representing the FBI's Lockerbie investigation team. He will watch the film on transatlantic hook-up. Producer Allan Francovich, not renowned for his dress sense, is this night bristling and arrogantly handsome. At the rear sits the stunningly beautiful Sheena McDonald, who will present the programme and chair a post-show discussion into the small hours.

The film makes clear that Iran had a strong motivation to attack America. Five months before the bombing of Flora's plane, an airbus carrying 290 pilgrims to Mecca was blown from the sky by the USS *Vincennes*.

Abul Hassan Bani-Sadr was president of Iran from 1979 to 1981: 'Shooting down an aircraft is a crime. Killing almost three hundred people is a crime. The people of Iran have never forgotten.'

* * *

Sheena McDonald reviews the evening and opens with a question as to who funded the film.[8]

Frank Duggan tries to hit the ball out of the stadium. 'This movie has been funded by Libyan interests. That's a violation of our embargo. It's more than a breaking of the law. It's disinformation by Colonel Gaddafi, to point the blame at everyone else.'

For an hour and a half Duggan has watched former DEA agents and drug runners talking straight at the camera. Two former directors of the US National Security Council have offered disturbing glimpses into America's covert history. Yet Duggan can only focus on who funded the film and stipulate that the world should obey *our law.*

Francovich rumbles into battle. 'There was no Libyan funding in this film. It's funded by a subsidiary of Lonrho. They
own the *Observer* newspaper and the Observer Film Company.
I was brought in because of my association with the *Observer*
and asked by Mr Rowland to do a film on Lockerbie. I said I
would as long as I had total control over it. And when Lonrho
withdrew its backing in December [1993], Mr Rowland stepped
in, and he completed the funding, and he owns the film.'

Until now the evidence against the Libyans seems strong;
I'm almost convinced of their guilt. Now Francovich has
pointed everything in an opposite direction. I lunge into the
discussion: 'One of the relatives who has seen this film told me
she doesn't care if it was financed by Adolf Hitler. What she
wants to know is, are these allegations true?'

Francovich defiantly rustles a letter from his pocket. 'I'm
going to read a letter, from someone in the CIA who knows Mr
Leppard. His name is Nathan Miller-Adams. Mr Adams was a
national intelligence officer. He sat on the CIA's group on
terrorism. And this letter is dated June 19th 1993. And he
says . . . "My conclusions are based on interviews I conducted
with several trusted sources, two of them who enjoy high-level
access with the Iranian government. Clearly the official report
was intended to focus blame on Libya rather than to identify
Iran, and Syria as sympathetic profiteer. Justice was sacrificed
in the interests of the 'Desert Storm' coalition." It goes on to
say—'

From Washington, Buck Revell interrupts: 'Who was this
from?'

Francovich: 'This was from Nathan Miller-Adams—'

Revell persists: 'Mr Adams was never a part of any of the
ranking structure of the CIA. I dealt with those people, and he
was not a part of it. I just don't know who this person is who
you are talking about . . .'

Francovich rattles back: 'Well, I do know who he is . . .' and
continues quoting Adams: ' "One expert who agrees with me is

David Leppard, deputy editor of the *Sunday Times* Insight team. We have both voiced our convictions on several forums." '9

I'm confused and getting nervous. Francovich has opened a stable door to inspect the muck inside, but they're all talking about a side issue.

Francovich continues, 'He was with the CIA as well. Yes, he was—'

Revell jumps in, 'He was never involved in Lockerbie, he was not—'

'He wasn't involved in Lockerbie, but he worked for the CIA,' Francovich fires back.

Well, maybe it's Tis and maybe it's Tisn't. I challenge Buck Revell: 'Two successive prime ministers have refused any kind of inquiry. And the name of Oliver North keeps cropping up. And to see Mr Cannistraro describing Oliver North as a professional liar doesn't fill us with confidence about American intelligence. Nor does it fill us with confidence when we as citizens cannot penetrate in any way what you guys are doing.'

In the back of my mind are the words of President Bush Sr when challenged by the White House press corps about the several warnings received prior to the attack. 'Sometimes, by going public, you achieve undue attention to what the terrorist wants to call attention to. But if you want me to say that if we have specific information that a specific flight was going to be specifically targeted and if that information had any credibility to it, then I think that widespread notices should be given. People should well know that they'd be putting their lives at risk.'

The plane had been less than two-thirds full. Flora had no difficulty in obtaining a ticket at the last minute. Many prominent people[10] were known to have cancelled their flight on Pan Am 103 and rebooked on an earlier flight, or cancelled their flights altogether. The warning was widely known, a lot of people had heard it, had acted on it. Only the mugs not on the inside of a system supposed to protect innocent people actually climbed on board. In Jane's words, a trusting Flora walked on board 'like a lamb to the slaughter'. Struggling to suppress my rage I ask: 'Buck, one other question. Your son was booked to fly on that plane. Why did he not get on the plane?'

There's an uncomfortable silence.

'Can you tell us that, Buck? I'm delighted he didn't catch the plane, but why didn't he?'

Revell recovers: 'My son was in Germany, in the army, and his wife came home early. He was able to get leave two weeks earlier . . . I mean, this was two weeks before . . . that he was able actually to come home. It had absolutely nothing to do with what happened. It was just a tragic – ironic – consequence. Obviously I'm delighted he was not on board. But I had absolutely no information – and I was in charge of FBI operations about Pan Am 103. Nor would I ever allow anyone's children to be on a flight that I knew was in jeopardy. Mr Cannistraro – although he was initially involved on the CIA side – he had retired a full year before the indictment was brought against Libya. So all of this is essentially a fabrication and has nothing to do with the facts of the situation.'

Sheena McDonald turns to Francovich. 'You also suggested a covert drugs connection which you allege was being run by American authorities, running drugs from the Lebanon to the United States. This is a fairly extraordinary thing. But you go further. You ask people to believe that there was an inter-agency cover up of a botched drugs operation. And then the US agencies compete with each other to the point where agents of one agency may have to be sacrificed. These are three incredible charges. And yet you claim to have the evidence.'

Francovich takes a deep breath and shuffles higher in his seat: 'Oliver North was running an operation in the Bekaa Valley using the Drug Enforcement Agency starting as early as 1984. I have with me documents from the National Security Council, in which they are discussing operations using Drug Enforcement Agency agents inside the Bekaa, which as Mr

Revell knows is a centre for terrorism and for drug dealing. And these operations were going on in 1984, '85, '86, and in '88, and Cyprus was the pivot point. That operation was penetrated very early on by the other side – the Syrians control the Bekaa – and they have inter-relations with Hezbollah, the Iranians have their bases there, and that's what happened.'

Is Sheena McDonald sensing a kill? 'The drugs connection which Allan Francovich describes, Buck Revell, can you refute that?'

Revell makes a startling admission: 'DEA assets were tasked by orders from the National Security Council to develop information on the American hostages in Lebanon.'

McDonald: 'So there was a legitimate drugs operation being run by the DEA between Lebanon and the United States?'

Revell: 'There was intelligence being gathered and operations being conducted against drug operations, but there was not a cross-over, except on the hostage issue, when all assets of the American government were directed to trying to determine the location of the hostages so that they could be freed under one means or another.'

What can Revell mean by 'cross-over'? And what is the 'one means or another'? What of Steven Donahue, who claimed in the film that he personally observed the transfer and processing of heroin, while working as a DEA asset-monitoring drug operations. He knew Khaled Jafaar and visited the home of the Jafaar clan in the Bekaa Valley.

McDonald is perplexed. 'Frank Duggan, I suggest this is an incredible thing, but is it not impossible that that kind of operation could not have been infiltrated in a way that is suggested in Allan Francovich's film?'

Duggan jumps in his chair: 'I can't . . . I don't know . . . I was not aware of that whole drug operation.'

McDonald: 'So this is fresh information to you. You weren't aware that there was such a legitimate – well, legitimate according to US law – covert operation and—'

Duggan back-paddles furiously: 'Well, subsequently from the public record, there ... there were ... there were drug ... anti-drug operations going on, but they were not going on at that time ... and it's just another ... another something that has been thrown into the pot, to keep stirred up. I mean, I just don't believe that these kinds of things are relevant.'

There it is again, that little word '*public*'.

Francovich is happy. He's dragged us all into his territory. He rumbles onward mentioning the 'Second Channel' group of Iranians used by US Security Adviser Robert McFarlane during the hostage imprisonment, the torture and debriefing of CIA Tehran station chief William Buckley and the sales of arms to Iran as part of the Iran-Contra activities. 'The United States had a back-channel co-operation with Iran, as you know, going back to Robert McFarlane. Oliver North was meeting with the Iranians. They were making deals with them. And there were several people who had very sensitive information about this, including a Brit by the name of Brian Spiro.[11] And all of whom died very mysterious deaths, and it went far beyond just trying to get the Iranians neutral. And I would like to point out that the Americans have intercepts, on radio, communications with the Iranian embassy congratulating the Iranian embassy in Beirut for conducting the Lockerbie operation. After it happened, there was a sum of money that was actually delivered to the PFLP-GC.'

Chubim suddenly asks, 'But if Iran is guilty, why haven't the United States reacted?'

Francovich: 'Iran is a very big country, and if you remember, in the film Mr Howard Teicher with the National Security Council makes the point that it's very easy to push Libya around. It's not so easy to push Syria around, or Iran.'

McDonald concurs, 'Buck Revell, the point that stings is that the focus is entirely on Libya and away from Iran and Syria. Now you suggest that Iran and Syria are still of interest to you, and yet what was very clear was that Iran and Syria were suddenly and – it seems – conveniently no longer in the picture. It does look fishy to say the least.'

Revell: 'Well, it doesn't really if you follow the sequence of the investigation. We were operating on the premise that [Iran] was the responsible party. But we simply could not bring to bear all of the information we had, and the evidence, and make it fit. And then when the microchip was found and identified we found the Libyan connection.'

Will there ever be a trial?

Sheena McDonald asks: 'All of these issues might of course be brought up in a trial. But no trial is currently planned. Do you actually believe there ever will be a trial?'

Teddy Taylor can't hide his dismay. There will never be a trial. The British and American governments aren't interested, for reasons they won't discuss.

Duggan, his disdain for me now quite open, retreats to first base: 'The American relatives want the trial either in the United States or in the United Kingdom, the way the UN resolution demands. They want Colonel Gaddafi to do all the things the UN has called for – to turn over the two suspects, renounce terrorism and to arrange some kind of compensation for the victims. Unless he does those, he's going to stay on that embargo.'

Leppard too cannot hide his disdain, declaring 'The issue here is whether two suspects – indicted for the murder of two hundred and seventy people – should be allowed to set the terms of their trial. There's only two places it can be tried, that's in Scotland or America.'

Revell too sees no need for a trial anywhere other than in Scotland or America. The men are guilty.

But Sheena refuses to see it his way. 'Then why has Libya offered to send the suspects for trial in a neutral country?'

I shoot back with quotations from a letter Prime Minister Thatcher sent to me in the early days of the investigation. She claimed that no specific warnings were received before the Lockerbie disaster, and that neither the Toshiba warning nor the Helsinki warning were found to be relevant. How could she deny there were specific warnings? I was given the Toshiba warning, with a picture of the bomb; my photographs went around the world. An inquiry is imperative, with parts of it in-camera to protect the nation's security. A trial will be the first stage on a journey to that truth.

The debate is over. Now I know for sure, having witnessed it first-hand, out there are the governing classes of Western and Eastern governments. Each use agents and spies of varying degrees of honesty to help them run their countries. Occasionally ordinary citizens get in the way and die. It may be a war, missiles from an aircraft targeting a sleeping neighbour-hood, or it may be a bomb in a plane full of travellers. Yet when the wounded folk try to find out how these untouchables contrive to kill innocents as proxies in their wars, society is denied all access on the grounds of 'national interests'. Whose nation? Whose interests? What is the state for if not for the trust of its citizens?

Revell's transatlantic head smiles. Does he know who killed Flora? He seems a kindly man, a family man, has a mother who makes great apple pie. He denies all knowledge of what has been revealed. His oath prevents it, sworn before the Stars and Stripes, hand on heart or on the Bible.

Sheena McDonald brings the programme to an end, softly the title music plays and we sit silent as the studio lights are dimmed. We've talked well into the small hours. Are any view-ers still watching? More importantly, does anyone care? The lights flood back to fullness, the producer thanks us and I politely say my goodbyes. Then I turn, walk through the studio doors into the polluted air of central London and inhale deeply.

Chapter 9

THE EARL OF Caithness assures all who enquire about airport security that things are safer, the cunning airline terrorist beaten at last. Sadly for the Earl, investigative journalist Roger Cook has never read his letters. Roger has reinforced my marzipan escapade of 1989 and smuggled a fake bomb through airport security across the UK and the Atlantic.[1]

Manchester Airport is said to be among the most secure in the world. Roger's October 1996 programme *The Cook Report* opens with covert filmed footage of a uniformed official taking a brief look at a car containing members of Roger's team and nodding it through into a secure area. Further down the road a second security guard with a wave of the hand allows them to pass even deeper into the complex.

During the 1990–91 Fatal Accident Inquiry, Andrew Hardie QC claimed that the Lockerbie bomb was in an unaccompanied suitcase. There was no evidence for this other than an uncertain record suggesting the existence of an unaccompanied bag. The bomb must have been in some kind of bag, so therefore the unaccompanied suitcase was the guilty one.[2]

Roger and his team decide to stress-test airline detection systems. They construct a dummy bomb based on my marzipan version. At Manchester the bomb is disguised as a parcel and collected onto a freight plane from Manchester to

Ancona in Italy. At Ancona Airport they collect the parcel. On the tarmac stands a large food container with a hole in its cover. Quickly they slide the parcel into the hole then covertly film as the container slides into the hold of a passenger plane.

According to the FBI, the Lockerbie bomb was concealed in a bag checked in by a passenger who then disappeared with deadly consequences. Modern technology – so the Department of Transport claims – prevents that happening again. Baggage tags are identified with barcodes, just like goods in a supermarket. If there is no match and a passenger does not arrive, the bag is taken off the plane. Immediately prior to the plane leaving the gate, a second check establishes whether an unaccompanied bag might have got through the system. That, at least, is the theory.

Yet at Logan International Airport[3] in Boston, Roger's cameraman watches, incredulous, as a bag containing the dummy bomb glides undetected through an X-ray scanner and onto a USAir flight to Buffalo. The operator is facing away from his screen with his feet up, reading a copy of *Sports Illustrated*. Roger's team fail to turn up for the flight, leaving the bag unaccompanied. A member of the team boards the next flight to Buffalo without having his boarding card checked, and collects the parcel at the carousel.

At another major US airport they do not even bother to check a bag in. They label it with a New York address, walk unchallenged into the luggage sorting depot, and put the bag into a container awaiting transfer to a passenger jet. They then travel to New York on a separate flight. The unaccompanied bag is duly delivered by airport courier to the designated New York address.

Cook interviews an airline security expert who admits: 'Every carrier out of the States is carrying unaccompanied baggage, and every bag is a security risk. It just amazes me that we've not lost more aircraft. The airlines admit to up to eight thousand unaccompanied bags a day worldwide. That adds up to several million per year.'

* * *

[Addendum by Peter Biddulph: When I contacted Roger Cook during the editing of this section, Roger kindly added the following information:

Following our programme, but still well before 9/11, one of America's most senior counter-terrorism officers, Bogdan Dzakovic, had his team run their own covert security tests at a number of US airports.

Dzakovic was a fourteen-year veteran of the Security Division of the Federal Aviation Administration in the United States. He began his FAA career as a field agent and Federal Air Marshal, then served as a team leader in the Air Marshal programme. From 1995 he served as a team leader of the FAA's Red Team, conducting undercover tests on airport security through simulated terrorist attacks.

They used not only dummy bombs as we had done, but also potential gunmen and suicide pilots. He testified before the National Commission on Terrorist Attacks upon the United States, discussing his experiences as well as FAA failures that may have contributed to the September 11th attacks.

Dzakovic had regularly reported alarming results to his bosses, and having got no response, decided to go public. He told journalists: 'We were extraordinarily successful in "killing" large numbers of innocent people in these simulated attacks. We breached security with frightening ease – around 90 per cent of the time – but the FAA suppressed our warnings. Instead, we were ordered not to write up our reports and not to retest particularly vulnerable airports to see if the problems had been fixed.

'Finally, the agency started providing advance notification of when we would be conducting our "undercover" tests and what we would be checking. Surprise, surprise: the airports started passing the tests and the FAA praised their progress. In other words, the government was unwilling to go beyond maintaining appearances. It was unwilling to back up the test results with measures that would disrupt the politically powerful air carriers.'

Mr Dzakovic was subsequently demoted to a junior clerical job in the newly formed organisation that has absorbed the FAA and the Transportation Security Administration. He was warned and threatened with criminal prosecution for going public with his concerns. None of his recommendations were followed.[4]

Chapter 10

A NORTH SEA wind whips across Edinburgh's South Bridge, swirling along the granite walls of the university law school. Waiting at the open door is a man who will change my life and, in his special way, help to move the world.[1]

'Jim! You managed to find me! Do come in!'

Robert Black QC, bearded, middle-aged Professor of Law, stocky, a quick mover, has a crisp appearance and an even crisper Scottish accent. He leads me along a corridor to a series of rooms squeezed into an ancient seat of learning. His office floor groans under an antique desk stacked with legal files. Apart from two big leather chairs, each bearing the impress of student rumps over the decades, the floor along each wall is heaped with more files. Almost up to the ceiling cling bookshelves stuffed with official tomes in blue, red and green.

We've come together strangely. William, instead of following me to Cambridge, chose Edinburgh for his degree. I'd heard of Robert's activities through media contacts and resolved to discover what was happening. All I knew is that immediately following the issue of the November 1991 indictments, a group of British firms approached him for his advice.

The coffee's ready. Robert leans over and pours two cups.

'So, Bob, what happened then?' I ask.

The professor sits back in his chair. 'They trooped in here and asked, "Why won't Libya hand them over? Can you help us? There are jobs at stake." They didn't know that Gaddafi's people had already approached the Lord Advocate just across the street from here. He sent them an outline of our legal system. But the Libyans were certain there must be a catch. The company people asked me if the system would work as the Lord Advocate said it would. I gave them my opinion. They in turn passed it to the Libyans as some kind of assurance. In the end, they and the Libyans trusted me. So, it seemed there might be a solution. But until it was signed and sealed, we had to keep things secret.'

'What happened then?'

'I was searching for a "best fit". I had to balance the conflicting needs of the Americans, the British, Libya and the United Nations plus the Arab League. Then it just came to me. Why not have a trial in a neutral country under Scottish law? The first scheme I drafted had the international judges acting as some kind of jury under the direction of a Scot. He would decide on legal issues and give directions on the interpretation of Scots law. I put it to the chief Libyan lawyer for the suspects and to the Libyan government's Lockerbie committee on the 10th of January 1994. Two days later the Libyans came back with a "*Yes*", in writing.'

Back home in Caspidge I relate Robert's words to the British relatives' group and then by fax and phone to the Americans. Gaddafi will never surrender the suspects for trial in Scotland or America. So, what is left other than Robert's formula? All agree it is the way to go.

Robert will become a sincere friend and wonderful travelling companion. From my first emergence as spokesman for the British group he must have seen me as a man obsessed. And now we understand each other well. To me he has been throughout the eminent Professor of International Law for whom I have the greatest respect. I feel I've known the man all my life. I'm told by his friends that he sees me as an honest and good man. Perhaps not entirely true, but I'll go with it.

* * *

SEPTEMBER 1997

Today's headline in the *Sun* newspaper reads: WE'LL NEVER BRING LOCKERBIE BOMBERS TO TRIAL. An anonymous senior government source is claiming, 'The chances of bringing the Libyans to trial are nil. The time has come to move on.'

What on earth are they up to? Are government ministers secretly ready to wash their hands of the Lockerbie dead? The government source concludes, 'What's the point, if it was the Libyans, or anybody else for that matter? It was all so long ago.'

The newspaper the *Scotsman* carries the same story with identical quotes.

For reasons which are patently clear, someone in America or Britain does not want a trial to take place. Hold out long enough and there'll be no trial, no inquiry, no public discussion of all that stuff about drugs and double agents doing their thing across Germany, North Africa and the Mediterranean. As Thatcher has tried to do in her memoirs, the leaders of the free world seem to be hoping that 270 dead people and their bereaved will disappear from history.

I immediately issue a press statement: 'We will never be fobbed off. The government may try to divert us, but they will fail. We and the world want a trial and the truth.'

Sure enough next day comes some back-pedalling, and in the *Mail on Sunday* a denial: 'A Downing Street spokesman claims: "Lockerbie is an issue of the highest importance to the British government."'

A welcome change of direction; but who on earth is that *anonymous senior government source*?

Quite a shock: it's Donald Dewar, First Minister for Scotland! He must have been ambushed by lobby correspondents at a recent Edinburgh dinner.

I aim a furious broadside at Dewar: 'What on earth are you trying to achieve? What of your government's promises?'

Dewar replies apologetically, reversing all his media statements. He assures me of his and the Lord Advocate's full support. Still, I wonder to whom he's been talking and why. People in his position do not make these things up, whatever the vintage of the wine. Somebody in government is testing public opinion, briefing the man and handing him a nicely designed kite.

Sadly, I discover that at a meeting of the UN General Assembly, Foreign Secretary Robin Cook rejected Robert Black's formula for a trial in a neutral country under Scottish law. Cook has made a counter-offer that a Scottish court sitting in Scotland should be attended by Libyan and international observers.

The question is to be discussed by Arab foreign ministers in New York on the periphery of a UN General Assembly meeting. They will examine resolutions adopted at a recent meeting of the Arab League, and consider the latest opinions of the Organisation of Islamic Cooperation (OIC) and the Organisation of African Unity (OAU). I'm greatly encouraged. The Lockerbie case has acquired a regional, Arab and African, dimension.

Three days later Libyan UN representative Abuzed Dorda asks the UN General Assembly: 'How can anyone expect the Security Council to solve the problem when our adversaries are permanent members of the Council and possess the veto power? My country calls on you to intervene so that we can reach a peaceful solution to this dispute. That is, for a trial to be held in any place to be agreed upon, or to be decided by, the Security Council.'

But Cook is adamant, telling the media that the suspects must face trial in Scotland: 'There is no legal authority in the law of the Netherlands for a court of another jurisdiction to sit in The Hague.'

Addressing the UN General Assembly, British UN representative Sir John Weston repeats Cook's stance, adding that observers from the Arab League, the OAU or any similar body would be welcome to attend the trial and monitor its impartiality. Additional facilities would be provided, including daily access to the accused.

My diary is jammed with travel and meetings and reminders. Then comes news that Libya has taken the case to the International Court of Justice (ICJ) at The Hague, accusing Britain and the US of exploiting the Lockerbie bombing for political ends.

Cancelling all those diary appointments I dash over to The Hague, there to witness five days of stubborn resistance by the British and American delegations. The Americans are at times strident, the Libyans always sure of their ground. In a surreal, atmospheric chamber the panel of judges listens intently.

After an adjournment of four months the ICJ conclude that Libya is correct in its claim. Britain and America put on a predictable and transparent show of anger. But even as they splutter and protest a new force is gathering. Deep in the Dark Continent lives a former terrorist-cum-freedom-fighter beatified through suffering, he who will further unlock the story of Pan Am 103.

* * *

In spite of Robin Cook's opposition, we relatives sense progress. Behind the scenes we continue to push Robert's proposal to Libya, the Foreign Office and onward to Washington.

But even the most informed media commentators remain unaware of the reality behind the intermittent media coverage. They speculate about a 'neutral' country, but nobody outside a small circle, which includes Robert Black, the British relatives and the Foreign Office, knows what that means. Libya has

quietly reaffirmed that they agree to Robert's formula. The
Foreign Office, however, remains in formidable lockstep with
the US State Department.

In Edinburgh, in one week's time, will be the October 1997
Commonwealth Heads of Government Meeting – CHOGM.
David Ben Aryeah is in touch with someone close to Nelson
Mandela. The South African president is making a point of
stopping off at Tripoli to meet with Colonel Gaddafi. He will
discuss Lockerbie, and then come to Edinburgh. He's not
forgotten the support he received from Gaddafi during his long
incarceration on Robben Island.

Reuters are reporting Mandela's stern dismissal of
American reservations. In Washington, at a US State
Department briefing by spokesman James Rubin, the questions get around to Lockerbie. A journalist asks: 'Mandela has
used some pretty strong words criticising directly or indirectly
the United States being the "Sheriff of the World". Can you
comment on that?'

Rubin replies, 'President Mandela is now in Libya. We
certainly hope that while he's there he will raise the issue that
has put Libya beyond the pale of the international community
– that is, their refusal to turn over the suspects responsible for
the murder of an enormous number of American and British
citizens over international – well, I don't know exactly – I guess
it was over Scotland, but an international act of terrorism . . .
it was not over that other place . . . (Laughter).'[2]

Following an urgent phone call from David, we British relatives are assembled in Edinburgh. For two days we've been plotting and are ready for action. Everyone's waiting for Mandela's
press conference, the only one during his visit. It will be on
closed-circuit TV in the press centre, and extracts will be
broadcast worldwide.

Mandela comes on screen. The first three questions are
about Nigeria. Then a journalist asks: 'President Mandela,
what do you think about Lockerbie?'

Mandela: 'I am always uncomfortable when a country is complainer, jury and judge.'

Back at the hotel we consider how to react to Mandela's words. A member of our group UK Families Flight 103, Pam Dix, has a letter just in from Tony Blair. He wants to meet us, but it will take time to arrange. Meanwhile, Robin Cook is ensconced in the local Sheraton Hotel. For months we've been badgering him for a meeting. Might he be amenable? We put the word about.

Next morning, at the Stakis Hotel, I'm in the car park with the news cameras. I've already done *Breakfast with Frost*: 'I'm more optimistic now of progress towards a trial. Mandela's view is that justice will not be achieved if the Lockerbie suspects are tried in Scotland.'

Suddenly David Ben Aryeah cuts in with whispered news that Robin Cook's officials are asking for a meeting that afternoon. I quickly change my sound bite: 'Under the previous government we could never have imagined an invitation to meet the foreign secretary at such short notice. The Blair government has inherited a complex problem, and Britain has been linked for years with the American position. To break with that would put pressure on the transatlantic relationship.

'Some American relatives already accept the Libyan view of a trial in a neutral country. Robin Cook has not been well-advised when he says it would be impossible. It's perfectly feasible to hold a Scottish court in a neutral country. The US would have to cooperate with the proposal, since it possesses much of the evidence.'

At five o'clock prompt, up rolls the official car. We squeeze into the rear seats and glide to the Sheraton. The FCO press officer arranges a photo-op in front of the fireplace lining us up like a row of tailor's dummies with Robin Cook in the middle; and then to business.

Robin seems nervous. He listens keenly to our views but struggles a bit when Jane taxes him in her own quiet way, 'Why is a trial in a neutral country so impossible?'

Robin pauses for a few seconds, and then confides in his unique undulation of voice: 'It's not impossible but it would be terribly difficult.'

Tomorrow will be Sunday; the leaders of the world – accompanied by a carefully selected group of journalists – are set to walk, talk and be filmed upon the hallowed fairways of St Andrews. Meanwhile the remaining 900 of the world's media will be kicking their heels in Edinburgh. David prints and distributes hundreds of flyers warning of a big Sunday afternoon press conference to be held at the Stakis.

The 900 duly attend and the hall is packed. Robert Black thunders from the stage; then we relatives break into groups with each of the main TV crews. The message flashes around the world.

Robert feels that the world has moved just a tad, but an important tad: 'I lay in bed all night, my adrenaline flowing, listening to the BBC World Service. It was on every bulletin, with discussions in-between. Every hour there I was, hearing myself saying, "Eventually the British government will do it."'

On his way back to South Africa, Mandela rubs salt in the wound by spending another day with Gaddafi. Twice within ten days, again worldwide publicity. The knives are out. 'What is that Jesus figure doing shaking hands with that evil bastard?'

Meanwhile, enthusiasm for UN and US sanctions is waning. Pope John Paul II enters the discussion, urging an end to all sanctions against Libya. Pressure comes too from President Robert Mugabe of Zimbabwe,[3] chairman of the Organisation of African Unity (OAU). He tells the UN General Assembly that sanctions against Libya are of great concern to his own and other African nations. All this resistance might well prove a clincher for Robin Cook and US Secretary of State Madeleine Albright.

The Foreign Office follows up the Sheraton meeting with a letter summarising the discussions. Cook is described as refusing to accept our view, yet, in our meeting, I really felt that he sympathises with our cause. So why does the Foreign Office persist with such an unwinnable strategy?

The phrase 'Turning the Tanker' comes to mind. Maybe Robin has to contend with more than the relentless American mantra. Perhaps in that Whitehall edifice built long ago to control a third of the planet there remain many Sir Humphreys who themselves must be convinced.

Nevertheless, Cook offers another meeting. And as we again sit around the table in the Foreign Office I sense that behind the friendly stonewalling things really have moved; by Foreign Office standards pretty quickly too. Robin briefs us in some detail, dealing with several *non-sub-judice* questions which we've been invited to submit in advance. As a bonus, he has arranged for us to meet Tony Blair.

Robin might be sympathetic, but when we later meet his Edinburgh colleague, the Scottish Lord Advocate, Andrew Hardie, we again face solid opposition. On 10 October, shortly before the CHOGM gathering, Hardie wrote to me saying – somewhat acidly – 'I do not agree that simply acceding to the wishes of suspected terrorists that they be tried in the venue of their choice presents the simple solution that you suggest, either in principle or in practice.' And in spite of Robin Cook's appearance of sympathy, when we meet Hardie his views are unchanged. I afterwards wrote in my diary: 'Hardie cannot see that history is on our side. He really ought to be more cautious in his dismissal of our campaign.'

* * *

18 March 1998. United Nations Headquarters, New York

On this day Deputy Secretary-General of the UN Louise Fréchette has invited me and several of the relatives to watch a General Council debate on Lockerbie, to be followed by a press conference in the UN press centre. Louise is most welcoming and apologises that Secretary-General Kofi Annan would have loved to be there, but is abroad for a few days.

The debate features an exchange of old discredited philosophies and some extraordinary mental acrobatics by the American and British ambassadors. Do they really think that we will ever give up? In a following press conference they make their determination crystal clear. Later, over lunch, we meet William Richardson, US ambassador to the UN, a man polite but decidedly frosty. We get the clear impression that we are not his favourite people.

* * *

Several more weeks have passed with seemingly no progress. In my darker moments I fear that the relentless mantra by Whitehall and Washington might wear me down. I'm losing touch with how many campaign groups there are, how many members remain in each group, how they feel about passing events. Some American groups are openly hostile. Daniel and Susan Cohen, who lost their daughter Theodora on Pan Am 103, never want to hear from me again. The number of relatives prepared to fight the authorities is reducing. Many have conceded the battle to fate, old age or death. Five other relatives have formed themselves into Terrorism Watch – Aphrodite and Peter Tsairis, Bert Ammerman, Joe Horgan and Peter Lowenstein. Their only wish is for justice and truth. They conclude that whatever arrangements for a trial the US and British governments might accept, Gaddafi is unlikely to release the suspects for trial – 'But if you Brits can persuade Gaddafi to send them to a neutral country for trial, we'll go along with it.'

In April 1998 comes a third meeting with Robin Cook. He is, as ever, courteous and welcoming, but his officials seem nervous. He appears to understand that an absence of truth and justice is adding to our suffering. He alludes mysteriously to 'diplomatic activities being pursued'. After the meeting he tells the press that he was pleased to see the families again. The

British government shares the families' need to see justice done, and he is determined to find a way.

I didn't reveal to Cook my intention to again meet Colonel Gaddafi. He'll get the story from MI6 so why spoil the fun? If the Libyans are using me for propaganda, everything will backfire. Still, nothing ventured, etc. Meanwhile, in the papers, on the internet, some describe me as 'The Man Who Does Not Give Up', and 'Admirable, but a Dupe'.

* * *

APRIL 1998

Out of the blue comes an invitation from Dr Esmet Meguid, Secretary General of the Arab League. The League are supporting Robert Black's proposal for the trial. Within days Robert and I are in hot, noisy and grid-locked Cairo. Somewhat dishevelled we step from the car into a crowd of cameramen and reporters. Holding high my photo of Flora, I remind all of the reason for our visit. The image of my dusty, grim face alongside that of the stunningly beautiful Flora flashes around the world.

Broad-shouldered and smiling, Meguid welcomes us to Arab League headquarters. For two hours we discuss the campaign and what we seek from the international community. Robert crisply adds: 'The British government has been shamed by Nelson Mandela's visit to Tripoli. The World Court and Mandela helped to crack Britain's granite-like stance.'

I study the faces around the room. Ten years have passed; the young reporters seem to know nothing of Lockerbie. Are the older ones listening? Some seem anxious to get away. I try to regain their attention. The British and American governments need their heads knocking together. The Libyans have made big compromises. 'It's about time all sides stopped shouting at each other from the touch-lines. I am not here to talk politics. I am here to talk truth and justice.'

We fly back to London for yet another press conference. At the centre of a circle of blank journalist faces Robert hammers onward undaunted. 'My latest proposal will be my last. If this proposal does not work, this may well be the end of the line. There's a slight chance it will be accepted, but any chance is better than no chance.' As the conference ends a message comes through. Colonel Gaddafi wants to meet us again; within minutes we are on a plane heading for Libya.

The following morning up rolls a Mercedes to take us into the vast Libyan desert, with rolling dunes, scorched rocks and the remnants of ancient civilisations. Out of the haze emerges a huge 4x4. We transfer to it and bounce even deeper into the wilderness.

After two rest breaks we perceive a line of tents shimmering on the horizon. As we get closer we can see it's a tented village. There we wait in an ante-tent with members of the Libyan government. The minutes tick away. The Libyans seem fearful, shuffling and twitching. Foreign Minister Montassa struggles to light a cigarette, his hands shaking.[4]

An attendant ushers Robert and me into a tent reminiscent of the sheikhdoms. Enter a bad-tempered Gaddafi, wearing his traditional brown robe and brown hat. He shakes hands with us, but instead of smiling as before, sits immediately, folds his arms and leans back in his chair, his eyes mere slits searching the roof of the tent.

Four years ago he agreed to a trial in a neutral country, but still Britain and America remain unmoved. Behind our frosty exchanges I detect his true feelings: *My people suffer from your sanctions. You smile and bring presents. What more do you want of me?*

We've travelled far. Failure is in the air. How to soften things? Hoping to bring back memories of our first meeting I try again the bereaved father approach. Gaddafi tosses his head in his unique nervous tick, his mouth curls to a hint of a smile, but his eyes remain dull. Of what is he thinking? Has there been another attempt on his life? Still, he has invited us, so surely he's convinced that we have something that he needs?

Next to Gaddafi, in preparation for light refreshments, stands a low table. As the conversation continues I lower my head and glance under it. A few seconds later I repeat the action, and then a third time.

Gaddafi stops mid sentence. The interpreter anticipates his thoughts: 'The Leader wishes to know why you are looking under the table. Have you dropped something?'

'Oh no,' I venture. 'I'm checking to see if Monica Lewinski might be present.'[5]

Puzzlement breaks across Gaddafi's face, then a dawn of understanding. His head goes back and he roars with laughter.

Soon he is focused on Robert's latest proposal, nodding agreement with each detail. Suddenly he breaks off the conversation and stands, mutters something to the interpreter, quickly shakes hands with us and sweeps out of the tent.

Montassa walks with us to the 4x4. As we settle into the rear he murmurs, 'You made him laugh today. Someone will pay for that.' What can he mean? Who in Gaddafi's entourage would enforce such a punishment, and why?

Back home I contact Reuters: 'Yesterday the Libyans not only renewed their undertaking for a trial in a neutral country – they reinforced it. I don't know what else the Libyan government can do to prove that they mean it when they say they will come to the court.'

The media have guessed that something is afoot so I add, 'Sanctions will never succeed. Why are the British so determined to hold to a position that will not lead to a trial? Could it be that there is material available which will destroy the prosecution case?'

As news of our latest meeting with Gaddafi reaches the US, the American relatives are again furious. Attorney Lee Kreindler tells the media: 'Swire has no authority to make agreements with anyone, least of all the arch villain Gaddafi. Dr Swire represents only Dr Swire. He's not speaking for any of my clients I know of, and I represent between twenty and thirty British families.'

One bereaved relative, Stephanie Bernstein of Bethesda, Maryland, laments that I once more have been duped by Gaddafi. 'Jim Swire must be some kind of fool. It's quite sad, quite tragic.'

The US State Department aims a kick at my shins in the form of spokesman Lee McClenny: 'Libya is obligated under UN Security Council resolutions to deliver the suspects for trial in either the UK or the US. We have no doubt that this latest agreement between Dr Swire and Libya reflects a desire to evade its obligations rather than a willingness to see justice done.'

Back in London a bemused Foreign Office spokesman mutters, 'We would stress that Dr Swire was acting in a private capacity. We hope to speak to him about it.'

I try to remain calm; almost every nation other than Britain and the US knows the sense behind Robert Black's proposal. Does America really believe that sanctions will ever result in the surrender of the accused to the US or the UK? Unless there is compromise over the venue there will never be a trial. We bereaved will go to our graves not knowing for sure who carried out the attack nor seeing them punished. Some American families are destitute, intend to sue Libya for civil damages. Am I harming them by cutting across civil actions they wish to pursue? Yet if the campaign for a trial is abandoned the dead of Lockerbie will be betrayed.

Chapter 11

JANE HAS BEEN so much out of my life lately. She doesn't deserve it. She murmurs, 'Yes, let's go to Skye, get away soon.'

As soon as what? So much left to do. Things are building both sides of the Atlantic. It's two months since that meeting with a frosty Gaddafi. Now I've written to President Bill Clinton to ask that the State Department look into Syrian involvement in the Lockerbie attack.

Clinton assures all that he will investigate President Assad's activities. He refuses to meet the British relatives but is happy for me to talk to his special adviser, Donald K Bandler, in June 1998, at the G7 summit in Birmingham, England.

Bandler welcomes me to the Marriott Hotel overlooking the busy circle of Birmingham's Five Ways interchange. He's a tall, broad-shouldered man, in the up-tick phase of a successful career. As we exchange a handshake, Bandler smiles. He seems well-briefed about this person of interest. As the conversation sours, his strong-jawed smile weakens to a hint of sarcasm.

I remind him that the idea of handing over the two accused for trial in a third country received a cautious welcome in Tripoli. 'Why is America still refusing to look at Robert Black's proposal? Why will you not trust the word of Colonel Gaddafi?'

Bandler looks at me politely but dismissively: 'The Libyans will never hand them over.'

'Then what plan does your president have to break the deadlock?'

Bandler can find no words to explain his position and we part coldly, each faithful to his own understanding of the world.

In the background, a process so far ignored by the Americans is coming off the rails. The Organisation of African Unity (OAU) recently met in Burkina Faso. They received a report from a five-man delegation that recently visited the UK and met with Robin Cook. The OAU threat is that if Robert Black's formula is not immediately accepted by both the UK and the US, the OAU will cease compliance with UN sanctions. Libya is surrounded on three sides by OAU member nations. Without their cooperation, sanctions will crumble rapidly. To help force things to a conclusion, Libya intends to challenge the sanctions resolutions in the International Court of Justice at The Hague, and will probably win.

* * *

21 JULY 1998

Jane has finally got her way; Skye at last. But, mind, it will be a short holiday, then back to work on *Justice for Flora*. We're relaxing in the lounge of our favourite hotel. Just before we left home I'd detected rumours that something was about to break. We raced through every speed trap between Bromsgrove and Skye. Will I be prosecuted? I can but hope that the powers that be are, for this most special day, kindly disposed.

'*This is the BBC news. A decision has been reached in the dispute over where the trial should be held of the two Libyans suspected of involvement in the Lockerbie bombing.*'

At last! America and Britain have agreed to Robert's proposal. In a complete reversal of policy the Foreign Office are not only accepting but promoting – and claiming credit for – the concept of a trial in the Netherlands before a panel of Scottish judges. Gaddafi won't agree to an all-Scottish panel. Still, after years of stonewalling, the governments of

Britain and America have conceded and final agreement seems close.

The American relatives have been alerted to expect an announcement but remain wary; the US and Britain might even now be stalling, hoping for some kind of way out. 'Sources' inside the Foreign Office are briefing journalists that it might take several years to arrange a trial. But Robert is sure that the authorities can set up a trial in a matter of days – if they want to.

The world's media are going frantic for news and quotes. David Ben Aryeah is filling the hotel office with faxes from all over the world. Messages are flooding in from members of the British group. *Is it all a dream?* At last I feel on home ground, among my ain folk. The phones are going crazy and the switch-board girl downstairs is having problems. Just in case, I brought along my mobile phone and a fax machine.

I tell every caller, 'I'm pleased . . .' It sounds so ordinary. But how dare a man say, 'I loved my daughter so deeply that I found a way to move the world'? No. Too vain, too presumptuous; many people have been involved, have struggled, have supported us in their own special ways.

The phones are ringing in chorus so I move out of earshot and try to arrange a few words inside my head. Too late; a phone fires off, then another and I'm into an interview, juggling landline, mobile phone and emotions. I'm on a roller coaster of triumph and sadness, sweet sadness that Flora will at last find truth and justice.

BBC Scotland journalist Shelley Jofre rolls in with a camera crew.[1] So often in defensive, protective mode with my family, this day I'm open-hearted, unfettered, elated yet calm, deeply calm. Jane goes willingly with Shelley's agenda and leads me by the hand. Such a strange feeling, so many friendships formed, a decade of anger, sadness, failure. At last we're on our way to achieving results. So just for Shelley and the cameras I re-play the phone juggling act.

Shelley wants to do some filming outside. Close by stands Orbost, a great lonely house that has moved in and out of the Swire family for generations. Here my parents met as children, became sweethearts and got engaged. It looks south across Loch Bracadale, and beyond its boundary walls lies a meadow that flows down to the ocean.

Shelley asks us to walk arm in arm down to the beach and round again while the camera rolls. A blue sea stretches to the Isle of Rum that Cathy, when still a tiny girl, christened 'Crocodile Island', after its twin peaks like a crocodile's eyes. A breeze rolls from the south, and beyond the bay the peaks of the Cuillins are crowned with wispy clouds. Suddenly, from deep within my boyhood memory comes a clear December night when my mother silently woke me, wrapped me in an eiderdown, carried me out to this same field white with hoarfrost, and we watched as Northern Lights danced among the stars.

We sit down, heads, arms, angles set by Shelley, me sitting on the warm turf, Jane resting on my shoulder, beyond us the sea and mountains, and the camera rolls again. Still on euphoric autopilot I'm rattling on about the media – '. . . you have to be prepared, and if you aren't ready like a proverbial Boy Scout and da de da de da . . .'

Jane cuts right across my ramblings. 'Well, *things* will settle down now . . .' Funny how she's been at my side all these years and I never guessed how she would see the moment. Now is Jane's time, on this meadow by a Scottish sea.

'We'll enjoy a *family* holiday,' she says.

I chip in, 'Oh, yes—'

She stops me short. '*And* we have William coming tomorrow evening and Cathy next week. So we're all with friends, we will enjoy it and have a family holiday in peace and quiet, I hope. We used to have lovely family holidays here with the children and they loved the freedom and the beach, and friends at the farm, and cousins to play with.'

Months later Shelley comes to Caspidge and completes the programme for screening just before the tenth memorial service in Westminster Abbey, scheduled for 21 December 1998.

She persuades us to dig out some family photographs and films. As my old 8mm-film clatters through its shutters I whisper, 'Glorious. I haven't seen these for years . . .' Splashing in tiny wavelets on the shore is baby Flora, eager to go deeper, me so much younger, paddling protectively between her and the deep water.

Jane smiles, 'This is Skye. I'm trying to keep her out of the sea. She wanted to go in. I'm sure it was cold. I'd completely forgotten how they walk in such funny ways when they're little.'

I cannot hide my feelings a moment longer: 'Flora was always wanting to know why something happened, why this, and why that. And eh . . . you know what dads are like about their daughters, and, urm . . . she really was a stunner because she had that lovely Celtic colouring of dark hair and blue eyes . . .' Suddenly I'm weeping.

Jane helps out: 'I wish I could feel anger. Anger is such a positive thing. It can help you through that terrible gutting sadness, the anguish. Jim felt anger. I envied him his anger. He's asking a lot of questions and he wants them answered.'

Now I can see it, Jane's heart. Squeezed into this moment, her anguish, the extra burden I've placed there, silently and lovingly born through the years. Torn between her anguish and what I must do for Flora, I've added to her suffering, always spirited away in search of something I could never clearly define. As I look into the camera, and behind it the puzzled eyes of Shelley Jofre, at last I understand. I'm humbled, all resolve gone; I've faced the world's press, robed judges, ministers, dictators, yet with a few glistening tears the true cost is revealed.

And what of William, grown to manhood, and Cathy soon to be married? William has been – throughout the campaign

– at my shoulder, hearing much, saying little. Cathy was so close to Flora. How can sisters embrace at the airport gate, kiss each other on the cheek, whisper goodbye, each murmur containing a lifetime of friendship, love, sisterhood – and part so cruelly? Cathy's final memory of Flora has been that moment of parting and an echo of their songs. And for Jane the eternal pain of the mother mourning her child, nurtured from that first creative moment through to a brutal death.

There is to be a trial, but what comes next? Even if found guilty the two accused are but minnows in a huge pond. Are more dark forces waiting to show their hand? If the trial is delayed I will not know what to do. Maybe the campaign will never end. Maybe those 270 poor souls will never find rest.

* * *

8 AUGUST 1998

At this critical stage, something our campaign can well do without, a former MI5 officer, David Shayler, is claiming that MI6 knew of a plot to assassinate Gaddafi. He says that an MI6 agent was present at a meeting when the plot was in its early stages. The attempt took place in February 1996. Shayler has been arrested in France at the request of the British government, but before the police could get to him he's talked to the BBC. His interview is to be screened on BBC's *Panorama*.

Shayler joined MI5 in 1994, working on the G9 Libyan Desk. At a joint meeting with MI6, he heard of an agent known as Tunworth. Also at the meeting was agent PT16B, who controlled Tunworth. Shayler tells of British collaboration with an extremist group in Libya trying to kill Gaddafi. He claims that he later learned that as the plot gathered pace, £100,000 was paid to Tunworth for his role. Shayler maintains, 'I was absolutely astounded . . . My thinking up to then on MI6 was that they were involved in a sort of *Boys' Own* comic, and suddenly this was very real.'

BBC journalist Mark Urban has evidence confirming that meetings did take place with PT16B, that Britain had advance knowledge of the attempt on Gaddafi's life and that Tunworth was a go-between with Islamic militant groups in Libya.

Foreign Office ministers at the time of the affair have been questioned by journalists and deny any authorisation for a murder attempt. Notably, not one of those interviewed has denied that MI6 knew of the attack in advance. Experts on intelligence suspect that the security services acted without political authority. Sources within the BBC claim that more evidence of Secret Intelligence Services activities exists, but is being withheld for security reasons.

An injunction to protect national security has delayed the *Panorama* broadcast. In this land of the free, the BBC is being allowed to transmit only after scrutiny and censorship by government solicitors and MI5. In the uncensored sections Shayler alleges that authority for the assassination came 'from the very top of the Foreign Office'. The prime minister's office states that such a plot is 'inconceivable'.

I call a press conference at Caspidge and issue a furious statement: 'It is now over five hundred weeks since my daughter was murdered at Lockerbie. As I speak, in Tripoli the head of the Arab League is meeting Gaddafi to persuade him to release the two suspects. The last thing we want are allegations that British agents have been in any way involved in a plot to kill him.'

I remind the media that in July 1986 Prime Minister Thatcher was part of an international attempt to assassinate Colonel Gaddafi, leader of a sovereign nation.[2] I follow up my statement with a letter to Home Secretary Jack Straw, reminding him that without a thorough investigation into the role of intelligence, conspiracy theories will prosper. I have no way of knowing how Gaddafi has reacted or whether it will destroy our efforts to bring about a trial of the two suspects. Meanwhile Robin Cook, on the *Breakfast with Frost* show, does his utmost to repair the damage, denying emphatically all of the Shayler allegations.

* * *

20 AUGUST 1998

Fortunately, Gaddafi seems to have handled the Shayler affair well. Perhaps he already knew it all through the efforts of his own security machine. Meanwhile Prime Minister Blair, while claiming a determination to make progress, assumes that Gaddafi will have no objection to a panel of Scottish judges. His assumption creates some puzzlement. Is he trying to delay matters?

A few days ago in Tripoli the team of lawyers representing Fhimah and al-Megrahi were dismissed, to be replaced by a new team including a former Libyan foreign minister. Washington and London interpret this as a sign that Gaddafi wants to accept Blair's new offer. They hint at a strengthening of sanctions if Gaddafi refuses. It is, they say, non-negotiable.

But Gaddafi does not trust Blair. He sits tight and says nothing. And one month later he again invites Robert and me to Tripoli. He wants to find out what we know, and explore what might be possible. Sanctions on air flights are still in place, and we have to land at Djerba in Tunisia for a long drive to Tripoli and Hotel Al Mahari. The hotel staff welcome us as if it's a homecoming.

Late at night we are whisked off for a midnight meeting at the Justice Ministry with Kamal Maghur, a member of the new defence team. The man is articulate, intelligent, friendly and professional. He listens intently to Robert's account of recent events.

Even as we meet with Maghur, news comes that the location for the trial is to be Kamp van Zeist, a former NATO base to which the United States still has treaty rights of access. Will this news cause the Libyans to renounce the 'neutral venue' concept? Fortunately, the Libyan Justice Ministry makes no reaction. Robert believes that this, more than anything, proves that the Libyans genuinely wish a trial to take place.

Next day a 4x4 takes us close to Gaddafi's home town of Sirte. We bounce through sand dunes to his latest tent, brightly coloured and surrounded by ruminating camels. As we enter he rises to greet us, leaning heavily on a silver-handled walking stick. On his head is a white straw Panama hat. He's touched when I ask if his recent hip operation went well.

Robert gives a concise analysis of the legal position and an outline of the British scheme. Gaddafi accepts their assurance that some of his concerns are unwarranted. All agree that should further clarification be needed, the most trustworthy route will be via the Secretary-General of the United Nations.

After two hours we rise to leave, with the clear impression that Gaddafi's almost ready to hand over the two suspects. On the table before us lies his Panama hat. I take off my tartan tie and suggest a trade. Gaddafi smiles and swaps trophies. I will later discover that the hat won't fit.

We drive back to Tripoli, then Djerba, then fly to London Gatwick. Robert takes an inland flight to Edinburgh. Meanwhile, David Ben Aryeah, with the help of Scottish TV, has arranged a car to speed me to Brighton to address a fringe meeting of the Liberal Democrat Conference. Fourteen Arab ambassadors are in the audience. I get a standing ovation and an invitation to dinner.

Poor Robert! He always misses the fun bits. He's never met Tony Blair, nor those American relatives still willing to speak to me. Nor did he meet Tiny Rowland, a man reviled by some in the British media, but a wonderful, kind – and strong – personality. In 1993, Tiny's personal funding of *The Maltese Double Cross* restored welcome momentum to the campaign just when we feared that the world had forgotten us. I never could work out how I found a way into Tiny's heart. By the time I summoned up courage to ask, Tiny had died,[3] leaving behind his lovely widow, Josie, who remains among our close friends.

Within days we enjoy a long and friendly session at the Foreign Office with Robin Cook. We make a special point of thanking him for Foreign Office help in bringing about this major shift in policy, particularly that of the US State Department. It's been no mean achievement. Robin admits that our campaign helped tremendously to move things along: 'It has been impressive.'

* * *

30 November 1998

UN Secretary-General Kofi Annan is to travel to Libya to agree final details for the handover of the suspects. Meanwhile, Gaddafi is under intense pressure from the Arab League and the OAU to formally and publicly accept the trial offer and release the two suspects. It is understood that Mandela and the Egyptian government are also advising him to accept.

Annan will go to Libya when it is certain that the two accused will be handed over. Only then will the Security Council be recommended to lift some of the sanctions. When talking to reporters Annan seems optimistic, but behind the scenes, however, his team are refusing to speculate as to how Gaddafi will respond.

A hopeful sign is that only one sticking point is coming from Libya: if convicted, the suspects must serve their sentences in either the Netherlands or Tripoli. Britain and the US, however, are adamant that the sentences will be served in a Scottish prison.

Before he leaves for his Gaddafi meeting, Annan expresses hope of an impending solution: 'I think we have offered most of the clarifications. I had hoped we would be able to bring the issue to closure.'

* * *

2 DECEMBER 1998

Today comes at last – our British relatives' visit to Downing Street. Prime Minister Blair speaks of the efforts he and his ministers have made over many months to try to bring about a trial. He fully supports the need to explore new avenues that might emerge from evidence to be revealed at the trial. He tells us, 'We thought that the Lockerbie situation was set in stone. Then we heard the voice of the relatives.' Flora would be proud to hear that.

The media is in hyperdrive. I tell the press of my hope that the suspects will soon be handed over for trial, but remain cautious. And today comes an invitation to again meet Excellency Abuzed Dorda, Libyan Permanent Representative to the UN. He invites our group to his residence in Geneva and explains his assessment of progress. Later, when back in London, I report to the Foreign Office on our visit, and in return discover that Kofi Annan wants to meet Dorda as soon as possible.

* * *

21 DECEMBER 1998

'You must clear the order of service with us,' say the Westminster Abbey administrators. John Mosey and I humbly comply. Nothing must be allowed to interfere with our tenth anniversary memorial service.

We park the car at the side entrance, unload my specially constructed ladder of candles, carry it into the hallowed nave and assemble it. The administrators inspect it, suck their teeth, and say, 'You'll have to make it fireproof.'

So we put each of the 270 candles into a new fireproof metal cup, securing each on roll after roll of aluminium kitchen foil. It stands before the centuries-old altar screen looking most out of place. An assistant helps as we rehearse the candle lighting ceremony. He offers a couple of oil canisters disguised as candles, each with long tubes and tiny wicks. They've been lighting candles at the Abbey for a thousand years, so surely they are the experts?

The BBC is reluctant to broadcast the service, but John has persuaded them to record it and hand over the film.

The cathedral fills rapidly. Robin Cook arrives flanked by officials. Tony Blair is followed by his deputy, John Prescott. Robin and Tony have delayed their Christmas holidays to be here.

Robin, Tony and John sit on the front row, with officials and detectives on each side. Behind John sits Cecil Parkinson, his silver hair bright in the half light. Just along from him is John Mosey's wife, Lisa, and beside her Tiny Rowland's widow, Josie. Finally, Prince Andrew, Duke of York, arrives, led to his seat by the Dean. Thus, facing John and me, ten feet away, are a prince of the realm, a prime minister, a foreign secretary and a deputy prime minister, and behind them a former secretary of state for transport.

There is to be a trial in a neutral country, but still the suspects wait in Libya. The British and Americans are turned, Gaddafi is almost turned. On this night all who might still harbour doubts will receive a little encouragement.

The searing cry of a mother's lament for a son lost in war, Gorecki's *Symphony of Sorrowful Songs*, rises to the great arched roof. Amid the shadows, stone faces of sinners and angels look down impassively as they have for centuries while humanity mourns.

Jane leads the opening prayer, written by Richard Phillips, Dean of Hendricks Chapel, Syracuse University: 'We are joined this night with the town and people of Lockerbie, the dead of Wilmington Virginia, the University of Syracuse and countries around the world. Once again we mourn the loss of two hundred and seventy lives. We pray for a terror-less world, and together affirm the beauty of life and love.'

Skye piper Hector McLean intones *Flowers of the Forest*. Then, in order, the world is reminded of the names of the dead. Each of the relatives present reads a section containing the name or names of their loved ones; Jane reads the section ending with *Flora MacDonald Swire* and passes the book to the next reader. The name of every victim is thus spoken firm and clear.

As the names echo across the aisles, John Mosey's son Marcus helps me to light – as each name is spoken – a candle on the ladder of candles. All rest upon a painted black wooden frame with a large mirror at each end, and as you stand before it a river of light flows away to infinity.

But as we light the candles, we forget that the oil canisters are designed only for use in an upright position. Something's gone wrong with Marcus' lighter and the fuel is running out, spreading in large puddles. I hurriedly light a wax taper, hand it to Marcus, and we resume, until the entire ladder gleams with lighting fluid below the menacing flicker of 270 candles.

Just in case, I've installed beneath it all a fire extinguisher. My problem is that if a fire takes hold I'll have to make a dive for it, and the security men around the prime minister will misunderstand. They'll bring me down with a flying tackle into a rolling scrum of bodies, a roaring ladder of candles will reach glorious to Heaven and a prince of the realm and a prime minister will find themselves at a memorial service they will never forget.

Quite unaware of the problem, John stands to deliver his sermon. The lights are set low. All eyes focus on John and the ladder of candles, while I sit trembling, rehearsing how to get to the extinguisher, which button to press, where to aim.

'It is not my normal habit to write out my sermons,' begins John. 'But it's good for you that I have written down what I want to say or else, because of the feelings and thoughts that are in my heart, you would be kept here far longer than the few minutes that I have permitted myself. In each memorial service for the Lockerbie dead I have spoken of the blood of two hundred and seventy innocent people crying from the Scottish hillsides, "Why?" Why was this preventable act of murder allowed to happen? I'm often asked if I am looking for justice. People assume that I am. They are wrong. In the world of international politics justice remains a difficult concept. It implies an eye for an eye, my pound of your flesh and retribution. And yet my daughter is dead because of retribution. You see, the real damage is to the heart. And no amount of retribution can heal it. So, how can the heart be restored? I believe that for the sake of civilised society we must continue to pursue the motto that is on our campaign badge, "The truth must be known".[4]

The camera cuts to a prime minister and foreign secretary on the edge of their seats, listening intently.

After the service, some come forward to admire the by-now safe ladder of candles. John Prescott slowly shakes my hand. 'Very moving . . .' he says.

Prime Minister Blair and Robin Cook talk hopefully of the trial and its aftermath. I stay chatting to Cecil Parkinson and Josie Rowland. Prince Andrew, Duke of York, is busy pressing the flesh in the main aisle. The departing crowd builds up behind him. Eventually he gets to John Mosey and shakes his hand. John, still running on adrenaline, jokes: 'So it's you that's holding things up!'

Prince Andrew grins sheepishly. 'Yes, this job does have its hazards.'

* * *

On this day, 16 June 1999, President Nelson Mandela of South Africa is to retire. He addresses his nation, and with the help of the media, the world:

There must be a kernel of morality to international behaviour. Of course, nations must place their own interests high on the list of considerations informing their international relations. But the amorality which decrees that might is right cannot be the basis on which the world conducts itself in the next century.

It was pure expediency to call on democratic South Africa to turn its back on Libya and Qaddafi, who had assisted us in obtaining democracy at a time when those who now made that call were the friends of the enemies of democracy in South Africa.

Had we heeded those demands, we would have betrayed the very values and attitudes that allowed us as a nation to have adversaries sitting down and negotiating in a spirit of compromise. It would have meant denying that the South African experience could be a model and example for international behaviour.

In many ways, our modest contribution to resolving the Lockerbie issue will remain a highlight of the international aspects of our Presidency. No one can deny that the friendship and trust between South Africa and Libya played a significant part in arriving at this solution. If that be so, it vindicates our view that talking to one another and searching for peaceful solutions remain the surest way to resolve differences and advance peace and progress in the world. We look forward with joy and anticipation to the full re-entry of Libya into the affairs of our continent and the world.

* * *

As Christmas 1999 approaches, Lord Advocate Hardie is rumoured to have regretted his decision to take on the Lockerbie prosecution and has resigned. Does he view the prosecution evidence as too weak? The Scottish Executive moves quickly, replacing him with Solicitor General Colin Boyd QC. In America, bereaved relatives Daniel and Susan Cohen ask: 'Does Hardie fear this is a bad case? What are we supposed to think?'

Boyd invites the British relatives to meet him at Dover House in London. He reassures us that things will proceed as before. He intends also to meet the American families and US Attorney General Janet Reno. He explains that two experienced senior counsels, Alastair Campbell and Alan Turnbull, will present the bulk of the prosecution case. The evidence, he claims, is sound.

The Trial

Chapter 12

OVERNIGHT WE DID not sleep. In driving rain I take the last of the bags down to the car. We're running late. The road to Harwich will be wet and tricky.

I pause to gaze at the portrait of Flora. Her backdrop is the Isle of Skye, where she is buried alongside her grandparents. In her hand she clutches a posy of wild flowers. Her image is as I remember her; her vitality, humour, her quick wit, that devastating smile that never failed to melt a father's heart. I whisper to her, 'This is it, the final piecing together.' Rightly or wrongly, I've pushed and pushed for this trial to take place. I need to know that Flora would be proud of what I've done: everything in my power to ensure that she and the other victims are not forgotten. I stand tall before the mirror and pin a badge to my lapel: *PanAm 103. The truth must be known.*[1]

As England fades into the mist, anger again swells within me. Why did they ignore those warnings of a bomb? How could they direct that a suspicious item should go into the hold six feet below sleeping passengers? Why do they still refuse to answer a father's questions? And yet today is a new day. A gust of wind washes over me carrying the scent of the sea, and suddenly I feel a loosening of anger, a sense of relief.

* * *

It has taken a day to get here. We are standing before a huge residential block in a municipal housing zone on the outskirts of Zeist. Somewhere here is a flat found for us by a friend, Ingebourg van Teeseling, a lecturer at Utrecht University.

As the door of the flat swings open Jane is speechless. Ingebourg has done all she can and has painted the walls of what should be a three-bedroom comfortable home. But there's hardly any furniture; there's no cooker, the electricity isn't working and the lavatory won't flush. In silence we tour the rooms. It's so dark that we can't see properly. Jane takes my torch, the one I used for peering down people's throats when a practicing doctor, and shines it across the kitchen. Its thin beam picks out dust and a broken sink. She sighs: 'Good job I brought lots of cleaning stuff.'

* * *

Overnight, again, neither of us slept. Kind friends have donated some furniture but still we must sleep on a mattress on the floor. There's also a cheap carpet so no need to sit on concrete any longer. Two kind journalists from the *Express* newspaper have purchased a kettle. There's a one-ring electric stove and Jane, like a resourceful trooper, makes porridge. We sit on the mattress and wolf it down. My back is aching.

The really good news is that Ingebourg has found us a sofa; but it's sixty kilometres away in Amsterdam and we'll have to go and collect it. We hire a van and drive with Ingebourg to Amsterdam and a quaint old house that stands beside a canal. The kind donor is happy for us to take the sofa. But it's in an upstairs room and the narrow twisty stairs of the old house mean that it will have to be swung out via a window onto a pulley and hook and lowered to the ground. With the help of the donor we load it into the van.

As we arrive back at the flat a message comes through on the phone that a preliminary trial hearing is to be held this after-noon. There's no time to get the sofa upstairs so we leave it in the foyer with a note saying it isn't junk and is not to be thrown out. When we arrive back at the end of the day the very respectable sofa has gone and in its place the most filthy broken-down sofa imaginable. Ah well, back to the mattress.

* * *

Kamp van Zeist's court building is constructed on the site of a former NATO military barracks. Some in the media comment wryly on the cost of its conversion from barracks to court complex, some £60 million.

It's modelled on the International Criminal Tribunal recently set up at The Hague to try suspected war criminals of the Yugoslavian wars. A spectator gallery faces the judge's bench. To the left of the gallery will sit the accused, each with his own entry door. They arrived at Kamp Zeist two weeks ago and have been processed and well prepared.

In front of them, on opposite sides, will sit the prosecution and defence teams; between all these, court officials, and above them, four judges. Three judges will hear the trial and deliver judgement; the fourth will be present in case any of the others fail to survive what is expected to be a long trial. On the wall above the judges' chairs, magnificent against a deep scarlet background, hangs the great seal of Scottish Justice.

More than 1,200 witnesses across several continents have been interviewed and many will come to court. Screens will protect the identity of those whose identity must, for security reasons, remain hidden.

Within the court will be two individuals of particular interest: US attorneys Brian Murtagh and Dana Biehl will represent the US Department of Justice. They will sit close to the prosecution team, passing to them advisory notes and legal papers, or leaning over with whispered advice.

For this preliminary hearing I discover that I am the only relative in court – the others (including Jane, who is back at the flat) want to wait until the trial proper begins next week.

As the two defendants are brought into the courtroom my heart starts to pound. I find myself staring at the men seemingly proved by a wealth of evidence to have killed my daughter. Expecting a flush of emotion I try to control it by digging my nails into my palms, but – astonishingly – feel no reaction. Perhaps I've studied them so many times in photographs and videos that I've grown numb.

Their families are here. Sitting in the spectator gallery tiny sons and daughters reach out in greeting to their fathers. A tremendous surge of hope wells up inside me that whatever happens in this courtroom over the coming months will be scrupulously fair. I will find no joy in seeing children separated from their fathers. There must be justice for the defendants as much as for Flora. My mind turns to thoughts learned long ago:

> . . . On a huge hill,
> Cragged and steep, Truth stands, and he that will
> Reach her, about must, and about must go,
> And what the hill's suddenness resists, win so.[2]

Amid this turmoil of emotion mingles a deep sense of relief. I've fought hard for the things that I might influence. Airport security is vastly improved. But what is about to transpire within this courtroom is out of my hands. The burden will be carried by others.

Part of my grieving process has been to see the perpetrators brought to justice. To achieve it, my family has become public property. No longer a country doctor and wife, we are defined by the night that murderers slaughtered our eldest child. Jane's way would have been to grieve in private, but I am driven to positive action, compelled to change the world for Flora. It was this trait that first attracted her when we met as students at Cambridge. To her credit, she's never tried to rein me in.

* * *

3 MAY 2000. THE TRIAL: DAY 1

Again for us both a sleepless night, tossing and turning, thinking of Flora. What has all this done to our family? Catherine and William loved Flora dearly. But there must have been times they felt frustrated that the focus was forever on Flora. Have they secretly wanted to scream '*WE* are still here!'? Jane is still plagued by those dreams of Flora. *If only I'd been there when Flora needed me in her final moments . . .*

We walk into the court holding hands and sit facing the two accused. It is stiflingly hot. When leaving England, and fearing the worst, we packed warm clothing. Thankfully, Jane has lately purchased some short-sleeved shirts.

I gaze again at the defendants. I've chosen my seat with care – directly behind the witness stand so that the judges will always be aware that I am here. Jane is surprised at how they have aged. She confesses to an overwhelming desire to walk over to them and whisper, 'Did you do it? Did you take my Flora from me?'

We listen to the details of how the bomb was allegedly planted.

I have prevented your death becoming a mere statistic. In that ice rink, that tiny room, I saw and touched the smoothness of that mole on your toe. I stood alone beside you for endless moments and you said nothing. I keep your lock of hair close to me always. How would you be now? A glittering career in medicine, husband, family, babies?

Anger wells from below. I reach for Jane's hand.

As the spectator gallery fills I spot that the witness TV monitor has an advantage over the two hanging above the spectators. I can see what a witness will see on screen, and watch the faces of the lawyers. The glass between the spectator gallery and the court is sound- and bulletproof. Only by wearing a closed-circuit headset may I listen to the words.

The American relatives are grouped to our right. John Mosey is to our left, leaning against the wall so as to ease his severe back pain. We will occupy these same seats for the entire trial. A few journalists have found a way to get in. Their colleagues will have to make do with a crowded press centre in a former gymnasium some distance from the courthouse.

Jane has gone back to the flat, cleaning and stocking up on food. Alone through the day she will worry about our cash. Our campaign has already cost us thousands. The flat costs almost £300 a month, every short visit back to England adding a further £100. She convinces herself that we will cope.

Al-Megrahi is represented by Alistair Duff, with advocates William Taylor QC, David Burns QC and John Beckett. Fhimah's solicitor is Edward MacKechnie, with advocates Richard Keen QC, Jack Davidson QC and Murdo Macleod.

The clerk to the court stands and addresses the judges. I am astonished when Duff and MacKechnie launch a special defence citing two organisations and ten individuals whom they say were responsible for the bombing. Some of the names are new to me. Most seem untraceable. The defence will not mention this again. They will give no reason for their omission.[3]

Memoirs can at times be tiresome to read. Detail takes over. If my account of this trial becomes in any way tedious I hereby apologise. I know, however, no other way of presenting to you what is probably the most complex mass murder trial in British history. Please be patient and all will, I hope, become clear.

The key elements of the prosecution's case are:

- In 1985, as members of the Libyan security service, Abdelbaset al-Megrahi and Khalifa Fhimah were involved in the receipt of a batch of twenty MST-13 electronic timers from the Swiss electronics company MEBO AG.

- Three years later, one of those timers was used in the construction of a bomb contained in a radio-cassette recorder which exploded in-flight over Lockerbie.

- On 7 December 1988 – two weeks before the bombing – al-Megrahi purchased a quantity of clothes and an umbrella from the shop Mary's House at Tower Road, Sliema, Malta.

- A witness to the purchase of the clothes was Maltese shopkeeper Tony Gauci, owner of Mary's House.

- On 21 December 1988 at Luqa Airport, Malta, al-Megrahi and Fhimah placed or caused to be placed on board Air Malta flight KM 180 to Frankfurt Airport a suitcase containing the said clothing and umbrella, and the said improvised explosive device concealed within a Toshiba RT-SF16 'Bombeat' radio-cassette recorder.

- The unaccompanied suitcase was tagged so as to be carried by aircraft from Frankfurt via London's Heathrow Airport to John F. Kennedy Airport, USA.

- An eyewitness to the insertion of the suitcase by avoiding the check-in desk at Luqa was al-Megrahi's co-worker at Luqa airport, Majid Giaka.[4]

- British forensic scientists Dr Thomas Hayes and Allen Feraday discovered that a fragment of an electronic timer found at the crash site came from one of the MEBO electronic timers delivered to Libya in 1985. The fragment was compared with sample boards supplied to the Scottish police by the original manufacturers, Thüring. Materially and structurally it exactly matched the samples.

* * *

4 May 2000. The trial: Day 2

Residents of Lockerbie tell of the night their town became a by-word in the history of terrorism.

Lockerbie resident Roland Stephenson recalls waiting for his daughter in the shadows of an empty car park at the town's railway station. As he listened to his car radio the train pulled in; after a few seconds, with a quaint *toot* it rumbled off into the darkness.

Just then he became aware of a strange noise that drowned the sound of the train. He got quickly out of his car to take a look, and from the north '. . . It was thunderous. It was coming at a shallow angle, travelling from the extreme right to the extreme left of the town. I could see objects descending. Black objects which I wouldn't know what they were, but they were black objects hurtling down towards the Sherwood Crescent end of the town from above.'[5]

One of those black objects was Flora. With her from above the clouds glided the wings still heavy with fuel. And then the huge white shape of the cockpit, the crew strapped in their seats, slams into the turf of the field of Tundergarth Mains.

More memories of horror from the skies replay. I force my mind into an un-hearing numbness. At the end of the day I face a round of quick-fire questions from reporters. I sat up late last night memorising a statement, but my bottle's gone and I have to read it. They react well to my trembling and become gentler. I am grateful for their restraint.

I travel back to the flat, eat scrambled eggs and fall exhausted onto the mattress. I knew today would be tough. There's a whole year of it to come.

* * *

5 MAY 2000. THE TRIAL: DAY 3

I'm grateful Jane is not here today. The names of 270 dead people are being read out. Eleven years ago I learned them by heart and can still remember. Some of their families are my friends; some are not. I know the intimate details of many of their lives. Nothing is said about the injured and maimed of the town. To my shame I do not know how many, nor any of their names.

As the list is read I lock my eyes onto the faces of the accused. I'm looking for signs of guilt, the slightest gesture. Their expressions remain impassive. I wait anxiously for Flora's name. Will the court officials stumble over it? I want it to ring out pure and true.

It takes three quarters of an hour to arrive. *Flora MacDonald Margaret Swire.* Gone in a second. Who in Holland, in this court, knows that her family, MacDonald, is linked to the rescue of Bonnie Prince Charlie from the English Redcoats by another Flora MacDonald?

As the day ends, Jane and I drive around Utrecht. Suddenly we spot another sofa. It's second-hand, but it is better. The Dutch have a tradition of putting out for use by others furniture they no longer require. I cheekily knock on the door and explain what Jane and I are about. The owner kindly helps us to load it onto the roof-rack. No more sitting on a mattress on the floor.

The Turkish families in our block of flats are charming. They practise their English on us with gusto. Their children dance and play in the hallway or on the grass outside. They remind us of Caspidge, its wood, its meadow, the laughter of Flora, Cathy and William.

* * *

Detective Constable Thomas Gilchrist[6] explains to the court how he was with a police team of some twenty officers on search and recovery in the crash area. Initially he was employed on body recovery. He then moved to debris recovery, based at the Dextar warehouse. Debris and luggage was assembled in large polythene bags and brought to the warehouse. It was laid out for searchers to sift, bag and label. It was, he says, a mammoth task.

In January 1989 he worked in Sector One around Dunnabie farm. 'When the large bags were brought in we would separate the items, place each in a bag, and complete the map reference where it was found. We were looking for electrical items and items that were charred.'

He and Thomas McColm came across a piece of a grey shirt collar. They placed it in a plastic evidence bag, completed a label with the date and Ordnance Survey location where found, and Gilchrist signed it.

He's being cross-examined by defence advocate Richard Keen, who invites him to look at the label on the overhead display.

'Mr Gilchrist, you wrote on the label the word "DEBRIS". If we magnify the image we can see that the word "DEBRIS" has been altered?'

'Yes, I can see writing underneath it.'

'Exactly. And if we look carefully at the writing underneath the word "DEBRIS", we can make out the word "CLOTH", with the C being under the D, the L under the E, an O under the B of "DEBRIS", and a T under the R, and an H under the S?'

'It's possible.'

'It's more than possible. It's perfectly obvious, isn't it?'

'Yes.'

Gilchrist says that until this moment he did not know that the label was altered. He's unsure as to how it's been altered or by whom.

Now it is the turn of prosecution advocate Campbell. He hands the label to Gilchrist to allow him to re-examine it. Suddenly its provenance becomes tricky. Gilchrist does not think the writing is all his, notably the word 'DEBRIS'.

'It's not the way I would do a "D" . . . The "DEBRIS" certainly appears overwritten. Part of the writing is mine, but I am not convinced it's all mine.'[7]

His evidence has confused me. Did someone other than Gilchrist change the label? He looks around the court. He's within the arc of an extraordinary tableau, one which the greatest of playwrights would find it difficult to portray. Around me are grieving relatives, some sworn enemies of all that I represent. In the spectator gallery and surrounding buildings are intelligence agents of at least four governments. Before me, wall-to-wall and floor-to-ceiling, stands a soundproof bulletproof glass screen. Beyond that is a silent moving tapestry, a mime show, an international game in which all search for advantage. At the centre sit two Libyans, said by two governments to be guilty of mass murder. Across from them sit the prosecution team, aided by two lawyers from the US Department of Justice. Arraigned above all is a D'Oyly Carte crimson and ermine-white row of solemn judges.

I promised Gaddafi that the suspects would receive a fair trial. But already the uncertain nature of Gilchrist's evidence, and apparent alteration by an unknown hand of an evidence label key to the prosecution case, has created within me a growing feeling of unease.

Each day, prosecution lawyers make themselves available in the relatives' lounge. It is clear to me that a grooming process is under way, steering all to accept a presumption of guilt. I resist the pressure; I'm convinced that whatever the lawyers might get up to in the relatives' lounge, the trial will be fair.

I draft a letter to Robin Cook: 'This week has taught me that I was right to refuse to allow the Lockerbie victims to be forgotten, and right to fight for a trial. I am deeply grateful to you and your colleagues for your efforts in ensuring that it is at last happening.'

Tomorrow, Jane and I will view the glory of the tulip fields before Jane returns to England. The thought of her not being here through the long nights to come fills me with dread. Images of Flora swim within my brain; I'm standing once more with Jane before the rasping television, Lockerbie is burning. I leave the courtroom to seek a quiet moment alone.

* * *

15 JUNE 2000. THE TRIAL: DAY 15

Dr Thomas Hayes was formerly head of the forensics explosives laboratory at the British Royal Armament Research and Defence Establishment (RARDE). He is now retired. And when did he retire? 'The exact date of my leaving is a little circumspect, but I believe it was in 1990.'

I wonder why he said it that way.

So what is he doing now? He's a chiropodist.

He actually resigned in 1989, a year that for him may be circumspect, but for this trial is significant. Early that year members of Parliament pressed for Hayes and two of his colleagues to be subjects of an inquiry about their role in another trial involving bombs.

In 1975, seven members of the same family – 'The Maguire Seven' – were jailed for assisting Gerard Conlon and others with a bombing attack on a Guildford pub in October 1974. Conlon, Patrick Armstrong, Paul Hill and Carole Richardson – known as 'The Guildford Four' – were convicted for the bombing; Anne Maguire, and six members of her family, were convicted for handling explosives prior to the attack.

A parliamentary inquiry under Sir John May into the trial of the Maguire Seven began in September 1989 and concluded in July 1990. In his interim report, Sir John discovered that the concealment of evidence by Hayes and two RARDE colleagues severely hampered cross-examination of witnesses for the prosecution. He concluded: 'The whole scientific basis upon which the prosecution was founded was so vitiated that on this basis alone the Court of Appeal should set aside the convictions.'[8]

In our Lockerbie trial, Hayes explains that on 12 May 1989 he examined the charred shirt collar found, bagged and labelled by DC Gilchrist. From the depths of the collar he teased out a fragment of multi-layered plastic 10mm². He categorised it 'PT/35(b)' and identified it as part of an electronic circuit board on page 51 of a 172-page loose-leaf notebook.[9]

Keen turns away, gathers his thoughts, turns again to face Hayes. 'You record in your notes that PT/35(b) was trapped in the collar of a shirt. So that fragment could not have come to light as far as the police were concerned, prior to it being extracted by yourself?'

'That's correct. Yes.'

Keen demands confirmation: 'So it could not have been seen by the police prior to it being extracted by you?'

'I'm sure that's the case.'[10]

Gilchrist could not have seen the fragment. So why was the label carefully overwritten from 'CLOTH' to 'DEBRIS' and by whom?

I am puzzled too by Hayes' inconsistent note-taking. He found PT/35(b) on 12 May 1989. His notes on that finding were written on page fifty-one. He made no drawing, undertook no testing.

Two pages before that, on page forty-nine, he recorded finding a similar sized piece of plastic. This he drew in precise detail and made notes. The date was 8 June, almost one month *after* his finding of PT/35(b). And he gave it an index number PT/30; that is five less than PT/35(b). Nevertheless he maintains that all his notes and drawings were contemporaneous.[11]

Furthermore, Hayes' notebook from page fifty-one onwards is re-numbered by hand.[12] There seems no logical reason for the renumbering. Why did he renumber the pages thus?

It is difficult to remember. He cannot recall.

At least not now; he will in due course remember. But only following review of his evidence under Advocate Campbell: 'Does that explanation of the way in which the items detailed in examination notes are listed help to jog your memory at all as to at what stage in the exercise you would, as a matter of course, fill in this document?'

Hayes replies, 'It has helped me, sir, in attempting to explain what appears a rather unfathomable mystery. And I think the solution is very straightforward. And it is this: That when I wrote these notes, I initially did not number the pages. And as I have commented earlier in my examination, my concern was that the pages were correctly dated, but not necessarily numbered, recognising that insertions at a later date could be helpful in reading the notes. When I then set about sorting the notes, the pages in approximately chronological order, I then set about numbering them.'[13]

Hayes and his colleague Allen Feraday concluded that fragment PT/35(b) might have been part of the Lockerbie bomb. So why did neither he nor Feraday conduct swab tests for explosive residues?

Hayes: 'I considered such testing to be unnecessary.'

* * *

8 June 2000. The trial: Day 18

When Hayes retired his immediate colleague Allen Feraday was promoted to head of the laboratory, took over the investigation and, with Hayes working with him on a semi-retired basis, produced the final Lockerbie forensic report.

Several pages from the report are displayed on the court overhead screen. Richard Keen turns to Feraday: 'On 18th July 1991, which is some five months before your report was completed, we have the words: "These are fragments recovered from the grey-coloured 'Slalom' brand shirt described in section 5.1.3 of the final report." Given that the final report was prepared over three and a half months to the middle of December 1991, and given your evidence that these are contemporaneous examination notes, was it not somewhat prescient of you to be able to decide that such an entry could be made in your notes in July of 1991?'

Feraday: 'Because those two sections on "clothing" and "luggage" were essentially completed. It doesn't mean that sections 1, 2, 3 and 4 were – 5 – 4 and 5 would have been easy to do. They were already essentially done by Hayes anyway and sort of numbered. This is a contemporaneous note. I mean, that's the date that I've put at the top of the page, and that's when I examined that item, PT/35(b).'[14]

So what is the substance of fragment PT/35(b)?

Feraday reads from page 130: 'The particular tracking pattern of the fragment has been extensively compared with the control samples of the [Thüring] MST-13 timers and circuit boards and it has been conclusively established that the fragment materials and tracking pattern are similar in all respects to the area around the connection pad for the output relay of the "MST-13" timer . . . The conducting pad and tracks present on the fragment PT/35(b) are of copper covered by a layer of pure tin.'[15]

So there we have it: materials, tracking pattern, similar in all respects. The fragment came from the batch delivered to Libya in 1985. My suspicions about the amendment of the Gilchrist label, of Hayes' uncertain record in his loose-leaf notebook, of the interchange between Hayes and Feraday during the preparation of the final forensic report – all must be misplaced. The two suspects are guilty; clear, undeniable.

And yet unknown to me, the defence team and the judges, one key aspect – the claimed metallurgy of fragment PT/35(b) – will in the coming years be shown to be false. For deep within his forensic notebook Feraday had recorded, in the margins of two separate pages, his concerns regarding metallurgical analysis results of the fragment, comparing it with a control sample board supplied to him by Thüring and the Scottish police. Of fragment PT/35(b), on 1 August 1991 he hand-wrote: 'Plating on the two thin lines is of pure tin (Cu [copper] breaking through from underneath). AF. 1/8/91.'

On the same day, of the control sample board, he hand-wrote: 'Tinning on the thin tracks is of 70/30 Sn/pb [Tin/Lead]. However this may be dipped or roller tinned on top of either the Cu tracks? Or the Cu tracks with a layer of pure tin? AF. 1/8/91.'

These statements are central to the conviction. We will return to them in later chapters.

* * *

19 JUNE 2000. THE TRIAL: DAY 23.
EVIDENCE OF EDWIN BOLLIER

The final witness of what has been a long hot day is Edwin Bollier, director and owner of Swiss electronics supplier MEBO. As he walks towards the witness box a smile creases his lips. Or is it a mild grimace? Did he spot my concern through the sheen of the glass? Above slightly jowled cheeks his face is round beneath a head of smooth combed-back hair. He seems to be a typical well-fed European businessman. His seeming involvement in the international game of terrorism, double and treble agents, and bought-and-sold politicians will prove central to the Lockerbie story. It will take the court five laborious days of exploration.

In opening exchanges prosecution counsel Turnbull asks Bollier about briefcases constructed for the East German secret police, the Stasi. Each was equipped with an electronic pager that could be remotely detonated, killing any person within range. Does he know that one was found in the Budapest flat of Carlos the Jackal?

Bollier knows nothing of Carlos. Of the briefcases he makes no comment.

Eventually the questioning moves to a central issue: PT/35(b). The prosecution maintain – and must prove – that this tiny fragment of an electronic timer said to be found at the crash site came from a circuit board supplied by Bollier in 1985 to

Libya. Turnbull invites Bollier to look at a photograph displayed on the overhead screen. Does it come from one of five timers he sold to the East German Stasi?

'It could be a counterfeit. It is not the same one shown to me by the Swiss police.'

Could be a counterfeit. Where is this taking us? What have the Stasi to do with Lockerbie?

Bollier's gaze for a moment locks on the photograph, then he turns away. He's restless, sounds flustered. Lockerbie has destroyed his company. His English is not good. The court translation is unsteady. Does he really understand where he is, what is happening to him?

More questions, more confusion. Hours later the court turns again to PT/35(b). Until now it has lain on the evidence table before the clerks, protected by an evidence bag. Bollier asks to look at it closely. He is permitted to put on protective gloves and examine the fragment with the aid of a magnifying glass.

He's bent over it, staring at it from different angles. Suddenly he turns to the judges: 'Your Lordships, this is not the fragment I saw in Scotland. It has changed. How many are there? This is why I would like to see the first photograph. And I would kindly ask you to show it to me, because the first photograph is determining for all of those concerned. The first fragment showed what we've seen, and then the case is clear. I've tried for eight years now to see this fragment. It was refused three times by Lord Advocate Hardie in all those years.'

I am stunned. I look around at the spectators. They're all awake, really awake. These are almost the exact words used by Bollier when interviewed in 1993 by Alan Francovich during the making of the documentary film *The Maltese Double Cross*. In that interview Bollier tells of his repeated unsuccessful attempts in Washington and in Scotland to inspect a supposed fragment from one of his timers. He was allowed only to view photographs, some of which – in his opinion

– appeared to differ. The court too, is unaware of these words, since none of those present are likely to have viewed the film directly or on Channel 4.

Defence Advocate Burns QC explores Bollier's earlier exchanges with the prosecution. He turns to Bollier's extraordinary claim of collusion by Swiss and Scottish police to switch photographs of the fragment.

In reply, Bollier claims that prior to 15 June 1990 the Scottish police showed him four photographs of prototype circuit boards manufactured by his company. 'Those photographs did not fit with the case against Libya. And it was said that this [i.e. PT/35(b)] was what was found at Lockerbie . . . And that is why the four photographs disappeared. That is where the Scots police came along, and they produced new photographs and said these are the photographs which will go into the records.'[16]

He seems to be a confused enigma. He swings back and forth between support for the prosecution case, and support for the defence case. It's not going well with the judges.

Who does he work for? Himself, the Americans, the Libyans, and, up to the 1989 fall of the Berlin Wall, the Stasi? He supplied to some of the world's secret services items possessing but one purpose – to dismember and kill. He stands before relatives of people killed by a bomb said to have been triggered by a device constructed by his company. He is trapped in a web of evil created by men whose trade is deception and murder. It extends across oceans deep into this court.

Eventually Bollier's evidence is complete, the tension – for a short while – reduced. But many more days, witnesses and evidence of unimaginable complexity are yet to come. My scribbled notes already spread over several folders. Head-down concentration on the whispering headphones has become my shield against reality. They are talking – and talking – about the murder of my daughter, the emotional destruction of my family. But it's happening to someone else, as in a play, the denouement of which will serve no penalty, no guilt. How have I become so detached? Where now is my dark rage?

* * *

11 JULY 2000. THE TRIAL: DAY 31. EVIDENCE OF TONI GAUCI AND THE HARRY BELL POLICE DIARY

At the beginning of the trial there were two identification witnesses for the prosecution: a Maltese shopkeeper, Tony Gauci, and a CIA asset, Majid Giaka. Giaka will shortly be exposed as an unreliable and discredited witness, leaving Gauci as the prosecution's only identification witness.

The indictment states that one of the accused, al-Megrahi, purchased a random set of clothes from Gauci's shop, Mary's House, in Sliema, Malta, on 7 December 1988. Remnants of those clothes were found at the Lockerbie crash site.

At this point my story becomes rather complex, for which I must apologise, for unknown to me, the judges and the defence team, behind the court exchanges lurked a sinister theme which would in time discredit all of Gauci's evidence. This is perhaps best explained as follows.

Earlier during the trial a short exchange occurred that went unnoticed by the defence and judges. Detective Chief Inspector Henry Wood Bell, known as Harry Bell, was the chief Lockerbie investigator for the Scottish police force. He was being cross-examined by Richard Keen QC: 'You presumably kept a record of your investigations on Malta, Mr Bell? Where is your record?'

'My personal record is in my diaries.'

'And where are those diaries?'

'They are in my office.'

'In?'

'Glasgow.'[17]

Bell seemed tense. I'd heard that tone of voice before, in my surgery, when a patient is afraid to confess what he most fears.

Why did the defence team or the judges not demand of Bell that he go and bring those diaries to court? I put the moment out of my mind.

From then onwards Bell's diary resided in a Glasgow office under lock and key. It would not be revealed until 2007, when the Scottish Criminal Cases Review Commission (SCCRC), after a three-year investigation, published its findings. They discovered two histories that had run in parallel: 1) Gauci's statements, and 2) The revelations contained in Bell's diary.

From Gauci's order books and records it was clear that someone did indeed purchase various types of clothing from his shop, Mary's House, on a day towards the end of November or in early December 1988. Fragments of such, and some complete items, were found at the crash site.

On 1 September 1989, Gauci was interviewed by a police team led by Bell. He said that he was working alone in the shop between 6.30 p.m. and 7.00 p.m. when the purchaser came in. Gauci recalled that the purchase took place on a weekday, 7 December 1988. He listed every item that the stranger purchased. Based on Gauci's information, police artists prepared photofit pictures of the stranger.

Within two weeks of this first interview of Gauci, Bell noted in his diary that discussions were under way with the US Department of Justice concerning massive rewards to Gauci. A letter addressed to Bell included the promise of '. . . unlimited monies, with $10,000 available immediately'. The purpose of the $10,000 was not explained.

Two weeks later, on 14 September 1989, Gauci went to police headquarters at Floriana, Malta, to be interviewed by Bell and Inspector Scicluna of the Maltese police. They showed him nineteen photographs. Gauci pointed to one of the photographs: 'The man is similar to the one who bought the clothing but the man in the photograph is too young to be the man who bought the clothing. If he was older by about twenty years he would have looked like the man who bought the clothing.' Gauci signed the front of the photograph of the man whom he identified as 'similar' to the purchaser. He claimed that the photograph looked like the man's features so far as the eyes, nose, mouth and shape of face were concerned. The hair of the customer was similar but shorter than that of the man in the photograph. The man he identified resembled a photofit of Mohammed Salem, known to be a colleague of acknowledged and convicted terrorist Abu Talb.

Twelve days later, on 26 September 1989, Gauci again attended police headquarters in Malta to be interviewed by the same two officers. He was shown more photographs. He thought that one of the faces was familiar. The man he identified was called Shukra, whose photograph was included at the suggestion of the BKA, the West German police force.[18] They suspected that Shukra might be the person whom Gauci had already described. Shukra, as with Salem, was, according to the police, unconnected to the Lockerbie attack.

Three months later, on 30 January 1990, Gauci was shown a section of a slalom shirt. He instantly recognised it as from a type he sold in Mary's House. He insisted, however, that the stranger had not purchased a shirt: '*I am sure I did not sell him a shirt. That man did not buy any shirts, for sure.*' [Our italics.]

On 31 August 1990, Bell and Scicluna showed Gauci a card containing twelve photographs. Gauci told them that none were of the stranger. He pointed to one of the photographs as similar in the shape of the face and style of hair, but it was not the stranger. Bell then opened another set of photographs. Gauci examined these but none were of the stranger.

On 10 September 1990, Gauci was shown an album containing thirty-nine photographs. Among them was a photograph of one of several suspects, the known terrorist Abu Talb. Gauci failed to recognise anyone. 'I have been shown many photographs. But I have not yet seen a photograph of the man who bought the clothing.' It was now two years and three months since the stranger purchased the clothes.

Then, for Bell and his team, came the vital breakthrough. On 15 February 1991 Gauci was to make his first vague identification of al-Megrahi. Bell asked him to look at some photographs, instructing him to picture the man in his mind. He warned Gauci that the face of the stranger may not be among the photographs. Gauci looked at all the photographs and concluded that they were of men younger than the man who bought the clothing.

But a decision was necessary.

Gauci is a smallish man, slightly crouched in his stance. His face is somewhat truculent, strong jawed with a broad forehead. 'I was then asked to look at all the photographs carefully to try to allow for age difference. I pointed out one of the photographs. I would say that the photograph at number eight is similar to the man who bought the clothing. The man in the photograph number eight is, in my opinion, in his thirty years. He would perhaps have to look about ten years or more older, and he would look like the man who bought the clothes. It's been a long time now, and I can only say that this photograph number eight resembles the man who bought the clothing, but it is younger.' At the conclusion of this February 1991 interview Bell recorded that photograph eight was of al-Megrahi. Gauci signed that photograph, but continued with: 'Photograph number eight is the only one really similar to the man who bought the clothing, if he was a bit older, other than the one my brother showed me.'

The 'other' photograph was of convicted terrorist Abu Talb, an early suspect in the Lockerbie case, and a man whose photograph Gauci had already rejected in his statement of 10 September 1990.

If we turn again to Bell's diary, Gauci's key interview was on 15 February 1991. Six days later, on 21 February 1991, a memo from Bell to DSIO Gilchrist[19] states that Tony Gauci 'expressed

Jane and Flora, 1966 (Swire family)

The Swires with Jim's parents (Swire family)

William, Flora, Jane, Cathy and captive lion (Swire family)

Flora Swire (Swire family)

Jim and Jane Swire (Swire family)

Flora's grave, Loch Caroy, Isle of Skye (Peter Biddulph)

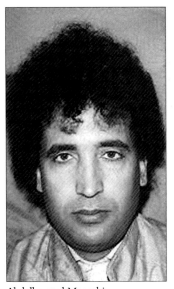

Abdelbaset al-Megrahi
(UPI/Alamy Stock Photo)

Jim Swire with co-author Peter Biddulph,
Flora's Wood (Peter Biddulph)

The Swire family with Nelson Mandela (Swire family)

an interest in receiving money at recent meetings' and that 'if a monetary offer was made this may well change his view'. We have to ask, *change his view from what to what?* I will return to the details of this sequence in a later chapter.

* * *

Immediately prior to the trial another key event occurred, an identification parade in which Gauci would select al-Megrahi as the guilty man.

The indictment against al-Megrahi was issued in November 1991. During the next eight years his photograph was prominent around the world with the caption of 'the Libyan suspect', 'the alleged bomber' or 'the Lockerbie bomber'. He and Fhimah were filmed with their family members, repeatedly protesting their innocence. Television pundits commented with his photograph or video as a backscreen. Newspapers speculated with his photo in colour or black and white. In the eighth year appeared another photograph of al-Megrahi wearing yellow sunglasses, and featured on the rear cover of *Focus* magazine.

Gauci purchased a copy, kept it for one month, then took it to Maltese police Inspector Scicluna, claiming that the photograph was of the man who came into his shop. Even then he couldn't be sure. 'I don't remember now . . . I don't know exactly what I said . . . His hair and glasses were not like that, the day he bought [clothes] from me. And he was much shorter than that, and he was without glasses.'

Within a week of taking the magazine to Scicluna, Gauci attended a police identity parade featuring al-Megrahi. Gauci's words to the accompanying officer were: 'Not exactly the man I saw in the shop ten years ago. I saw him, but the man who look a little bit like exactly is the number five.'

Meanwhile, in the courtroom, prosecution advocate Campbell asks Gauci to point out the stranger who walked into his shop more than twelve years ago. Accordingly, Gauci points

a finger at al-Megrahi; a ridiculous display of courtmanship of
which Campbell should be ashamed.

Can I, a general practitioner, remember a particular patient
on a particular day at a particular time with a particular condition, from twelve years ago? Can I remember his hair, his face,
his nose, his clothes, his waist measurement, his diagnosis, his
accent and whether he carried an umbrella? Can I recall the
exact weather conditions as the man walked out of my surgery?
Are my powers of recall so finely tuned that I can not only
remember such events, but what was happening down the street
in the way of Christmas street lights?

But, after being offered his photograph several times by
investigating officers, all with the assumption that the guilty
man is somewhere in the pack, and month after month seeing
his photograph in newspapers and magazines alongside the
word 'bomber', and having him standing before me in a row of
volunteers – several quite unlike him in terms of age or nation-
ality – would I not choose 'the Libyan al-Megrahi'?

The most extraordinary feature of Gauci's role is yet to
come. In his written and spoken judgement Lord Sutherland
will explain Gauci's astonishing feat of memory thus: 'The
clear impression that we formed was that he was in the first
place entirely credible, that is to say doing his best to tell the
truth to the best of his recollection ... Mr Gauci applied his
mind carefully to the problem of identification whenever he
was shown photographs, and did not just pick someone out at
random ... We accept of course that he never made what could
be described as an absolutely positive identification, but having
regard to the lapse of time it would have been surprising if he
had been able to do so.'

A vague, numerously qualified and uncertain judgement,
but one which condemned a man to a lifetime of
imprisonment.

What would Lord Sutherland now make of the revelation
that from the earliest stages of the police investigation Gauci

was offered – in the words of the US Department of Justice – 'unlimited rewards . . . *only if he gives evidence*'? [Our italics.]

* * *

7·AUGUST 2000

I'm back home at Caspidge. Yet another adjournment; the judges are on holiday for a while. It's one of those August nights when autumn whispers a warning with a clearing sky and a crescent moon. The old iron fire is cosy again. It's hard to stay awake. Batty the Burmese cat is stretched out on the carpet. Kala the dog slaps her tail against the leg of the chair. Two hours ago Jane served Scottish beef stew with apples and cherries from the wood. We silently ate our meal. Exhausted, Jane went to bed.

I feel myself still in an underworld peopled by phantoms. The phone is ringing again. It's a Swedish journalist seeking 'The Wisdom of Jim'. Don't they ever sleep? My media record is twenty-four interviews in a day. I will not stop until the truth is out.

The second hand sweeps past the midnight line. Kala's rolled over, legs akimbo, snoring gently. Of what does she dream? I fear to sleep. For into my dreams will slide that burning Lockerbie cottage, roof gone, walls crumbling, glowing timbers streaming sparks like errant stars. What was it like for Flora? What did she see and feel? As the stars spun around, how long, how long?

People wince at my gaunt frame, my deep-set eyes, my untidy mop of hair. Some think I'm mad. You can see it in their eyes. Sometimes even I will wonder. This desk, this computer, this fax, files and tapes and discs and papers, phones and mobiles, envelopes I haven't opened, opened letters I haven't yet read. Still onward to the truth. One more letter . . .

What? Have I been asleep? Kala's whining, tail wagging away the heat. Let her out, poor thing, into the night. Soon I'll be abed. Then darkness with screaming jets and baggage check-ins and a warm, comfy aeroplane at three minutes past seven and Flora looking at the stars and the burning cottages and a great glowing wound gouged into a sleeping town. Thank God Catherine didn't buy that ticket. We were a hairsbreadth from losing them both.

Aphrodite Tsairis, a board member of the American Victims of Pan Am 103, once sent me a letter:

Dear Jim, I was not certain you have heard the news about the Bermuda press conference . . . On Friday 14th April at about 4.15 New York time, towards the end of the press conference, President Bush suddenly removed from his breast pocket our jointly signed letter, and began reading it.

He mentioned both Bert's name and yours, and then spoke several minutes to the families on the issues of state sponsored terrorism. Sitting next to him, Margaret Thatcher responded in kind.

Needless to say, those of us on this side of the Atlantic are overjoyed that we have come to the forefront of our leader's political agenda. We are certain that you and the other families of the UK share this sentiment. After many such letters to our President, this is the first one to be so acknowledged. A sure sign we are making progress. With affection, Aphrodite.

Poor Aphrodite, so fondly deceived by the Iron Lady. Her president too, in spite of his legerdemain of sympathy, spoke weasel words.

Flora's photo looks down from the shelf, a jaunty smile, raven hair flowing. It smiles too from the front of my briefcase whenever I meet civil servants and security men. They can't miss it. Their hackles rise. *Who is this country doctor? What does he know about airport security? He's lost a daughter.*

Hasn't everyone at some time? Why doesn't he stick to doctoring?

But the men I am talking to allowed Flora to be killed and I am there to tell them that they might have stopped it. I remember the cold of that Lockerbie mortuary. My skin tingled with the smell. These civil servants, these officials, they can never know that. I will lead them to an understanding. Long ago our society had simple rules, anger channelled into revenge, a head on the block, the closure of the axe. Now our freedoms are dissipated; but justice seems now powerless to discover truth in a crime that fell like a glowing Satan from heaven.

'Yours sincerely . . .' I sign the latest letter, address the envelope and stretch like a worn-out cat. Kala is back, friendly and enquiring. The descending moon brushes the high window edged with wisteria's skeleton. The lights of Bromsgrove glitter through the blackness of the wood. Beneath a starlit horizon the Malvern Hills brood away the night.

* * *

25 AUGUST 2000. THE TRIAL: DAY 44

During the 1991 Fatal Accident Inquiry, Crown Solicitor Hardie claimed there had been no opportunity on the Heathrow tarmac for anyone to plant a rogue suitcase into Pan Am 103. His conclusion was therefore that the bomb must have arrived on Pan Am 103A flying from Frankfurt to Heathrow.

His submission completely ignored the following vital issue: during the early evening of 21 December 1988, luggage container AVE4041, destined for Pan Am 103, was unguarded and unsupervised for at least forty-five minutes. It stood adjacent to the office of the luggage loading team leader, a Mr Walker, and next to the terminal and baggage area for Iran Air. Inside the container, and partially visible, were several interline bags and cases originating from the baggage processing and X-ray line of Heathrow's check-in system.

Luggage loader John Bedford left the area for a thirty minute tea break. When he returned, he noticed in the container two additional cases, both hard-shell. Pan Am 103A then arrived from Frankfurt, and passenger luggage was transferred to container AVE4041, and from there into the hold of Pan Am 103. Both Bedford and his colleague Sultash Kamboj[20] gave statements to the police, and these have been repeated today. Bedford claims that Kamboj told him that it was he who put the two hard-shell cases there. Kamboj, however, denies that he said those words.[21]

Defence advocate Davidson QC explores matters further: 'So far as the interline shed was concerned, Mr Bedford, am I correct in thinking that overnight it was left open, unsecured?'

'Yes, sir.'

'At the point outside the shed where bags were put on the belt to be fed into the interline shed, there was no security guard?'

'No, sir.'

Staff, known and unknown, could wander anywhere in the proximity of AV4041. Up to seven airlines operated from the interline shed, among them Iran Air. People of several nationalities were coming and going whom Bedford did not recognise.[22]

A joint minute is read to the court: It is admitted that '. . . in 1988, of twenty thousand airside passes issued to non-flying staff, nine hundred were missing or destroyed'. In January 1989, one month after the attack, the figures rose to more than 30,000 issued, and almost 800 lost or destroyed.[23]

In the trial verdict and judgement, extracts from the words of a confused and forgetful Maltese shopkeeper, Tony Gauci, will be believed. Of him the judges will argue that even though his evidence was worryingly inconsistent, he was a sincere man who tried to help the court. Yet the evidence of this equally sincere Bedford, consistent throughout a long trial, will be dismissed as irrelevant.

* * *

The fuller picture of Heathrow security has proved terrifying. On 21 December 1988, 70,000 airside passes were circulating across Heathrow, distributed to many nationalities and construction workers busy with major changes to terminals and roadways. During the police investigation which began within days of the bombing, the head of Heathrow Security, Norman Shanks, possessed that information. I cannot understand why the police seem unaware of it.

Shanks was soon to retire. On 10 March 2012 a *Sunday Express* journalist contacted him to seek his views about the al-Megrahi conviction. After all these years, did Shanks have any reservations about the Lockerbie verdict? Was it possible for a rogue suitcase to be placed into a luggage container by an unknown person?

Shanks was candid: 'Any country that flew into Heathrow could have done it. Several airlines had engineering stores brought in and transferred to various areas without having to go landside. Equally it would have been easy for somebody to take something through to airside. There was no screening of staff, no restriction on people walking through with bags. There was no reason for anyone to be stopped and questioned about anything they were carrying.'

Shanks believed that there remained 'legitimate questions' concerning the Lockerbie verdict. He claimed that he informed the police about a security patrolman's report of a break-in on the day of the attack, but could not recall when or how that information was conveyed.[24]

Cool August slips into colder September with yet another adjournment. I again fly home for a longed-for respite with Jane, Cathy and William. But rest does not come. A shell of uncertainty and anger surrounds me. They too suffer, and not always in silence.

* * *

26 September 2000. The trial: Day 50.
Evidence of CIA asset Majid Giaka

Of the next person to give evidence, billed in 1991 by some in the media as 'a star witness', the CIA's Vincent Cannistraro observed: 'Majid Giaka is a former member of the Libyan Intelligence Service who defected to the United States. He will be used in the trial of Fhimah and Megrahi.'[25]

In November 1991 the Lord Advocate assured us British relatives and the world that the indictments relied on evidence from reliable witnesses who would prove the case beyond doubt. Today, within the context of Scots criminal law, 'reliable' will be exposed as a meaningless word.

Throughout 1999 the defence team have possessed twenty-five CIA cables concerning Giaka; these have proved difficult to assess due to heavy redactions. In November 1999 they interviewed several CIA agents, and in one of the interviews an agent under the assumed name of Stauton claimed that the defence possessed all existing cables concerning Giaka.

One of the cables is of special interest. A long section has been redacted, and in the margin William McNair of the CIA, or someone acting on his behalf, has written in longhand 'Filing details'. Upon this section Giaka's credibility is about to turn.

Before he is allowed to enter the court, however, an angry exchange takes place between the heads of the two teams: Bill Taylor for the defence, and Lord Advocate Colin Boyd for the prosecution.

On 1 June 2000, three months previous to Giaka's appearance at this trial, the CIA had secretly arranged a meeting at the US embassy at The Hague between several CIA officials, and Alan Turnbull and Norman MacFadyen of the prosecution. Turnbull and MacFadyen were there on Boyd's instruction.

The CIA officials showed the two a set of cables with much of the censorship removed. Why that was done was unclear. Perhaps the CIA felt that by revealing to the prosecution the reality of Giaka it might strengthen their hand in the court-room. Whatever interpretation we might choose, someone in the CIA was trying to prevent the judges and defence team from seeing the uncensored information. To all appearances the Lord Advocate had become part of that process.

On 21 August 2000, news of the CIA/prosecution team meeting leaked out, but only through the honesty of one member of the prosecution team: Advocate Depute Campbell. On that day Campbell told Bill Taylor of the uncensored versions of the cables.

Boyd now defends his actions. He claims that he simply wished to study the uncensored versions, to judge their relevance to the defence position. His honest conclusion is that they are not relevant.

In court, an angry Bill Taylor challenges Boyd: 'Giaka is a crucial witness in this case. It is vital to the securing of a fair trial that the defence is not disadvantaged when Giaka is cross-examined. It is obvious, in Scots common law, never mind the European Convention, that the Crown and the defence must be on the same footing. And if a view has been formed by the Crown . . . that what is contained in the blanked-out sections is of no relevance to this trial, I emphatically do not accept that it is of no interest to a cross-examiner. Further, I challenge the right of the Crown to determine for the defence what is or is not of relevance to the defence case. It is a novel and an alarming statement that it is for the Crown to determine relevancy. And I go further and say that if that proposition is advanced, it is plainly untenable in the law of Scotland.'[26]

Giaka has been brought from the United States at great expense. He is here with the single purpose of providing eyewitness evidence. He tells the court that during the hours prior to the Lockerbie bombing, al-Megrahi and Fhimah walked through customs at Luqa Airport carrying an unchecked brown hard-shell suitcase to be routed to the United States via Frankfurt and London Heathrow.

He has a history to grace a Walter Mitty story. In August
1988 he was working at Luqa Airport as a motor mechanic.
Having been disciplined for bad behaviour, and feeling angry at
his   employers, who included Abdelbaset al-Megrahi, he approached
the American embassy in Malta offering his services as an
agent. From thence he worked as a double agent for the CIA
and the Libyan secret services – the JSO.

In January 1990, in statements to his CIA handlers and,
subsequently, FBI and Scottish investigators, he claimed that
Fhimah had spoken of ten kilos of TNT delivered to Luqa
Airport by al-Megrahi. And when Fhimah opened his desk
drawer, Giaka saw two large boxes containing yellowish material. He recalled that the explosive was accompanied by airline
rush tags,[27] and that the TNT was later taken to the Libyan
consulate in Malta. Fhimah, stated Giaka, also stored in his
office $10,000 in traveller's cheques. It sounded useful for the
Lockerbie evidence file. But for the CIA it was not enough.
Irrefutable eyewitness information was required.

Within days Giaka was taken aboard the USS *Butte*, moored
as a permanent intelligence outpost in international waters
twenty-seven miles off Malta. There he was told that unless he
came up with something of worthwhile intelligence value, he
would be hung out to dry above a Mediterranean swarming
with intelligence officers from Libya, a country he had betrayed.
And so, late in January 1990, Giaka duly delivered the required
information.

He was interviewed repeatedly, from 21 July 1990 on eleven
consecutive days, by two US Department of Justice lawyers.
Why was he so interviewed? Perhaps the answer lay in the fact
that he was scheduled to be interviewed one day later by
Scottish police. At that interview, Giaka told Scottish detectives of a December day at the Malta airport as he watched
al-Megrahi and Fhimah walking past customs carrying a
Samsonite suitcase.

Today, in court, Giaka opens his testimony by describing something of his work from January 1984 for the Libyan secret services as a motor mechanic. His chief was al-Megrahi, at that time head of the airline security section of the JSO. Also working in Luqa was the second accused, Fhimah.

Now Bill Taylor cross-examines. He notices that Giaka is smiling past him towards US Department of Justice representatives Bhiel and Murtagh. I'm wondering why Giaka is smiling. Over his shoulder I can see the faces of the two Americans.

Unfortunately for Giaka, Lord Boyd and the Americans, the judges are now aware that the now unredacted CIA cables reveal a motivation other than a search for truth. His handler writes: 'Giaka will be advised in no uncertain terms, on 4th September [1989], that we will only continue his $1,000 per month salary through to the end of 1989. If Giaka is not able to demonstrate sustained and defined access to *information of intelligence value by January of 1990, the CIA will cease all salary and financial support until such access can be proven again*.' [Our italics.]

He's scared for his life, his presence here weakens the prosecution case. The judges agree: Giaka is an unreliable witness; all he has said until now must be discounted.

The defence must indicate only a probability of reasonable doubt. The prosecution must prove an unbroken chain between the two Libyans, the bomb and its appearance in the luggage container of Pan Am 103. For me, nothing has yet emerged to prove such a connection. For Lord Advocate Colin Boyd and his distinguished team, things seem to have fallen apart.

In 2009 I will discover that eight years prior to the trial chief police investigator DCI Harry Bell noted in his diary the words of Dana Bhiel: 'The US DoJ will give Magid [Giaka] $2 million dollars, *provided he gives evidence*.' Thus the reason for his smiles; and thus would a humble car mechanic become rich.

* * *

It is seventeen years since Jane and I came to Caspidge. We fell in love with it even as we walked up the pathway towards the front door. We followed distinguished footsteps: the world-famous Sir Adrian Boult lived here when conductor of the City of Birmingham Symphony Orchestra. The house brings memories of Orbost,[28] the great farmhouse on the Isle of Skye where, as a boy, I played along the shores. With thick sandstone walls and high mullioned windows Caspidge has Edwardian style, yet it could not protect us from the harshness of a general practitioner's career. Medicine is forever rewarding, but ever demanding and emotionally draining. Day and night the ringing phone carved itself into our psyche. Even today it speaks to us of illness or of death.

When William was born, Flora and Cathy loved him dearly. They were all gifted children, but from the start Flora was my darling, wrapping herself around my heartstrings; a bubbling personality with interests close to mine; a jaunty step, brilliant at maths, a wonderful singing voice. She chose medicine as a career. Sister Cathy has always been gifted, arts and writing oriented, highly talented in a unique and independent way. William too has grown with an enquiring mind; like me he is interested in electronics. With Flora gone, Jane's gentle patience has kept us together and we've grown ever closer.

As the agony of the trial grinds onward we sense that life at Caspidge soon must end. Not only are her rooms large, they are many, with seventeen acres of woods and fields to match. A new, more manageable home must soon be found.

Before that time comes, BBC cameras again fill our family room. For an interviewer too young to remember Lockerbie we re-live the night of the bombing. Twelve years have passed since that terrible night. Still angry beats the heart, but grief has mellowed to reflect on that part of the human condition that creates every Lockerbie.

The Sermon on the Mount says, 'Blessed are they that mourn, for they shall be comforted.' That's a comfort in itself, but there's also one about 'Blessed are they that hunger and thirst after righteousness' and the promise that the search will be fulfilled. Most devastating for me is the discovery of how those in positions of power behave. There seems no concept of right or wrong, no ethical structure to inform a government's decisions. Am I too naïve in hoping that there might be change? All those Lockerbies since aviation terrorism became fashionable carry such fundamental lessons that mankind ignores them at its peril.

Lord Advocate Boyd maintained that CIA redactions in cables referring to Giaka were irrelevant to the defence case and were 'made on the basis of what is in the interests of the security of a friendly power'. That power was and remains America. And when the sections were revealed it became clear that they had nothing to do with America's security. They were redacted to hide embarrassing facts that would weaken the prosecution case.

The history of Lockerbie is littered with UK public immunity certificates signed by secretaries of state, and American objections to the revealing of FBI and NSA reports that weaken a prosecution case. Those that have – with great difficulty – finally emerged for public scrutiny, hold nothing of significance for American or British security. The truth always hurts most those who most of all want the truth to be hidden.

Again into the cold eye of a camera I restate my determination to discover who killed Flora, why they did it, who paid them to do it and why she was not protected. I believe that God set in motion a complex universe and does not meddle. If Pan Am 103 had fallen apart through metal fatigue it would have been just bad luck. I would not have blamed God for it; I would have accepted that Flora was in the wrong place at the wrong time. Lockerbie was enacted by a person or persons acting with free will and evil intent. Still, somehow, I must force goodness out of tragedy. If I'd not been consumed throughout with a passion to discover the truth, grief would have broken me. I must never fail Flora. The heart will not allow it.

The BBC put the 'Wisdom of Jim and Jane' on their website. The story features for six or seven weeks then disappears.

* * *

10 November 2000. The trial: Day 67. Evidence of Abu Talb

Across the spectator gallery the whispering fades away. Six feet ahead of me stands the man whom many believe to be part of the Lockerbie murders.

Mohammed Abu Talb: a man serving life imprisonment in a Swedish jail for the bombing of airline offices in Copenhagen and Stockholm; a man identified by 'intelligence sources' and David Leppard of *The Sunday Times* as the Lockerbie bomber.[29]

Why is he a prosecution witness? Many suspect that he is guilty; how might he help the Crown case? Will he by his evidence dispel those same suspicions? Perhaps that is why the prosecution team arranged for him to arrive at Kamp Zeist one week ago; and each evening as late as 10.00 p.m. they have discussed with him whatever prosecution advocates do discuss with a chosen witness.

Over Talb's shoulder I watch defence advocate Taylor's face and reactions. What of Talb's commando training in Armenia and the Soviet Union in the use of shoulder-launched rockets? Talb's shoulders tense. He does not answer. He hates all within this court. If he were holding a machine gun all would be dead.

When instructed to answer by Lord Sutherland, Talb finally admits membership of the PLO's armed wing, Al Fatah, but claims that from 1982 he withdrew from terrorist activities.

If that is so, why is he in prison in a Swedish jail?

Talb's head turns towards the judges. 'I was convicted on one charge only, a bombing in Denmark of a Jewish site, not of anything else. I was convicted even though I was not there, and I did not confess to the crime.'

Why did Talb hold three forged passports, all in false names? Why did he have a suitcase containing money used to finance the Danish bombings? Why was 21 December 1988 marked in his diary? A list of terrorist associates was found in his house. Some of those names are listed in the indictment for this trial. Did Talb meet with Hafez Dalkamoni, PFLP-GC member and Jibril's right-hand man? Talb admits to being in Cyprus from 3 October 1988, and Dalkamoni was in Cyprus at the same time.

Throughout, Talb has stonewalled Taylor. Nothing is proved or successfully challenged. Richard Keen steps forward.

Talb was to be interviewed in 1989 by a Swedish investigation team accompanied by FBI Special Agent Hendershot. Talb walked into the interview room and spat furiously at Hendershot. He refused to talk at that interview, but gave a great deal of information to the Swedes at other times.

Keen: 'Mr Talb, on 30th October 1989, United States government officials announced: "Mohammed Abu Talb has admitted to [Swedish] investigators that between October and December 1988 he retrieved and passed to another person a bomb that had been hidden in a building in West Germany used by the PFLP-GC."'

'This is not true.'

Talb is here under the European Convention on Mutual Assistance in Criminal Matters. He has full immunity.[30] Even if the defence proves his guilt he may stand silent and safe.

The word-game of death ends without resolution. The Talb convoy sweeps back across Europe to a Swedish jail. *A bomb that had been hidden in a building in West Germany used by the PFLP-GC.* Was that the bomb that murdered Flora?

* * *

17 NOVEMBER 2000. THE TRIAL: DAY 71

Rainer Gobel worked for the German BKA as a specialist in the electronics of explosive devices. He examined and reported on one of two improvised explosive devices captured in October 1988 during the arrests of the PFLP-GC group. The second device was being examined by his officer colleague in a separate section of the BKA laboratory at Weisbaden when it exploded, killing the officer.

Prosecution advocate Turnbull leads Gobel through his evidence. Gobel describes the 'ice-cube' timer: 'This detonating device is designed in such a way that it could automatically trigger an explosive device in a plane. Once the necessary altitude has been reached, and the pressure drop occasioned thereby has started the timer to run, and once the timing delay has been reached, detonation takes place ... The required altitude to commence the initiation of the timer by the pressure gauge would take about seven minutes. The delay time after the pressure gauge was activated must have been about thirty to thirty-five minutes.'

Gobel adds, 'The course of the operational sequence of the detonators ... fits in very well with the conditions during take-off and the initial flight phase of PA 103 from London to New York. It would have been impossible for a primed explosive to have been carried on flight PA 103A from Frankfurt to London without detonating ... If we assume that an explosive of similar design was used for the attack, it must have been put on board in London, or at least primed there by plugging in the main switch.'[31]

Put on board in London? Exploded thirty-eight minutes after take-off – therefore in the centre of the time window of the combined delay of a pressure switch and the type of ice-cube timer used by the PFLP-GC!

I stand, lean forward and frantically scribble across a piece of A4 paper '103 EXPLODED AFTER 38 MINUTES!' I press it against the glass in full view of the court, waving wildly with a free hand to attract the attention of Keen and Taylor. They glance vaguely towards me but give no reaction. The security guards hovering in the aisles are not amused; nor the much-puzzled spectators.[32] Mumbling an attempt at an apology I sit down. Two days will pass before my darkness subsides.

* * *

5 DECEMBER 2000. THE TRIAL: DAY 76. EVIDENCE OF FBI SPECIAL AGENT EDWARD MARSHMAN

During the first year of the investigation Iran was believed to be the instigator of the attack. The foremost intelligence organisation in the history of the world, the CIA, assembled a portfolio of evidence from sources which, in the words of Robert Baer, a former CIA Middle Eastern specialist, were 'as good as it gets'. Thus the authorities were keen to establish that the radio-cassette recorder containing the bomb came from a PFLP-GC group arrested by German police in October 1988.

The May 1989 discovery of PT/35(b), however, switched the focus towards Libya. To justify that brutal reversal, the prosecution must now prove that none of the cassette recorders used by the PFLP-GC contained the bomb.

They also must establish that the cassette recorder was of the type sold primarily to Libya – i.e. the 'Bombeat' – in the years prior to the attack. Furthermore, they must establish that the PFLP-GC's bomb maker, Marwan Khreesat, while working in Germany in 1988 for the PFLP-GC, did not use the Bombeat type of recorder for any of the bombs he constructed.

Their hope lies not in the design of the Bombeat, but upon several fragments of paper discovered by Thomas Hayes: 'On the 30th of June 1989 some explosively damaged paper fragments, which bore indications that they originated from the owner's instruction manual for a Toshiba RT-SF16 radio-cassette player, were received at this laboratory, thus conclusively establishing which of the seven models of the Toshiba radio cassette had been employed in the Lockerbie bomb.'[33]

The question, however, remains: was this the type used by Marwan Khreesat to construct his bombs? He remains a proven terrorist bomb maker and an expert in the craft of mass killing, a double agent working for Jordan and a CIA asset. He was twice interviewed by an FBI agent in the presence of several US intelligence officers and the top Jordanian security general watching and listening to his every word. Such a man is certain to give an honest answer, is he not? Especially when – if he so much as hints that he might have made the Lockerbie bomb – he will stand on trial in this court.

But Khreesat is not a suspect. Nor is he a witness. Instead, we are obliged to listen to FBI Special Agent Marshman reading pages of hearsay statements compiled during those two interviews of Khreesat held in November 1989 at Jordanian security headquarters in Amman.

'Khreesat advised that he does not know what type of device was used to bring down Pan Am Flight 103. Khreesat advised that he does not think he built the device responsible for Pan Am 103, as he only built the four devices in Germany which are described herein.'[34]

He does not think he built the device. Is that as good as it gets? In other interviews, Khreesat admitted to making five bombs. One of his devices, hidden in a flat in Neuss, was recovered and exploded during an examination at the BKA's headquarters, killing an officer scientist. Khreesat is therefore guilty of the manslaughter or murder of that officer, but will be neither arrested nor tried for the offence.

In addition, as the defence team assembled their evidence in preparation for this trial, two members of the team – Alistair Duff and Edward MacKechnie – travelled to Amman, Jordan, with the purpose of interviewing Khreesat. There they were escorted to an interview room by a member of the Jordanian secret police. Khreesat recalled for them that the PFLP-GC leader, Ahmed Jibril, had in September 1988 personally asked him to construct bombs for some kind of operation involving aircraft. And when he visited a house in Syria used by the group he witnessed several already prepared radio-cassette bombs.

Some of the radio cassettes had one speaker, some had two. The items definitely included Toshibas. 'There is absolutely no doubt in my mind', added Khreesat, 'that Jibril wanted a Pan Am flight out of Frankfurt blown up.'

I am confused, puzzled and furious. How can Marshman's hearsay evidence be allowed without challenge? Khreesat wrote no statement, signed no statement written down by others and swore no affidavit. There was no interrogation by lawyers, no cross-examination, no checking of facts.

Unknown, however, to me, the defence team and the judges, a personal and classified letter written in 1989 by King Hussein of Jordan to British Prime Minister John Major contradicts the FBI spin placed upon Khreesat's evidence. King Hussein indicates that the real culprits for the Lockerbie crime were indeed the PFLP-GC, using a bomb constructed by Khreesat and used by his colleague Dalkamoni and others. It will prove to be yet another example of important evidence concealed by government to prevent a fair trial.

King Hussein's understanding of Khreesat's role differs markedly from Marshman's account. Was the king advised of the discrepancy by his chief of security who was present at the interviews?

At the time of this trial the letter lies concealed in police, Crown Office and Whitehall files. It will be discovered by the Scottish Criminal Cases Review Commission (SCCRC) during their three-year investigation following the failure of al-Megrahi's first appeal (see chapter 14). At the time of its discovery, officers of the SCCRC will be forbidden to take copies, make notes or discuss the letter's contents outside of police presence. The letter will be subject to a public immunity certificate signed by Foreign Secretary David Miliband.

In 2012 the Scottish *Herald* will learn of the letter's contents and try to publish them. The British Foreign Office will threaten to close down the newspaper for one day to prevent publication. The sequence of events will be exposed in the memoirs of Scottish Cabinet Minister for Justice Kenny MacAskill.

MacAskill will state that at the time of the *Herald*'s threatened publication he took a phone call from Tory MP Alistair Burt, at that time working for the Foreign and Commonwealth Office: 'He threatened not just to pull the *Herald*'s story, but to pull the whole edition of the newspaper . . . I was incredulous. I told him that the people of Scotland would definitely notice if there was no *Herald* next day . . . It really showed the extremes the UK government was prepared to go to stop the publication of something fundamental to Scotland's leading criminal case.'[35]

* * *

During an adjournment of several days, John Mosey and I fly to London to meet members of the British relatives' group. We then go to meet Robin Cook at the Foreign Office and repeat our demand for an inquiry. Robin seems more relaxed than before but holds to the official line. No inquiry is possible until all criminal proceedings end.

No point in taxing him with what form an inquiry might take. It's not his department. But when asked, he agrees to reconsider matters. He will convey to the Cabinet, to the PM, and specifically to John Prescott, the relatives' view that what is being revealed in the trial greatly increases the need for an inquiry when the trial is over. He concludes with, 'We will need time to assess the situation after the trial, before any inquiry is defined in law.'

Has he registered an 'out', just in case things prove nasty? Can we trust him? He adds: 'The political consequences of an inquiry might be a difficulty.' Difficult for whom? Are the Americans dictating what a British foreign secretary may or may not do?

We leave him in no doubt: 'In the event of an acquittal, the British relatives will not tolerate further delay.'

* * *

6 DECEMBER 2000

The trial is ended. In spite of their opening sweep of a 'special defence that implies the guilt of others and might incriminate the following', the defence have called only three witnesses. They missed obvious opportunities throughout the trial. As they offer their submissions they seem tired, out of ideas and ready to retire.

I'm deeply uneasy; more than 230 witnesses have been interviewed and cross-examined. Their evidence spans more than 12,000 pages of transcript. My hand-written notes stretch for 500 pages. Reasonable doubt has surely been established. Will a not-guilty or unproven verdict against either or both suspects allow a deeper, more trusted investigation and a long-overdue inquiry?

My mind runs hot with questions that were never asked. Why was the initial defence of incrimination not pushed to a conclusion? Why were FBI and CIA Lockerbie investigators Buck Revell and Vincent Cannistraro not asked to come to court, or at least forced to make depositions? The judges sail upon a sea of contradictions. I fear that their decision will serve neither justice nor truth.

As the court empties, John Mosey and I say the fewest of words to waiting journalists.

'That should do it.' We are too dog-tired to explain what *it* might be.

Chapter 13

BETWEEN THE HOURS of 5 a.m. yesterday and 2 a.m. this morning I gave continuous media interviews. This morning I rose at five and again began a series of interviews. A tiny, bitter breakfast, then what has seemed an endless journey, each step towards the courtroom longer than the last, a creeping numbness slowing the thoughts, confusing the body. I open and close my briefcase again and again; open and close my diary again and again. The judges must agree; reasonable doubt: there can be no other way.[1]

'*Court!*' All stand.

The court usher enters, followed by Lord Justice Sutherland as steady as a priest, then his three colleagues glorious in white and scarlet. They sit; the usher courteously checks their robes, starting with Sutherland, each moment of protocol used to full extent. Sutherland looks right, then left, then down to the clerk of the court and nods. The clerk stands, turns to face the bench, and speaks.

'My Lords, have you reached a verdict in respect of each of the accused?'

'We have.'

'What is your verdict in respect of the first accused [al-Megrahi]?'

Each day and night since that first news of Flora's murder, rationality has waltzed on a membrane below which my emotions have writhed in agony. Have I trusted too much in the steadfast judges, my champions for truth and justice?

'*Guilty.*'

My world rips apart. Anger and despair flood upward, a dark whirlpool fills the room until all slowly spins.

A voice echoes, 'Is your verdict unanimous or by majority?'

Another replies, 'Unanimous.'

The court starts to empty. Suddenly amid the buzz of conversation comes a coldness, a tingling, the tableau before me jigsaws to a white mist, a voice repeats again and again from the depths '. . . *Guilty* . . . *Guilty* . . . *Guilty* . . .'

Then the lights go out.

* * *

'I hope I didn't say anything silly.'

'Not a word.' A photographer stands above me. Behind him hovers William, his face white with shock.

I ask for whisky. The doctor gives me water, slopping it into my mouth, and moment by moment a week of sleepless nights is eased.

They help me to a wheelchair and trundle me to an ambulance for a check-up. Gathering my strength I stand, swaying, then walk airily back into the court muttering, 'I'm OK, I'm OK, don't worry, I'm OK.' William at last seems comforted. Still shaking, I ask about the second accused, Fhimah. A voice from somewhere in the press pack mutters, 'Not guilty'. Very strange, how could that be?

As I leave the court, out of the media chaos come hands poking microphones into my face. I force a joke: 'I blame you lot for this.'

Nobody laughs.

In the shocked silence, David Ben Aryeah mutters something beginning with 'F', but, God bless the man, he's never stopped me saying anything I wanted to, and he isn't going to do it now.

As we head for the cars John Mosey and Barry Berkley tell the press: 'Some of us came here not looking for an innocent or a guilty verdict concerning two people, but looking for honesty and truth about Lockerbie. For twelve years we have demanded to know what happened before and immediately after Lockerbie, and why the public were not protected or warned by Western governments and their agencies. We intend to continue to seek answers to these important questions.'

American bereaved relative Susan Cohen sees it as an enormous relief. 'There's no way that Libya can now say they were not involved. That bloody murderer Gaddafi has destroyed my life.'

Her American colleague, Bert Ammerman, adds: 'The families got some justice today. The verdict leads right to Gaddafi's doorstep. The Scottish justice system has proved excellent, and I hold Gaddafi personally responsible. World leaders should now take a stand against state sponsored terrorism.'

Suddenly I realise I've forgotten Jane and reach, still shaking, for the phone. She's frantic with worry. Hearing my voice comforts her a little. 'Jim, all the TV channels are talking of an appeal, and you must eat properly.'

We arrive at London's Park Lane Hilton close to midnight. The story is running around the world and I'm still gaga. They won't let me near my laptop. Instead, Charles Norrie, an adopted member of the group – his brother was killed in the 1989 French airline UTA bombing – grabs it and sets to work. Is he zapping all my files? I'm frantic, almost out of control. Arms reach out to restrain and calm me. Next day I discover that Charles has successfully downloaded the trial transcript; a labour of love for which all will in time be deeply grateful.

The following afternoon we set up a press conference. I'm still groggy, warbling on about ice-cube timers. For the media people it's all too complicated.

David Ben Aryeah's press friends take him aside. 'What's this ice-cube thing? And what's this "All your fault" business?'

David manages to salvage something from the wreckage called Jim Swire. 'Come on, fellows. It's been a rough time. Can't you cut him some slack?' And they do.

The relatives all chip in: 'We don't feel any further forward than on 21 December 1988. Given what we've heard in the trial, the verdict is unsatisfactory.' Everyone anticipates an appeal. That's a good thing.

But the Devil hasn't finished with my emotions. If there is an appeal will my globetrotting have to continue? How will Jane react?

The BBC persuade me to host one of their website forums. 'As a Libyan intelligence officer begins a life sentence for the Lockerbie bombing, families of the dead are to step up their fight for justice. Jim Swire, who represents the UK families of those who died, is to launch a campaign calling for a full public inquiry into the disaster. What is his reaction to Wednesday's verdict? What next for the families of the dead? When will he be satisfied that justice has been done? To watch the forum, select the link below . . .'

Since that night of 21 December 1988 the years have flown by. In spite of news of an impending appeal, Lockerbie is fading from the headlines. With gentle massaging by the spin doctors of Whitehall and the Scottish Crown Office, closure of the public mind seems inevitable.

* * *

Even as Jane and I were in 1998 relaxing in Skye, hugely relieved at the news of international agreement for the trial, others were working to a contrasting agenda. Through their actions we may learn something of the governance of our 'free nation', Britain.

Immediately after the July 1998 announcement, the University of Glasgow set up a Lockerbie Trial Briefing Unit under director Ms Clare Connelly and Jim L. Murdoch, Professor of Public Law. The unit would be a resource for those with a professional interest in the trial. The unit's Briefing Handbook explained 'This is to be the international trial of the decade and the Scottish trial of the century.'

As the unit was formed, a talented recruit appeared. Professor R. Andrew Fulton, former diplomat and Visiting Professor at the University of Glasgow School Of Law, expressed a willingness to help with this worthy task. He'd worked as a legal counsellor at the UK's Washington embassy and came with good reports by the British and Americans. And so he put his administrative skills to work in the critical and powerful post of coordinator of the unit.

Meanwhile, Michael Scanlan, President of the Law Society of Scotland, expressed his and his Society's pleasure to be associated with the unit. 'The trial of the Libyan suspects will be one of the most important criminal trials in Scottish legal history and will have a truly global effect. Our sincere sympathies go out to the bereaved relatives.'

Whether sincere sympathies were also in the mind of Professor Fulton seems doubtful. In May 2000, shortly after the commencement of the trial, a journalist checked out a website containing a list of members of the intelligence services. He spotted the name R. Andrew Fulton, a former MI6 officer who, when he retired a year prior to the commencement of the trial, was head of the MI6 station in Washington.[2]

We may ask to whom Fulton was reporting, and for what purpose. When challenged he said not a word and hurriedly departed.

Members of the Briefing Unit were devastated. They felt betrayed. And so they were, by their own government. Or perhaps, more worryingly, the government knew nothing of it. Had MI6 become so powerful as to drive its own agenda while ministers watched, powerless to intervene?

Whatever the case, the Glasgow University unit set up with a brief including support to bereaved relatives was, in the eyes of many, discredited. Could anyone now fully trust an educational organisation in which the intelligence service of a government had a role? Were other MI6 informants already within the organisation? It is easy for intelligence agents to pressurise and recruit members of staff within a large and complex organisation. Few people have cupboards empty of a skeleton.

Memories of the 1991 Fatal Accident Inquiry flooded back into mind. More than that, we British relatives knew for sure that we were under scrutiny by our government and others, certain that we were – still – *persons of interest*.

* * *

5 AUGUST 2001

Today comes an invitation to meet Foreign Secretary Jack Straw. He speaks of negotiations under way between Britain, America and Libya regarding current UN resolutions. One condition is payment of appropriate compensation, together with public acceptance by Libya of guilt for the bombing.

We ask, 'What if al-Megrahi is freed following an appeal?'

Straw smiles: 'We are conducting negotiations.'

His evasive answers infuriate me. I look him square in the face: 'We've repeatedly requested and been refused an inquiry over the last twelve years. Each time we raised the issue we were told that no inquiry could be held because there was a criminal investigation and a possible trial. The trial is over, yet now there is further delay. What more does it take?'

Straw does not know that in my pocket is a copy of a document dated 31 January 1995, signed by Harry Ditmas, head of TRANSEC, the security section of the Department of Transport. Prime Minister Thatcher agreed extra funding for improvements in airline security. Before leaving office, however, she reversed the policy and forced through a major budget cut. In a letter to his department, Ditmas explained how he was required to implement a 30 per cent cut in his security staff.

To be fair to Jack Straw, his brief had never included transport so he's unaware of the Ditmas letter. Meanwhile planes from a myriad of foreign airports are flying in over the Thames and central London, some of them loaded with unaccompanied baggage and unchecked freight.

* * *

11 SEPTEMBER 2001

New York's Twin Towers and the Pentagon building have been attacked by hijacked passenger planes. Every journalist in the world is focused on it. Some 3,000 people are said to have been killed. 'The people who knocked down these buildings will hear from all of us soon,' mutters a traumatised President George Bush Jr, as he stands amid the ruins surrounded by firefighters and police. Now he prepares to lead his people into an act of overwhelming revenge against an Arab nation, yet to be selected, in the quiet of the Oval Office. The world stands paralysed as the strongest nation in the world prepares to destroy one of the weakest. A rampant media feeding on CIA misinformation will persuade 60 per cent of the American public to believe that Iraq's Saddam Hussein is responsible for the Twin Towers attack. He, his entire family and hundreds of thousands of his army and people must die.

Meanwhile, a recently convicted Libyan Arab is the same focus of that anger; his future as a convicted person seeking an appeal against what he and others believe to be an unjust verdict does not look at all promising.

A Desperate Appeal

Appendix

Chapter 14

WITHIN WEEKS OF the issue of the verdict, Abdelbaset al-Megrahi's defence team obtained leave to make an appeal, but a further year of delay and obfuscation elapsed before its commencement today in the same courthouse in Zeist.

American bereaved relative Kathleen Flynn, her chin jutting proudly, tells journalists: 'We are here to make sure the Libyan gets his just deserts.' Tired and emaciated I force out my mantra: 'We hope that the cause of truth and justice will be furthered by the appeal.' In the coming days, people who watched the interview will ask 'Are you OK? You didn't look too good.' I will blame bad lighting.

Beside the pathway to the courthouse stands a pathetic Libyan family group holding photos and placards. In broken English al-Megrahi's son Khaled mumbles: 'My father is innocent.' In the spectator gallery John Mosey and I are the sole representatives of British relatives.

In the opening exchanges, defence advocate William Taylor describes the Lockerbie night. He recalls the testimony of John Bedford, the baggage handler in the interline shed who went for a tea break. On his return he found in the baggage container two brown Samsonite suitcases that were not there previously. He looked at the suitcases in a way that enabled him to remember the event. Was that the moment upon which Lockerbie turned from possible to probable, killing Flora and 269 other innocents? My body shudders with anguish.

Four days after the commencement of the appeal, the *Mail on Sunday* publishes extracts from tape recordings of trial identification witness Tony Gauci boasting of holidays in Scotland at the invitation of Scottish police.[1] It emerged that as early as 1991, as detailed investigations were still in progress, the police took him to Lockerbie and several cities and towns around Scotland. Should anyone ask how he could afford such visits, the police advised Gauci to say that he had won money on the European Lotto.[2] He admitted to salmon fishing and sightseeing in the final week of March 2001, eight months after his testimony in the trial. With him on one visit were four members of his family. He mentioned luxury hotels in Glasgow, Perth and Inverness, and added that at all times he had been accompanied by police officers.

A senior retired judge is concerned: 'If Gauci was taken on visits or was promised such visits, it suggests that the police were attempting to influence his evidence.'

A spokesman for Strathclyde Police explains: 'We never comment on matters relating to witness protection.' Why witness protection required a spell of salmon fishing, a further visit to Scotland eight months after giving evidence, or what danger Gauci might face once the trial was concluded, the Strathclyde spokesman does not explain. A sad point for me is that not a single journalist has insisted that he does explain.

New evidence is offered by a former Heathrow security officer, Raymond Manly. On the night prior to the Lockerbie attack, while on routine patrol he discovered that a break-in, or break-out, had occurred at terminal three. The event has lain in Manly's memory and hidden in police files for almost fourteen years. The story featured in the first editions of some British newspapers[3] only to be smothered by on-going news coverage of the destruction of New York's Twin Towers.

Manly's cross-examination by the prosecution proves unfortunate. He is on a regime of medication causing periods of vomiting. He breaks off his evidence, retires to a corridor to vomit, then returns pale and breathing with difficulty. He's carrying a bucket which he places by his feet.

He insists that between 10 p.m. and thirty minutes past midnight on 20 December, a padlock on double swing access doors at terminal three was cut or broken. The doors were made of reinforced rubber and locked by the insertion of a steel bar. The bar was sealed into place by a strong padlock. The door, named T3:2A (Terminal Three, Door Two Alpha), allowed access from the landside area of terminal three to part of the tarmac area, the baggage assembly area, and the gates for Pan Am and Iran Air. At the time the door was forced, members of the public were freely present within the landside of terminal three. Manly immediately reported the matter up the security chain, and next day completed a written report.

Alan Turnbull QC takes advantage of Manly's distress. Manly gets angry. Turnbull demands to know why, confusing the man, leading him down blind alleys. Heathrow management witnesses claim there is nothing of concern. They claim that disgruntled baggage handlers damage similar doors when taking short cuts. It's an easy explanation that excuses management of all responsibility.

The judges will note Manly's evidence, having allowed the break-in evidence to be heard, but the prosecution case was a very weak and circumstantial one and was further undermined by the additional prosecution concession that they had not been able to prove how the bomb that destroyed Pan Am Flight 103 got into the interline baggage system and onto the aircraft.

Taylor, Megrahi's lawyer, must have felt that the prosecution could not succeed, for the most that the Maltese shopkeeper Tony Gauci would say (either in his evidence in court or at an identification parade before the trial or in a series of 19 police statements over the years) was that Megrahi 'resembled a lot'

the purchaser, a phrase which he equally used with reference to
Abu Talb, a proven terrorist and one of those mentioned in the
special defence of incrimination originally lodged on behalf of
Megrahi.

Gauci had also described his customer to the police as being
six feet (183 centimetres) tall and over fifty years of age. The
evidence of the trial established (1) that Megrahi was five feet
eight inches (173 centimetres) tall and (2) that in 1988 he was
thirty-six.

As the appeal judge wrote: 'When opening the case for the
appellant before this court, Mr Taylor stated that the appeal
was not about sufficiency of evidence: he accepted that there
was a sufficiency of evidence.'

Perhaps this complacency explains why Mr Taylor never
developed his original ' special defence' to the point where the
break-in evidence heard for the first time by the appeal court
could have been seen in conjunction with the evidence of the
Heathrow baggage loader Mr Bedford as an insuperable
'reasonable doubt' as to how the bomb might have reached the
hold of Pan Am Flight 103 before it took off from Heathrow on
its final flight, rather than being accepted as having come via
Frankfurt on the smaller feeder Flight Pan Am 103A. At last
both the Bedford evidence and the break-in evidence could
have suggested that the entire prosecution story, including
Malta, Frankfurt and Pan Am 103A itself might be challenged
by the theory of direct insertion at Heathrow.

As Professor Robert Black wrote:

Until such time as an appellate court (perhaps on a reference from the Scottish Criminal Cases Review
Commission) is required to address the fundamental
issues of (1) whether there was sufficient evidence to
warrant the incriminating findings, (2) whether any
reasonable trial court would have made those findings
(and could have been satisfied beyond reasonable doubt

of the guilt of Megrahi) on the evidence led at Camp Zeist and (3) whether Megrahi's representation at the trial and the appeal was adequate, I will continue to maintain that a shameful miscarriage of justice has been perpetrated and that the Scottish criminal justice system has been gravely sullied.

I retire to the relatives' lounge for a rest. Colin Budd, British ambassador to the Netherlands, is there. He seems personable, gives an impression of doing his best to be helpful. But the evening brings a hint of menace. Crown QC Norman MacFadyen tells assembled American relatives how well things are going. Then he turns to the opposition: me. A strident Kathleen Flynn joins in. The Americans, riding the Twin Towers war horse, cheer and high-five. In the background stands a much-comforted Lord Advocate Colin Boyd.

As they leave, I buttonhole Boyd: 'This is an appeal hearing. What you are doing is not appropriate.' I later try but fail to counter the anti-Iraq, anti-Arab war hysteria with an interview for CNN. In vain I hope that in the Lockerbie case they might retain some objectivity. The reporter, too young to know about Lockerbie, is rocked on his heels by what I tell him. 'My God,' he says, 'I didn't know it was like that.' I reassure him it won't be the end of the world if al-Megrahi goes free. Nevertheless, at CNN headquarters in Atlanta, an establishment proud of its record of accurate reporting, closure of the Lockerbie story seems to have occurred long ago. The focus now is Iraq, and the term 'Kill 'em all' walks abroad among military and political classes. Those few independent minds who dare to question are overwhelmed by the thunder of war drums and the ranting of Fox News.

For Jane, for Robert Black, John and Lisa Mosey, for all the British and some of the American relatives, for David Ben Aryeah and all who've supported the campaign over the years, it's been an endless labour of love. Meanwhile, the US and British governments remain locked in denial of anything that might embarrass or challenge their activities. Knowledge is power, and power, as ever, corrupts. Democratic nations forget at their peril that intelligence services work for governments who should be the servants – not the masters – of the people. Even as *Maid of the Seas* was blown apart on the night of 21 December 1988, the wall of secrecy surrounding government actions was steadfast. When, not if, airline security systems again fail, will anyone be held accountable for anything?

* * *

14 FEBRUARY 2002

Lord Justice General Cullen hunches his shoulders around the microphone: 'We have concluded that none of the grounds of appeal is well founded. The appeal will accordingly be refused.' He ends proceedings thus: 'To all those people named and unnamed in our trial and appeal we give you thanks. And now we make avizandum.'[4]

Al-Megrahi shows no emotion. They fly him by helicopter to Barlinnie jail in Scotland to serve the rest of a twenty-year sentence.[5] Outside the court his lawyer, Havid Jhoja, intimates the possibility of a further appeal. He murmurs something about human rights. He seems confused.

The trial judges got it badly wrong; the appeal has been a boring repetition of weak defence arguments; Manly's evidence was ridiculed and the outcome predictable. Even commentators who once held some objectivity are now saying 'Told you so. End of story.' If I or anyone of like mind dares to persist it will be a lonely battle. Most of the American relatives who have doubted the verdict are sure to desert our campaign.

Even my staunchest American supporter, Peter Lowenstein, is undecided. He will continue to applaud the British relatives' campaign for an inquiry, but '. . . if it is going to be an attempt to change this [appeal] ruling, then that would be foolish. Al-Megrahi was guilty, and it may go as high as Gaddafi himself.'

American Kathleen Flynn feels 'a great day for justice has arrived'. According to Lockerbie councillor Marjorie McQueen, the people of Lockerbie have today found some closure. The repeated raising of appeals will only extend their sorrow.

In Downing Street, Jack Straw walks confidently to the microphone. 'I will be speaking to representatives of some of the families later today. We will study the judgement and announce our decision about a government inquiry. It remains for Libya to fulfil its international obligations in respect of Lockerbie. Libya has shown a desire to turn away from international terrorism, but I urge the government of Libya to comply fully with the terms of Security Council resolutions.'

But we campaigners know in our hearts there will never be an inquiry. Amid a sea of intrigue, assassinations, illegal renditions, bribery and lies, Britain has signed contracts with America's main intelligence organisations and has unsigned acknowledgements with members of Gaddafi's entourage and security services. Any undue revelations by America's so-called allies will result in withdrawal of US security and intelligence cooperation. Straw knows it, so did his predecessors and so will his successors.

Concealed Evidence,
False Evidence

Chapter 15

DURING ONE OF his several visits to Britain, Nelson Mandela insists on meeting al-Megrahi in Barlinnie prison. The two chat for a while, and al-Megrahi's family take several photographs.

Al-Megrahi is much encouraged, writing in his memoirs:

> That the world's most respected statesman should again take the trouble to demonstrate his solidarity gives me a great lift. We chatted mainly about the unjust guilty verdict. Before he left I introduced him to my family, who thanked him and presented him with a bouquet of flowers. I was allowed to take photographs of him in the reception area and he signed my Arabic version of his book *Long Walk to Freedom*, which describes his prison years. In it he wrote: 'To Comrade Megrahi, Best wishes to one who is in our thoughts and prayers continuously. Mandela.'

Following his meeting, Mandela holds a wide-ranging press conference. Of al-Megrahi he comments: 'The man is all alone. He has nobody he can talk to. His solitary confinement is nothing short of psychological persecution.'

Meanwhile I'm midway through a book by a former CIA Middle Eastern specialist, Robert Baer, entitled *See No Evil:*

The True Story of a Ground Soldier in the CIA's War on Terrorism.[1] It brings back memories of the time before the pronouncement of the November 1991 indictments. Baer was a significant part of the CIA's investigation up to August 1991. He writes with authority based on insider knowledge.

He and his CIA colleagues obtained information from a wide range of sources. Those sources were, claims Baer, 'as good as it gets'. When the investigation turned to Libya he was surprised and unconvinced. But he was no longer on the case so there was nothing he could do.

He confirms all that was said to have happened in Germany in the weeks prior to the bombing. Iran was set on a course to bring down American aircraft as revenge for the USS *Vincennes* incident. The PFLP-GC group devised a means to plant the bomb, and Abu Talb was part of the operation, for which he was paid $500,000 on 25 April 1989. An $11 million transfer took place into a PFLP-GC account two days after the Lockerbie attack.[2] Talb and Dalkamoni were honoured by Iran as heroic martyrs.

In the 1994 film *The Maltese Double Cross*, Baer's CIA associate Vincent Cannistraro was interviewed on camera. Of the Hayes/Feraday fragment PT/35(b) he said: 'Grey timer boards were used by the East German Stasi. Green timer boards were used by Libya.' At the time of the Channel 4 debate about the film, therefore, I had no reason to doubt the provenance of the fragment.

Yet Baer's central premise is that the bomb did not come from Libya. If he is correct, fragment PT/35(b) is of unknown origin, and perhaps a planted fake.

* * *

16 AUGUST 2003

Within a year of the conclusion of al-Megrahi's unsuccessful appeal come signs of a Libyan return to international respectability. Without an admission of guilt, sanctions will continue indefinitely. They have already cost Libya many billions of dollars. Her economy is seriously damaged.

Today the logjam is breached by a letter from Libya's UN Envoy, addressed to the Security Council:

> I am pleased to inform you that the remaining issues relating to the fulfilment of all Security Council resolutions resulting from the Lockerbie incident have been resolved. In this context, and out of respect for international law and pursuant to the Security Council resolutions, Libya as a sovereign state has facilitated the bringing to justice of the two suspects charged with the bombing of Pan Am 103, and accepts responsibility for the actions of its officials.

Britain's UN ambassador, Emyr Jones Parry, has announced that within three days the UK will circulate a draft resolution for the lifting of UN sanctions. Nevertheless, a suspicious American administration demands that Libya must go further. Not until full access is granted to UN weapons inspectors, and all terrorism and programmes for the acquisition of weapons of mass destruction renounced, will America consider any changes to its own sanctions programme.

Some within the White House claim Gaddafi's change of heart has come following the destruction of Saddam Hussein's regime in Iraq. Gaddafi fears for his position. There are rumours of dissent in parts of Libya.

Gaddafi's timing supports that suspicion, but it's clear that other forces are at work. I am convinced that Gaddafi wants to ensure a safe transfer of power to his sons – primarily Saif al-Islam – and the survival of the Gaddafi dynasty.

* * *

3 DECEMBER 2003

The Travellers Club in Pall Mall, London, has been for decades a favourite haunt of spies. On this day a somewhat interesting group gathers to discuss a special kind of bargain: a Prisoner Transfer Agreement (PTA) which might enable al-Megrahi to return to Libya, and a Libyan renunciation of all nuclear weapons ambitions. Whitehall sources will later confirm that the subject of al-Megrahi is part of the discussions.[3]

The meeting includes the Libyan head of external intelligence, Moussa Koussa, Libyan officials, nine top-level MI6 officers, CIA representatives and Foreign Office staff. The Foreign Office are keeping Tony Blair informed of progress via Downing Street. Koussa remains banned from the UK following accusations of plots to assassinate Libyan dissidents, but has been allowed safe passage because of his closeness to Gaddafi.

On 5 December 2003, Prime Minister Tony Blair telephones Gaddafi. Within a fortnight London and Washington declare that Libya has come in from the cold.

And yet, is Libya really admitting guilt for the Lockerbie bombing? The enigma is strengthened by an interview given to BBC television by Libyan Prime Minister Shukri Ghanem. He claims that the August 2003 declaration of guilt is not real: 'After the sanctions and after the problems we have [been] facing because of the sanctions, we thought that it was easier for us to buy peace and this is why we agreed compensation.'

The BBC seek clarification: 'Is Libya now denying guilt for the Lockerbie bombing?'

Ghanem stands firm: 'I agree with that and this is why I say, we bought peace.'

There seems no hope of progress with our demands for an inquiry. With a sad heart and mixed feelings I withdraw into father mode. In frequent visits to the summer house in Skye I start to repair winter's attrition to roof and windows. The boat house has huge pebbles slammed against its doors by winter's waves; they take a lot of shifting. At Caspidge, each day's agenda is topped by William and his wife, Julie, Cathy and her husband, Johnny, and their new home in Malvern, and a growing tribe of grandchildren.

* * *

12 NOVEMBER 2006

On this day a US State Department lawyer, Michael Scharf, alleges that the CIA manipulated the Lockerbie trial and lied about the strength of the prosecution case to get a result that was politically convenient for America. The case was 'so full of holes it was like a Swiss cheese. It should never have gone to trial'.

Scharf joined the State Department's Office of the Legal Adviser for Law Enforcement and Intelligence in April 1989, just four months after Pan Am Flight 103 was downed and at the height of the CIA's Lockerbie bombing investigation. He was counsel to the US counter-terrorism bureau at the issue of the indictments against al-Megrahi and Fhimah. He was also responsible for drawing up the UN Security Council resolutions that imposed sanctions on Libya in 1992 in order to force Tripoli to hand over the two suspects for trial.

He claims that the CIA and FBI had assured State Department officials there was an 'iron-clad' case against al-Megrahi and Fhimah, but that in reality the intelligence agencies had no confidence in their star witness, Majid Giaka, and knew well in advance of the trial that he was 'a liar'. The case was '. . . a whitewash. Everybody agreed ahead of time that they were just going to focus on these two, and they were the fall guys.'

Scharf adds: 'The CIA and the FBI kept the State Department in the dark. It worked for them for us to be fully committed to the theory that Libya was responsible. I helped the

counter-terrorism bureau draft documents that described why
we thought Libya was responsible, but these were not based on
seeing a lot of evidence, but rather on representations from the
CIA and FBI and the Department of Justice about what the
case would prove and did prove . . . It was largely based on this
inside guy, Libyan defector Abdul Majid Giaka. It wasn't until
the trial that I learned he was a nut-job and that the CIA had
absolutely no confidence in him and that they knew he was a
liar'.

Scharf, now an international law expert at Case Western
Reserve University in Ohio, is convinced that Libya, Iran and
the Palestinian terrorist group the PFLP-GC were involved in
the bombing. But the case had a 'diplomatic rather than a
purely legal goal . . . Now Libya has given up its weapons of
mass destruction, it's allowed inspectors in, the sanctions have
been lifted, tourists from the US are flocking to see the Roman
ruins outside of Tripoli and Gaddafi has become a leader in
Africa rather than a pariah. And all of that is the result of this
trial.'[4]

* * *

28 JUNE 2007. REPORT OF THE SCOTTISH
CRIMINAL CASES REVIEW COMMISSION (SCCRC)

In 2002, al-Megrahi's newly appointed solicitor, Edward
MacKechnie, was convinced that a miscarriage of justice had
occurred. He recruited a team of legal, police and administrative experts to prepare a request for a review by the Scottish
Criminal Cases Review Commission (SCCRC).

In September 2003 MacKechnie presented to the Commission
his 400-page application. The Commission's estimate was that
their own review would take at least a year. It would take, in
fact, almost four years, during which time MacKechnie would
be succeeded by Tony Kelly, and al-Megrahi's health would
deteriorate severely.

Today the Commission has issued its report. A statement of 820 pages and thirteen volumes of appendices identify six grounds for referral back to an Appeal Court. All who support a second appeal for Abdelbaset al-Megrahi are of one mind. Not only has new evidence emerged, the Commission has discovered that several important items of evidence available at the time of the trial were not put before the judges nor disclosed to the defence.

To withhold or conceal from a defence team evidence which may cast doubt on a prosecution case is an offence in law. At best it seriously hampers an advocate's ability to cross-examine a prosecution witness; at worst it can falsely imprison an innocent person. British legal history has suffered several such events, including the Guildford Four and the Hillsborough Inquiry. Will Lockerbie join the list?

* * *

WITNESS STATEMENTS AND OFFERS OF REWARDS

Deeply significant, the SCCRC finds no reasonable basis for the trial court's conclusion that the purchase of clothes from Mary's House took place on 7 December 1988. Newly discovered evidence indicates strongly that the purchase took place prior to 6 December 1988; in other words, when al-Megrahi was not on the island of Malta. The implication of this fact alone presents a major flaw in the prosecution case: *if al-Megrahi was not the purchaser of the clothes, then Gauci never met him. How then might Gauci recognise him from photographs, at a police line-up, and in the trial courtroom?*

There is also evidence not made available at the trial indicating that only four days prior to the police identification parade at which Gauci picked out al-Megrahi, he was familiar with a photograph in *Focus* magazine which identified Megrahi as the bomber. Gauci purchased the magazine a month prior to the identification. In the Commission's view, his long exposure to that photograph undermined his reliability then and at the trial.

A further important discovery has been the diary of Harry Bell, the senior Scottish policeman who headed the investigation team. His diary and related HOLMES[5] entries contain several references to massive rewards for Tony Gauci, his brother Paul, and CIA informant and Crown witness Majid Giaka.

Apart from a brief exchange during the trial, the judges and defence were unaware of the existence of Bell's diary. The Commission does not comment on the role of the prosecution team in this. In summary, Bell's diary reveals that:

- Within two weeks of Bell's first contact with Gauci, an 'unlimited' multi-million dollar payment was on offer from the US.[6]
- The first occasion on which Tony Gauci identified al-Megrahi coincided almost exactly with insistent demands for money by Tony and his brother Paul.
- In the words of the US Department of Justice, the reward would be paid 'only if he [Tony Gauci] gives evidence'.

Gauci's first encounter with Bell's police team was on 1 September 1989. He met them again on the 14th and 26th of that month. Two days later, Bell recorded that the US were prepared to offer 'unlimited monies to Tony Gauci, with $10,000 available immediately'.[7] It is a reasonable conclusion that the offer was based on discussions that had taken place throughout September.

Further entries by Bell reveal repeated demands for money by Tony Gauci. He writes that Tony's brother Paul 'has a clear desire to gain financial benefit' from his and his brother's cooperation. Another example includes 'reward money as a last resort'. We might ask: a last resort for what? One entry records that a discussion took place regarding 'reward money and the Maltese reaction'. Another records proposed payments to the CIA's witness Majid Giaka. Bell writes: 'The DoJ will pay Giaka $2m ... I also clarified with them about the Gauci reward and the response was "only if he gives evidence".'[8]

There is a significant time correlation between an entry concerning Gauci's further insistent demands for money, and his first formal identification of al-Megrahi from a photograph.[9] On 15 February 1991 Gauci gave his first identification in a written statement. Six days later, on 21 February, a memo from Bell to DSIO Gilchrist states that Tony Gauci 'expressed an interest in receiving money at recent meetings' and that 'if a monetary offer was made this may well change his view'. We might ask: change his view from what to what?

The SCCRC have also discovered entries in Bell's diary about Gauci's visits to Scotland. The first visit took place shortly after Gauci's first identification of al-Megrahi from photographs on 15 February 1991. When discussing the arrangements, DCI Harry Bell writes: 'Scicluna spoke to Gauci today. He is not keen on going to [*redacted location*] ... However, he would consider ... [*redacted alternative location*] but would like his father with him even though they may argue. He wondered how he would explain the cost of such a trip. He was told to suggest the National Lotto as having won a prize.'[10]

Professor Robert Black QC advises that under Scots law payments or other incentives do not automatically disqualify a witness. Payment is one of several factors to be considered in assessing credibility. In order for this to be done, however, it is necessary for the court to know that payment was promised and/or made. Failure by the Crown to disclose a promise and/or payment is a serious breach of duty to the court and the administration of justice.

In the trial the judges dismissed Majid Giaka's evidence as a mixture of fantasy, self-preservation and pecuniary interest. They did not know that he and Gauci were each being offered

$2 million for their cooperation. If I had known it at the time, I'd have sprinted from the court to grab the first available journalist.

* * *

In addition to monetary issues Bell records in his diary and other undisclosed police records, there is an interview in which Gauci told him that 'the Libyan' had returned to his shop on 25 September 1989, ten months after the claimed original visit.

Then on 2 October 1989 Bell met again with Gauci who stated that he was 'only 50% sure that it was the same man'. In a note attached to his record of this interview, Bell records concern over Gauci's accuracy in that he 'may be trying to please us'. Since Gauci was aware of the possibility of huge rewards, such would explain his willingness to please.[11]

On 11 October 1989, Bell met Gauci in the presence of co-investigator DCI Henderson. Bell records: 'Tony's judgement of age may be questionable. The number of photographs being shown to him may confuse matters.'

On 21 February 1990, Bell interviewed Gauci again and recorded the following: 'Gauci states he may have seen the suspect before in May 1987 when he made a purchase of two or three blankets from the Sliema shop. Tony delivered the blankets to room 113 of the Hilton Hotel where he handed them over. He could not state positively that it was the same man but he was similar.'[12]

One day later DS Byrne entered in his personal notebook that '. . . Grech and Godfrey Scicluna found it difficult to believe Tony's story about the Hilton Hotel and were of the opinion that he had become confused about things'.

Two weeks later, on 5 March 1990, Gauci recalled a further sequence of events. Bell notes: '[Gauci] was sure this event was in 1987, maybe June 1987. He had moved shops in April 1987 and it was sometime after that. The room number was 113. The manner of purchase was the same which is one of the reasons he thought it was the same man. He was similar to the purchaser if not the same man.'

DS Byrne then re-interviewed Gauci: 'Gauci was adamant it was room 113 and an Arabic name on paper. [He recalls that the] receptionist used [a] push button type phone . . . in addition his explanation for recall of the Hilton is that he feels the man had been in his shop before . . .'

Six months later, on 10 September 1990, Bell records that Gauci, when pressed, refused to repeat all that he had previously offered, stating: 'All I can say about this event is that the man who bought the blankets was similar to the purchaser.'[13]

Matters were wrapped up by the Maltese police who carried out their own inquiries. They discovered that no Libyans were resident in room 113 during 1987, and that one Arab male guest was in that room in January 1987.

* * *

During the trial I learned that another witness was offered rewards for his cooperation. At the time of the bombing in December 1988 Vincent Vassallo was duty manager in the cafeteria at Malta's Luqa Airport. He was a colleague of the accused al-Megrahi. More than two years later, on 18 April 1991, Harry Bell and his team went to Luqa to ask Vassallo about the suspects al-Megrahi and Fhimah.

Vassallo said of Bell's visit: 'Harry Bell asked me, he said: "Try to remember well. You know there is a large reward, and if you wish to have more money, perhaps go abroad somewhere, you can do so." '[14]

Defence advocate Bill Taylor briefly mentioned the Vassallo episode in his closing submission. And the trial judges gave equally brief attention to his words.

* * *

Not contained in Bell's diaries, but held on other undisclosed police files, was information concerning David Wright, a possible second identification witness to the purchase of clothes in Gauci's shop.

On 6 November 1989 the BBC Six O'Clock News showed footage which mentioned for the first time that a suitcase containing the bomb was introduced in Malta's Luqa Airport. Images of Gauci's shop, Mary's House, were displayed. The commentary said that fragments of clothes were found at the crash site, and that the clothes were purchased from Mary's House by an Arab man.

Watching the programme was David Wright. A week later he contacted Dumfries and Galloway police. One month later he signed a statement.

He claimed he was a frequent visitor to Malta and a friend of Tony Gauci. He would spend time in Tony's shop. During one of his visits, made between 28 October and 28 November 1988, he was in the shop when two men entered saying they were interested in purchasing some clothes.

With Gauci offering guidance they proceeded to buy various items of clothing. They were smartly dressed, one wore a dark suit and he had swarthy skin. Both were aged over forty-five years. They spoke English, said they were Libyan, and claimed they were staying at the Holiday Inn. During the purchase, Wright recalls Gauci boasting that he could tell the size of people just by looking at them.

Wright gave descriptions of the two men, neither of which matched al-Megrahi. He said that he subsequently recognised the younger of the two men from a TV programme when the man appeared as a spokesman for the Libyan government.

Wright claimed that Gauci described the two as 'Libyan pigs' and that when he spoke to Gauci around the time of the BBC news broadcast, Gauci appeared not to remember the event.

The SCCRC traced the police records of Wright's contacts and interviews. His statement was initially flagged for action on 18 December 1989 but was changed to 'filed' on 13 February 1990.

Seventeen years later, on 5 December 2007, Wright was interviewed by officers of the SCCRC and signed an affidavit confirming his previous account.

The key feature of Wright's statement is the date of the purchase. The Crown made much of al-Megrahi's presence in Malta on 7 December 1988. The judges accepted the Crown argument on the premise that unproven inferences elsewhere in the Crown case indicated that al-Megrahi might be the culprit.

Yet if Wright's statement is correct, a significant purchase of clothes occurred on a different day, possibly but not necessarily 23 November. Whatever day it was, al-Megrahi could not have been one of the purchasers, since his passport records showed he was not in Malta on any of the days when Wright was present.

There is no evidence that the items purchased when Wright was in the shop were the source of clothing found at Lockerbie. It might be that two purchases took place. But Gauci made no reference whatever to the 23 November purchase throughout his two years of contact with Harry Bell. He did, though, as explained above, talk freely about a stranger who resembled the purchaser of the Lockerbie clothes coming into his shop and purchasing blankets as far back as 1987.

Wright's statement was given to the Dumfries and Galloway police at the height of their investigation. 'The most intensive police investigation in Scottish legal history' was daily news throughout the force. It is inconceivable that the officers recording Wright's statement were unaware of its significance, and surely they must have sought advice from senior officers.

There are, therefore, serious questions which must be put to those who recorded Wright's statement and filed it. Who did you inform about the David Wright statement? Were they aware of its content? What instructions did they give you as to what to do with the statement? Unfortunately, without a further appeal or inquiry, these questions will never be addressed.

Wright's statement remained undisturbed in police archives for seventeen years. The trial and appeal judges and the defence team were unaware of its existence.[15] We can though be sure that if the defence had been aware of Wright's statement they would have invited him to give evidence. If credible he would have undermined Gauci's reliability. Stronger cross-examination of Gauci would have followed, which might have changed the course of the trial.

Were officers of the Scottish Crown aware of Wright's statement? If so, failure to inform the defence and the court would be a breach of the Lord Advocate's obligations in law.[16]

* * *

During the trial I watched with some suspicion the evidence by DC Gilchrist, Hayes and Feraday regarding fragment PT/35(b). This tiny item – ten millimetres by four – holds the key to what many believe to be the reality of Lockerbie. It would be wrong to simply state that it is a planted fake; nevertheless, so much information has come to light regarding its structure and materials that nagging doubts have emerged through the years regarding its manufacture and origin.

The SCCRC appears to share those doubts. In September 2006, members of the Commission went to Dumfries police station to read two secret documents. The documents were supplied by an unnamed country, said not to be the United States. They were not allowed to make copies. They could make their own notes, but were required to leave them in the keeping of the police.

Nevertheless, in their statement of reasons, the Commission indicate two clues to their contents. In a letter to the Commission dated 27 April 2007, the Crown Office claimed that 'It has never been the Crown's position that MST-13 timers were not supplied by Libyan intelligence to other parties, or that only the Libyan intelligence services were in possession of the timers.' In other words, Libya may have supplied MST-13 timers to other nations and their intelligence organisations.

What nations might they be? And who was working for them on the date of the Lockerbie attack? Does the Crown have any evidence to support this innuendo? They made no mention of it throughout the trial and appeal.

Secondly, '. . . failure by the prosecution to disclose one of the two documents to the defence team indicates that a miscarriage of justice may have occurred'. The Commission cross-refer this startling observation with sections of the written judgement at the trial. All of those sections concern MST-13 timers. The mystery deepens.

The Commission's conclusion is that a second appeal is justified. When hearing that, appeal the judges must surely reflect on the Commission's words: '. . . *a miscarriage of justice may have occurred*'.

* * *

The Commission's report devastates my emotions. The black rage has returned not only against Heathrow's management and the faceless ones of the Department of Transport; now there are new opponents: prosecutors who obfuscate and conceal; policemen who hide their diaries; a Maltese shopkeeper who can identify a complete stranger from photographs up to two years after apparently never meeting him.

Yet even as I reflect upon these events, at the heart of the prosecution case lies a falsehood greater than any revealed so far. Deep within the forensic notebook kept by Allen Feraday are two hand-written comments. Within the files of the police and prosecution team lie three reports by reputable scientists. All suggest that the central feature of the prosecution case is based on a falsehood. They concern PT/35(b) and the timer boards manufactured by Thüring and supplied by MEBO to Libyan intelligence. I am not to discover this amazing truth until December 2011; the full story will be revealed in February 2012.

* * *

19 December 2008

Three years ago, in an out-of-the-blue moment, Peter Fraser, Scotland's Lord Advocate at the time of the 1991 indictments, admitted to doubts concerning Tony Gauci. In *The Sunday Times* Fraser was quoted: 'Gauci was not quite the full shilling. I think even his family would say [that he] was an apple short of a picnic. He was quite a tricky guy. I don't think he was deliberately lying but if you asked him the same question three times he would just get irritated and refuse to answer. You do have to worry, he's a slightly simple chap, are you putting words into his mouth even if you don't intend to.'[17]

Lord Advocate Colin Boyd attempted a carefully phrased rearguard action. Ignoring what were accurately reported quotations Boyd protested: 'Lord Fraser has indicated to my officials that he did not intend to attack the credibility or reliability of Mr Gauci. At no stage has he conveyed any reservation about any aspect of the prosecution to those who worked on the case or anyone in the prosecution service.'

Well, your Lordship, Fraser may not have said anything at the time, but he was certainly saying it in 2005.

Did Fraser's words cast a new light on the resignation shortly before the trial of his predecessor Lord Hardie? There were rumours that Hardie feared the prosecution case would not pass muster before the Kamp Zeist judges. Was Hardie of like mind regarding Gauci's credibility?

Now today, 19 December 2008, Fraser becomes more candid.

'Could the CIA have planted the evidence?' asks a *Times* journalist.

'I don't know,' says Fraser. 'No one ever came to see me and said "Now we can go for the Libyans." It was never as straightforward as that. The CIA were extremely subtle. For me the significant evidence came when the Scottish police made the connection with Malta.'

'So what is your own view?' presses the reporter.

Fraser cites the case of Patrick Meehan, in which it was alleged that the prosecution case had been 'improved' by the planting of evidence. So, is there a similarity?

'I don't know,' says Fraser.

Tam Dalyell MP talks to Fraser and asks him a similar question.

'If there was a conspiracy,' says Fraser, 'then I am in it up to the neck. I have to be involved. The only other possibility is that I've been so naïve that bits of evidence have been planted, and I have swallowed it hook, line and sinker. But four other Lord Advocates have also examined the evidence and they have all concurred with it.'[18]

Fraser accuses me of suffering from Stockholm Syndrome (a condition where surviving victims of terrorist outrages develop an empathy with the cause of those who attacked them). Indeed, he's said it to journalists. Still, I find some comfort in the man's words; at least he did not say 'one apple short of a picnic'.

* * *

A second appeal is imminent. Al-Megrahi is seriously ill. He's complaining of prostate problems. Escorted by security vehicles they've taken him to hospital for tests. The doctors report a cancerous condition. Will it spread?

The outing features in British tabloids who scream about a £20,000 waste of money on a terrorist. Long and lonely separation from family and all things Libyan is taking its toll. The attitudes of fellow prisoners and staff, subtly and daily revealed, force his separation to a specially designed secure unit. The criticism mutates from hatred of the man to cynical comments about a comfortable life in Greenock prison and the 'Gaddafi Café'.

Risking the anger of politicians and the media, Robert Black and retired MP Tam Dalyell have separately visited al-Megrahi. Two months later it is my turn, accompanied by Tony Kelly, al-Megrahi's solicitor. The prison gate closes behind us. I glance at the staff. Eyebrows are raised.

Tony Kelly has arranged today's visit. He's well known here, visiting frequently over the last eighteen months. Today I am news; will tomorrow bring a shower of brown envelopes from the press to be handed to prison staff for exclusive stories? Into my mind flow wild and damaging headlines.

The prison governor stretches out a welcoming hand and leads us to his office. Al-Megrahi is there already, easing his pain in a comfortable chair. I sit facing him, to enable relaxed conversation.

It's the first time I've seen him since he was taken down at the end of the first appeal. The man has aged a lot but seems secure in himself and at peace. He's followed every step of our campaign and is deeply pleased to see me.

'Jim,' he says, 'it is good to meet you. Thank you for coming to see me. Please, call me Baset.'

We talk about his family, the difficulties they face so far from Tripoli. His wife, Aisha, lives with their children in Newton Mearns, some way from Glasgow. They've been moved there for their own safety. Their first home was attacked with bricks. When on the streets in Glasgow they were spat on and abused. I recently visited their temporary home. He is grateful for that.

He makes no request of me. His demeanour betrays loneliness. He looks the forgotten man. As we talk, my suspicions return. Surely, he and Khalifa Fhimah were persuaded to offer themselves for trial on a promise that they were bound to be acquitted?

We've talked for over an hour. Finally he hands me a card on which is written a personal message. A devout Muslim requests that Jim Swire the Christian prays for him. As we say goodbye I offer a clumsy attempt at encouragement, but each of us knows the truth; political and intelligence forces are gathering to destroy a second appeal.

* * *

I'm in London, in a taxi.

'Dorchester Hotel, please,' I say.

In a luxury suite in the hotel, Libyan Deputy Foreign Minister Obeidi is most polite. What are my thoughts about Baset's second appeal? Obeidi is worried about a poor prognosis. Is time our greatest enemy?

I say, 'It's not looking good. He needs treatment and care at home among his family.' As I'm speaking Obeidi glances up and over my shoulder. Someone has entered the room.

I turn to face the impassive gaze of Moussa Koussa and my heart chills. Koussa nods politely, moves to the side of the room and sits down. His silence is uncanny. I regather my thoughts and resume our conversation as Koussa watches with an occasional nod of understanding.

Obeidi seems grateful for our campaign. He gives no hint of anxiety for al-Megrahi's repatriation, in spite of the Blair/Gaddafi Prisoner Transfer Agreement. I take care not to mention Libya. There are deep suspicions about the trial evidence, but it's still possible that others are working to a Libyan agenda. I keep in mind that in 2002 Abu Nidal boasted to a gathering of his group's council that he'd carried out the Lockerbie attack. So I stay with the doctor theme, recalling the politeness with which, in 1991, I was received in the hospital in Tripoli. Laying on heavily the issue of primary care for cancer in Scotland, I assure Obeidi that Baset will get the best available treatment. To keep him in prison for the final months of his life would be distinctly cruel.

At the back of my mind also runs the thought that in a recent CNN interview Gaddafi's son, Saif, claimed that the Lockerbie story is 'all a game'. And so to Baset; is he a part of Gaddafi's game? Might Libya prefer him to fade away, his appeal rejected? Best not to mention that. I stand and say farewell to both. Koussa stands, silently shakes my hand and sits down. He is clearly staying. But why is he here?

* * *

23 January 2009

After almost three years of extraordinary delaying tactics by the Crown Office the opening skirmishes preceding a second appeal have begun. Meanwhile, Baset's terminal cancer is steadily advancing.

Early court hearings focus on the secret document concerning PT/35(b) discovered by the SCCRC. Because its contents were not disclosed to the defence prior to or during the trial, the SCCRC concluded that on the basis of that alone a second appeal is justified.

Scotland's new Lord Advocate, Elish Angiolini, tells the judges that her office will not object to the document being disclosed to the defence. It seems a generous offer but is worthless. For behind the scenes, British Foreign Secretary David Miliband has signed a public interest immunity certificate to ensure that it remains hidden.

A worse example of inequality of arms is difficult to imagine. Margaret Scott QC, who leads the defence team, accuses the British government of interfering in a Scottish court process. Why has Miliband stepped in? Is it his own decision, or is it forced upon him by the Americans? The British government, the Foreign Office, the Justice Secretary, the Scottish police, the Scottish Crown Office all know the contents; but not the plaintiff, his defence solicitors, nor the public.

What is Miliband's reason? 'National Security', two words that are the cause of excessive government secrecy in our so-called democracy. Does America's national interest trump all other values? Are the dead of Lockerbie not to be weighed in the balance?

Away from the High Court an angry Tony Kelly protests: 'This is the first time we've ever had a PII Certificate signed in this way in Scotland. Why aren't Scottish ministers screaming from the rooftops about United Kingdom interference in a Scottish criminal trial? This document is so important that it could form the winning point of the second appeal.'

Robert Black is deeply puzzled: 'If this document has been in the possession of the prosecution since 1996, how can it affect British national security in 2008?'

Former CIA agent Robert Baer steps in with what many believe to be the truth: 'It may include some kind of contract,' he explains, 'not to reveal the channels of co-operation between MI6 and the CIA.'

In spite of our anger we relatives are powerless. The nearest we may get to discovering the contents is an agreement – imposed after weeks of stubborn resistance by the Scottish Crown and David Miliband's office – for a security-vetted defence representative. This solicitor or judge – his or her appointment agreed behind closed doors – will study the document and decide whether its contents are relevant to the defence case. Does that not sound familiar? It smacks of the legal tricks used by every tin-pot dictator since the law was invented.

When the Scottish *Herald* discovers the contents and wants to publish, the British government threatens legal action, forcing the *Herald* editors to sign a gagging order. An unnamed source tells the *Herald* 'The document itself is historical . . . it is hard to believe it presents any risk at all to national security. It originates from Jordan and incriminates the PFLP-GC. It does not rule out the Libyans but it does indicate that others were involved. It shows the lengths the UK Government is prepared to go to ensure that any evidence undermining their case against Al-Megrahi will never see the light of day.'[19]

Meanwhile, on a mid-winter day in 2009, as we gather in Edinburgh's High Court to watch yet another page of history unfold, the defence do their best, but are severely limited in what they can raise with the judges. After several days of presentations the court adjourns, with the judges promising that they will consider carefully what they have witnessed.

* * *

But their adjournment is overtaken by momentous events. On 30 August 2009 it is revealed that the British government, in the persons of Tony Blair, Gordon Brown and Jack Straw have all along been using al-Megrahi as a bargaining chip in oil industry negotiations with Gaddafi and his son, Saif al-Islam.

Two years previously Straw wrote to Scotland's Justice Minister, Kenny MacAskill, regarding the Prisoner Transfer Agreement (PTA) signed in March 2004 by Blair and Gaddafi. Journalists named it the 'Deal in the Desert'. At that same meeting, and at a later meeting, Blair agreed with the Libyans an $11 billion trade agreement involving British Petroleum.

In 2007 Straw had been challenged about the deal and its links with al-Megrahi. He told MacAskill that he favoured an option to leave him out of the PTA. But as the months passed and back-channel negotiations proceeded, Straw reversed direction: 'I previously accepted the importance of the al-Megrahi issue to Scotland. I said I would try to get an exclusion of him in the face of the agreement. I have not been able to secure an explicit exclusion.'

Straw did not indicate where the resistance had come from. Was it from the British government, or was pressure coming from Libya with threats of withdrawal from the BP agreement?

He continued with the bombshell: 'In view of the overwhelming interests for the United Kingdom, I have agreed that the PTA should be in the standard form and not mention any individual.' In other words, it could include al-Megrahi.

Two years later, on 5 February 2009, Straw seemingly cleared the matter up entirely. In an interview given to the *Daily Telegraph*, he admitted that his original requirement was that the PTA would exclude al-Megrahi. But, following a warning by British Petroleum that failure to include al-Megrahi could hurt BP's Libyan interests, Straw capitulated. 'Yes. It was a very big part of that. I'm unapologetic about that. Libya was a rogue state. Trade is an essential part of it, and subsequently there was the BP deal.'[20]

To counter the ensuing furore, Prime Minister Gordon Brown made a special point of interrupting a school visit to claim that there had been 'No deal, and no private assurances by me.'[21] The important words were '*by me*'.

* * *

Meanwhile, as the appeal adjournment slowly unwinds Baset knows that there is another option – compassionate release. A 1994 Scottish law allows a prisoner compassionate release if the circumstances are appropriate in terms of health or family circumstances.

Four lawyers representing Baset have visited him in Greenock prison. For me the news bears a frosty sound. If the second appeal is withdrawn and he goes home to die, our relatives' campaign might be forcibly ended.

My fears are soon realised. On 6 May 2009, Abdel el-Ubaidi, leader of the visiting Libyan delegation, makes a statement. The Libyan government has requested of the Scottish government that Baset be transferred to their custody under the PTA. An appeal hearing is due in six days time, but at its commencement, Baset will ask the judges to drop his appeal. 'He is sick. He has cancer. He wants to die among his family and friends. He is ready to drop the appeal if it is guaranteed that he will be transferred to Libya.'

It's a clear invitation to Scottish Justice Minister Kenny MacAskill. Accompanied by two senior civil servants MacAskill travels to interview the dying man in the presence of his solicitor. The official minute, notable for its precision, includes: 'The prisoner insists that he has been unjustly convicted. He is deeply sympathetic for the terrible loss of the victims' families. He feels there is little prospect that his appeal will be concluded before his death, and that his dreams of returning home clearly no longer exist.' An unofficial addendum, hand-written by Baset, offers a variation: 'I'm a very ill person. The disease I have is incurable . . . I have a short time left. I have a burning desire to clear my name. I think now that I will not witness that ultimate conclusion. As I turn now to face my God, to stand before him, I have nothing to fear.'

Worldwide reaction and anger against what seems an inevitable decision is on every television channel. The FBI's Richard Marquise and Scottish police officer Stuart Henderson take MacAskill to task. 'The release of Al-Megrahi will nullify the dedicated work of dozens of law enforcement officials around the world.'

My priority is for Baset to return home to his family. If new evidence proves he was not involved in the attack, so be it. It would be unfortunate indeed for him to die in prison awaiting a further appeal and later be judged innocent.

And so MacAskill sends him home. The world's cameras coldly watch as a frail middle-aged man wrapped in a heavy coat, a thick scarf hiding his face, woollen hat covering his head, struggles up the steps of a specially commissioned jet. Then he is gone.

But not quite; a row of Scottish saltires waves at Tripoli Airport as Baset stands at the door of the plane beside Gaddafi's son, Saif al-Islam. Below them a hundred or so of Baset's tribe sing and shout in ecstasy at the return of the family hero. Saif ensures that he and Baset are photographed together for history's sake and beckons the official photographer up the steps to get better focus. Compared to the 1988 ecstatic homecoming of the USS *Vincennes* it is but a small affair.

For his homecoming Baset has taken the trouble to put on a dark suit and tie, with a pocket handkerchief. His tidiness and respect for his family will in the coming decade be deliberately misinterpreted as proof that he really is not seriously ill, and that his struggling departure from Scotland has been part of a public relations stunt.[22]

Within hours, FBI Chief Robert Mueller publishes a letter attacking MacAskill. The Labour, Conservative and Liberal Democrat parties in the Scottish Parliament do likewise. To this is added vitriol and ocean-to-ocean coverage on US networks of the views of the Cohen family and Bert Ammerman, and the condemnation of someone I met in 1994 in the Channel 4 studio, Frank Duggan. 'We thought it was a mistake,' says President Obama. 'I'm deeply disappointed,' says Secretary of State Hillary Clinton.

But is it all phoney, a choreographed display? I am convinced that the American and British governments are heartily relieved that Baset is at last off the Western stage. A second appeal has been abandoned; pressure for an inquiry has been dissipated; all embarrassing revelations and suspicions concerning the activities of American and British intelligence communities can be safely consigned to their appropriate archives.

My suspicions are reinforced when, on 7 December 2010, a series of formerly secret diplomatic cables is released by the Wikileaks organisation to the *Guardian* newspaper, including documents concerning exchanges between the Libyan and British governments.

The Tripoli administration made a series of threats concerning trade and diplomatic relations should Baset's release not be handled in a manner favourable to Libya. 'Thuggish' and explicit statements emerged from Colonel Gaddafi's office, indicating that all trade deals with Britain would be halted, and embassy staff subject to harassment. At the same time, 'a parade of treats' was offered to the Scottish government in exchange for his release on compassionate grounds.[23]

* * *

9 SEPTEMBER 2010

Yet another invitation arrives from Colonel Gaddafi for me to visit Libya, this time via the Libyan ambassador, His Excellency Omar Jeliban. Officially the message is about a visit to the al-Megrahi home, but behind the scenes it's an opportunity for Gaddafi to discover from me directly the latest developments.

In Tripoli, at Baset's villa, I talk with the dying man for one and a half hours. He is coping well with his pain and can walk unaided. He's exasperated by the British media: stories telling how US senators are in paroxysms of rage at his release, and how British Petroleum fixed his exit from prison. Nothing, however, about the evidence and witnesses who put him there. So he's prepared a dossier of material that will prove his innocence when the opportunity arises.

Then, for me, onward to Benghazi – this time in a private jet – for a fourth meeting with a now aged Colonel Gaddafi. Gaddafi explains that contrary to daily rumours about Libya's international stance, he and his government remain determined to clear Libya's name. He does not indicate how this might be achieved. He leans back in his chair and casually asks: 'As part of that process, would you be willing to make a statement that would have an international impact?'

I feel a tremor of adrenalin in my veins. Given the reputation of the Libyan regime and recent events, does Gaddafi really think that the world's press and governments will listen to little old Jim Swire? I try to remain calm. 'I'll consider your request carefully. When the time is right I will speak with as much authority as I can.' I am not hopeful.

Gaddafi arranges for me a second visit to his former home, now derelict. During my first visit in December 1991 it seemed that the 1986 American attack included a missile targeted directly at the house. And yet an ironic tragedy occurred; the primary target was not the house, but the reinforced underground bunker where Gaddafi spent his night hours. The missile glanced off the roof of the bunker and shot forward into the main entrance of the home in which Gaddafi's mother, son and daughter were sleeping.

The minder guides me into the bedroom where once stood the picture of Flora with the message: 'The consequence of the use of violence is the death of innocent people.' The message is still there, but the picture of Flora has changed from her aged eighteen years to one in full womanhood. Unknown to me, events are already in train that will destroy the house and all within.

* * *

NOVEMBER 2010

Yet another relentless year has passed with me on a treadmill of frustration and hope. Hundreds of emails flood in daily with requests for interviews, questions rasp from an ever-ringing phone, polite invitations arrive for me to attend plays, speak at book launches, make speeches in my own right, plus all the quiet plotting that campaigners are forced to do in this age of government monitoring of each and every citizen.

Today is a cold autumn day. On the M74 heading south I'm well in need of a rest, so I pull into the services at junction thirteen. Peter Biddulph, my co-writer, tracks me down on my mobile and we talk about what has been a busy day.

'Jim, you sound exhausted.'

I can't keep up this momentum. I long to be once again the family man surrounded by daughter, son and grandchildren, Jane at my side, doing what fathers do when they are not some kind of celebrity. How does Jane feel, after more than twenty-two years, almost half of our married life together? Yet she's still there, allowing a man to do what a man believes he must do. Coping with intermittent bouts of media attention, cameras in the hallway, me closeted away composing sound bites for all-consuming news channels; Cathy well into her life and family, mentoring other bereaved and troubled folks; William, with two sons of his own, solid in his overcoming of cancer, his career surviving. All must surely wonder, *Is it not time, Dad?* Jane ponders it all within her heart, and as she does so I jump on the next plane to Libya, William again horrified, *Mum, what's Dad up to? The media will tear him to pieces.* But they don't, just the story of my meeting with Baset a footnote on page four.

We British relatives believe we are so close to proving the need for an inquiry. We cannot give up; we owe it to the Lockerbie dead. Jane never questions. Always that shy smile: *Jim, see it through to what you see as a conclusion, that moment when you will be content with Scottish justice and your conscience.*

Libya Destroyed,
a Deathbed Farewell

Chapter 16

It was 2001. About ten days after 9/11 I was in the Pentagon. I saw Deputy Secretary Wolfowitz and Secretary Rumsfeld. Then I went downstairs to talk to some of the people who had worked for me and one of the generals called me in. He said. 'We've made the decision. We're going to war with Iraq.'

I said, 'Why?'

He said, 'I don't know. I guess they don't know what else to do. We don't know how to fight terrorists, but we've got a good military and we know how to take down governments.'

I came back to see him a few weeks later. I asked, 'Are we still going to war with Iraq?'

He said, 'It's worse than that.'

He picked up a piece of paper from his desk. He said, 'I just got this down from Secretary Rumsfeld. It's a memo that describes how we're going to take out seven countries in five years. Starting with Iraq, and then Syria, Lebanon, then Libya, Somalia, Sudan, and finishing off with Iran.'

[General Wesley Clark, Commander of Operation Allied Force and Supreme Allied Commander Europe of NATO from 1997 to 2000. Filmed Interview, *Democracy Now.*]

FEBRUARY 2011

A well-armed uprising has begun against the Gaddafi regime. Similar events are occurring in Egypt and Tunis, with the eventual removal of dictator presidents. In Bahrain and Qatar security forces have quickly and brutally suppressed all dissent, with many murdered on the streets and in their homes. The same is happening in Yemen and Syria. Massive Western and Arab funding has been channelled into groups opposing Gaddafi. Western politicians are embracing the lies and false promises spread by opponents of the regime, and arms are being channelled via Jordan with support from other Arab states.[1]

The Western media rejoice in the words 'Arab Spring'. With Iran an eventual and final target, some American commentators express hope that the Arab Spring might become a Persian Summer. Others ask whether new evidence about the Lockerbie attack might emerge from Libya's turmoil. The numbers of citizens and entire armies killed in such overseas adventures will count for nothing when weighed against American and Western exceptionalism, the God-given belief that France, Britain and America have the right to do whatever they wish, when and where they wish.

On 16 February 2011, inspired by the revolutions in Tunisia and Egypt, demonstrators gather in the eastern Libyan town of Bayda, calling for the overthrow of Gaddafi. A police car is set ablaze at a road junction now known as 'The Crossroads of the Spark'. Gaddafi foolishly reacts with blood-curdling threats of extermination of the rebels. Immediately, British Prime Minister David Cameron takes to the world stage, warning that 'Gaddafi must go'. Our purpose, he claims, is to prevent genocide and 'protect innocent civilians'. During a parliamentary debate he adds that it is 'contrary to Britain's overwhelming national interest' that a rogue state should exist on the shores of North Africa.[2]

A United Nations Security Council resolution is composed with words meaning all things to all men. The stated aim of a no-fly zone to protect innocent civilians is undermined by the addition of the phrase 'all necessary means'. In other words, NATO will be the air force of the Libyan rebels. What are described by government press releases as 'defensive operations against Libyan planes' prove to be nothing less than attack sorties with precision-guided bombs and high-explosive missiles.

Codenamed 'Operation Unified Protector', over 26,000 strike sorties are being flown, and over 400 artillery batteries and 600 tanks or armoured vehicles destroyed.[3] 'Our intention is not to assassinate Gaddafi,' declares British Defence Secretary Liam Fox. Gaddafi's several homes are, however, classified as 'command and control centres' thus justifying attempts to kill the entire Gaddafi family in a single strike. Several such attacks take place and Gaddafi is lucky to survive them. News conferences by NATO Secretary General Anders Rasmussen at which he proudly announces the day's kills – he calls them 'missions' – become a regular feature. As predicted by General Wesley Clark, and as early as 3 March 2011, the game has been a simple one: regime change, the killing or deposing of Gaddafi, and the installation of an initially paid-for government friendly to Western interests.[4] NATO, established in 1948 to resist Soviet expansion in Europe, has discovered a new role: the pursuit of American and British campaigns of regime change across the Middle East.

The distinguished American investigative journalist Robert Parry writes as follows:

Today's third deadly myth is Washington's certainty that Libyan dictator Gaddafi was responsible for the Pan Am 103 attack and thus must be removed from power by force and possibly by assassination.

The alternative option of taking Gaddafi up on his offers of a cease-fire and negotiations towards a political settlement has been rejected out of hand by both the Obama administration and by nearly all of the influential pundits in Washington, in part, because of the Pan Am case.

Repeatedly citing Gaddafi's killing of Americans over Lockerbie, the US debate has centered on the need to ratchet up pressure on Gaddafi and even chuckle over NATO's transparent efforts to murder the Libyan leader (and his family members) by bombing his homes and offices.

President Obama apparently sees no choice. After all, the conventional wisdom is that Gaddafi is guilty. All the leading US news organisations, such as the *New York Times*, and prominent politicians say so. 'The blood of Americans is on [Gaddafi's] hands because he was responsible for the bombing of Pan Am 103,' declared Sen McCain, R-Arizona, after an early trip to rebel-held Benghazi.[5]

Libyan Minister for Justice Mustafa Abdel-Jalil is the first major figure to defect to the rebel cause. Setting up an office of the 'New Libyan Coalition Council' in Benghazi, he claims that Gaddafi personally ordered the Lockerbie bombing. To journalists he declares 'I have proof.' When asked for the proof, he remains silent.

Only days after being sent by Gaddafi to violently suppress the Benghazi uprising, next to defect is Gaddafi's public security minister, General Abdel Fattah-Younis. He is effectively number two in Gaddafi's inner circle, wielding more power than anyone except Gaddafi, and perhaps even his sons. His value to the rebels comes from the information he brings with him. From his headquarters in Benghazi he claims that Gaddafi ordered the Lockerbie attack: 'I have proof.' When asked for proof he too remains silent. He is later shot and killed in circumstances that are not clear.

During a conflict lasting a further eight months, Gaddafi's forces are pounded by NATO missiles, and from all directions rocket and artillery fire from rebel forces supported by Egyptian, British and French Special Forces based along the Egyptian and Libyan borders. One rebel group is reported to be summarily executing all foreign mercenaries captured in the fighting.[6] Minute by minute coverage is provided by Sky News reporters embedded with the rebels. As Tripoli falls, a laughing Sky News reporter features in the back of a rebel pick-up truck bouncing through the rubble towards the city centre.

On 21 October 2011 comes the inevitable end. Gaddafi, fighting to the last man in his home town of Sirte, is cornered hiding in a large drain pipe with one of his sons. Dragged out and badly beaten by rebel fighters, he and his son are executed on the spot. Gaddafi is slaughtered like an animal by a highly brutal method from which I will spare you the details.

The rebels have proclaimed themselves to be the 'National Transition Council', and now produce the first lie of their existence: 'Gaddafi and his son were killed by crossfire between rebel and Gaddafi forces.' How the new government will react to future internal dissension has yet to be observed. We should recall that many in the new regime were fully active in the old one, and that the prisons and torture chambers they employed are – many of them – still intact. The skills of suppression of dissent are not rapidly dissipated.[7]

Mustafa Abdel-Jalil is now the unelected *de facto* senior minister in charge. Facing a huge gathering of ecstatic Benghazi citizens he stands between French President Nicolas Sarkozy and British Prime Minister David Cameron. Joining hands the three raise their arms to heaven. All are featured on the world's television screens; all promote their own agendas. Above the cheers of the crowd Cameron roars: 'Your friends in Britain and France will stand with you as you build your country and build your democracy for the future!'[8]

US Secretary of State Hillary Clinton adds a footnote in an interview on CBS News. Mimicking the words of Julius Caesar concerning his conquest of Britain, Clinton says 'We came, we saw, he died.' She claps her hands and roars with laughter at her own joke. Her adrenaline-fuelled hilarity says much about the American mindset, the great enjoyable game, the long inbuilt assumption that America is the new Rome and all nations are its subjects.[9]

* * *

As the Libyan conflict subsides, Gaddafi's minister for foreign affairs and former intelligence chief, Moussa Koussa, arrives in the UK. His whereabouts during the conflict have been uncertain. All that the media are permitted to know is that he has come voluntarily and is accommodated in a secret safe house.

One month ago, in Koussa's former office, Human Rights Watch announced that they had found files confirming that his relationship with Britain and America has been even closer than the media might have guessed. Over the previous decade senior officers of MI6 and the CIA have had regular dialogue with their counterparts in Libyan intelligence.[10]

One file records that MI6 officers assisted Koussa with the draft of a speech to be made by Gaddafi during a visit in 2004 by Prime Minister Tony Blair. Another, that it had been Downing Street's idea for Blair and Gaddafi to meet in a tent while negotiating the 'Deal in the Desert'.

Most damning is a file containing evidence that the US used Libya as a base for its Middle East rendition programme, transporting prisoners for further interrogation on foreign soil in so-called 'black prisons'. Human Rights Watch claims that the purpose was to enable the torture of prisoners outside US jurisdiction.

Other revelations have emerged. While Britain was – to all appearances – not itself involved in torturing, MI6 provided up to 1,600 questions to be put to captives while under torture.

MI6 officers were reported as being present while torturers employed by other nations performed their evil trade. The arrangements would ensure that at some future date, if found out, MI6 and the British government could claim 'we do not use or condone torture'.

There are references to 'interviews' in the prison at Guantanamo Bay, and one letter details arrangements for the rendition of Sami al-Saadi[11] with his wife and four children via Hong Kong. It includes chilling advice that agents should ensure that the plane landing at Hong Kong be fully insured.

Another example of Britain's assistance is the rendition of Libyan dissident Abdel Hakim Belhaj and his four-and-a-half-months-pregnant wife. He would spend six years imprisoned with periods of systematic torture within the tender mercies of Moussa Koussa.[12]

With this 'gift' of Belhaj and his wife comes a covering letter from Sir Mark Allen, the head of MI6's counter-terrorism unit, to Moussa Koussa offering congratulations on the safe arrival of the 'air cargo'. Allen writes: 'This was the least we could do for you and for Libya to demonstrate the remarkable relationship we have built over the years.'

Several years previously, shortly after the 9/11 attack on New York's World Trade Center, Koussa visited the UK. He was invited to meet William Burns, US Assistant Secretary of State for Near East Affairs. The British Foreign Office refused to disclose the names of all those Koussa was allowed to meet; but Libyan ambassador to the UK Mohamed Azwai confirmed that Koussa had not only met with British and American officials, he provided them with a list of more than a dozen Libyans living in the UK suspected of links to Osama Bin Laden.[13]

This extensive history of coordination between Libyan, British and American intelligence explains why, instead of being arrested during his visits to England, he was politely absolved from all his sins by kindred spirits accompanied by MI6 and Scottish police officers, and allowed to go on his way.

Within days of his final visit to the UK his multi-million-dollar assets were unfrozen from sanctions. From London he travelled initially to Qatar, then Jordan, and onward to lonely luxury in other hiding places, his record of atrocities fading quietly from history. As with all such matters, the Foreign Office have declined to comment other than to remind the nation of the need to protect United Kingdom intelligence and national security.[14]

Exposure of the hypocrisy of the British government's position continues. Journalists who can read between the lines, and those with a nose for weasel words, still comb Libyan security files amid the ruins of Gaddafi's former homes and offices. Their discoveries might be described as horrific, and are closely detailed in a meticulously researched feature by the *Guardian* newspaper.[15]

I find the history of the time, especially the details listed by the *Guardian*, deeply disturbing. It reveals the enormity of the system of international behaviour that has hampered our Lockerbie campaign group for many years. The story of Pan Am 103 is but a twig of debris twisting upon a flood of deceit. We have learned much about the behaviour of our own and US intelligence, sometimes modified by the input of ignorant politicians. Some who are immersed in this frenetic world of international behaviour seem inured to any concept of right or wrong. They will claim that they are working for the benefit of their nation, freedom and democracy. A few may actually believe that to be true.

* * *

DECEMBER 2011

I am in Tripoli for what will prove to be my final visit. The NATO bombing campaign is over, but still the conflict continues in outlying parts of the country as those warring groups that combined to destroy and murder Gaddafi now fight each other for territory. From the Saharan night echo distant rattles of AK47s and deeper explosions of something more sinister.[16]

I am here with the permission of the new self-styled Provisional Libyan Government. They have asked to meet me, and ITV are making a documentary about my visit. Prior to my talks with ministers, the producers ask me to stand amid the remains of what once was a street with homes, blocks of flats, offices and shops. I hold across my heart my famous photo of a smiling Flora. With eyes half-closed with emotion and travel weariness I attempt a look of determination, but twenty-five years of campaigning have taken their toll. Behind me, wandering across a confusion of shattered walls and floors and homes is a young girl aged perhaps ten. Did she live here? Where are her parents, sisters, brothers? Will she survive, find somewhere else to inhabit, or become a refugee to wander the Mediterranean nations or northward to Europe?

Ashour Shamis, an adviser to the new Libyan prime minister, tells me that Gaddafi personally was involved in the Lockerbie attack. 'There is no doubt about it. Al-Megrahi was involved in the bombing: He was a small player. As an employee of Libyan security if he was told to do something, he would have done it.' Shamis seems to be speculating and extrapolating. He offers no evidence to back up his supposition.

Leaving the government offices I look for Gaddafi's former home in a huge complex on the outskirts of Tripoli. I'm hoping to recover that photo of Flora. As the road opens onto a square all comes as a severe shock. The walled park that once contained a military barracks and Gaddafi's home is now a huge street market. The walls that used to surround the complex are demolished. Of Gaddafi's home nothing remains but low heaps of rubble. Those citizens who speak English and are willing to talk seem relieved that Gaddafi is gone. They are anxious to pin on him every crime under the sun.

I will later discover that American intelligence and some within the American administration have been considering the illegal rendition of the dying former prisoner. One agent quotes my own misgivings from a recent newspaper report: 'I am worried for Baset. I can just see the unit they sent to kill Osama bin Laden being sent to extract him. Presumably, they wouldn't extract him but kill him on the spot.' Five days later the CEO of a US government-employed security agency emails to his staff that he is considering that Baset be murdered by switching off his oxygen.

Meanwhile, in Tripoli, I am relieved to move onward from the destruction. To avoid drawing attention to myself I hire an anonymous taxi and with an American bereaved relative, Ken Dornstein, travel incognito to Baset's villa. Baset's wife Aisha offers me a welcome reserved for friends, but does not wish Dornstein to meet her husband. Instead, her son Khaled asks him to wait in the porch.

Years later I will discover from American reports that Dornstein is secretly wired-up with a microphone with the intention of making a documentary. Is he perhaps hoping to persuade Baset to make a whispered deathbed confession?[17]

Aisha leads me up a flight of stairs to a bedroom set up for intensive care. I've seen brief and shaky images of Baset on television over the previous months, but now the man has clearly deteriorated. Propped up on pillows and covered by a thick floral blanket, his eyes are sunk deep into his face. He seems in severe pain.

We shake hands and embrace softly. I carefully sit where he can look at me without having to turn his head. He speaks slowly, his voice strained and hoarse. Sometimes he closes his eyes when considering his next words. He sympathises with my impossible situation. He's well aware that Jane and the children have suffered as I pursued our campaign.

Suddenly I hear voices from outside the door. Dornstein has asked to use the toilet, which is situated next to the bedroom. Dornstein will later admit in an interview with the *New Yorker Magazine* that he considered barging into our meeting and recording the reaction of both Baset and myself, but decided against it.

As our meeting continues, Baset rasps: 'You had no choice. You saw a wrong that had to be challenged. You did what you thought was right.'

'And Gauci—?' I halt mid sentence, wishing I hadn't mentioned the man.

He stirs and raises his voice: 'Gauci made fifty-five statements. I have them all. Sometimes they conflicted. The police said nineteen. They lied.'

'Yes,' I offer, not wanting to burden him. 'But out of this evil I just hope for something good to emerge.'

His eyes close for a few seconds. He seems uncertain. He whispers, 'I have something to tell you. But you must promise to say nothing until John's book is published.'[18]

My mouth goes dry. I lean forward almost onto the bed. Something extraordinary is coming.

He makes a huge effort: 'Feraday swore the fragment was similar in all respects to the circuit boards sold to Libya. But Tony Kelly and John have discovered that those boards had coatings of tin/lead alloy. PT/35(b) was coated with pure tin. Feraday knew the fragments were different when he spoke in the trial. He deceived the judges.'

Twenty-five years, and now the final truth? Is the fragment a fake, planted in a tampered police evidence bag to make the connection to Libya? No wonder they forced the man to drop his second appeal. Suspicions about the Gilchrist testimony; the Hayes finding and recording of PT/35(b); Feraday's flustered explanations concerning his forensic report; the confusion of Gauci, his seduction by promise of millions of dollars; and now the falsity of PT/35(b) itself – all merge to a gigantic mosaic of deceit. I sink back exhausted.

But the question remains: who murdered Flora? He's still out there, turning over in his mind his life and achievements. Or is he dead, with only surviving colleagues to honour his memory in obscene worship? Will we Lockerbie bereaved go to our graves having never heard his name? My pulse thunders in my ears, I can hardly hear his next words: 'For this I am sorry. Almost as much as giving up clearing my name, I regret letting you down.'

No, he has not let me down. The combined might of three governments and their twisted and corrupt systems of justice have let me down, and let down Flora, all the Lockerbie dead and Baset himself.

We look into each other's eyes. We know what the moment holds. He clasps my hands. 'I am going to a place where I hope soon to see Flora. I will tell her that her father is my friend.' Tears in my eyes, I can only nod.

Aisha leads me towards the door. As I reach the head of the stairs I look back. One of his grandchildren is kneeling on the bed. Grandfather and grandson are in a loving embrace.

Abdelbaset Ali al-Megrahi died on 20 May 2012.

Truth Will Find a Way

Chapter 17

JOHN ASHTON IS a skilled and authoritative writer on Lockerbie. In 1993, five years after the attack, he commenced research into the investigation. In 2000 he teamed up with journalist colleague Ian Ferguson, and together they embarked on a forensic study of the trial evidence and conduct of the trial.

When, on 31 January 2001, the verdict was announced, the two were astonished. At that moment they were on opposite sides of the Atlantic; John in the UK, Ian in the US. As the judgement came over the wires their emails told it all:

Ashton to Ferguson: 'Can you believe this?'

Ferguson to Ashton: 'This has to be a joke!! I can hardly believe what I'm reading.'

Their amazement turned rapidly to determination. Thus, in 2001, emerged what many believe to be a major contribution to the history of criminal law: *Cover-up of Convenience: The Hidden Scandal of Lockerbie.*[1] Only when justice is finally achieved in the name of Baset al-Megrahi will its significance be fully understood.

Yet today, 26 February 2012, John tells me of another book he's written – *Megrahi: You Are My Jury – The Lockerbie Evidence.* John was a close friend to Baset, visiting regularly over several years, and more frequently as Baset's cancer advanced. He has been preparing an important book based on Baset's solicitor Tony Kelly's investigation of the now fully available prosecution files. The book is to be published tomorrow, the 27th.

'Jim, there's something that you will find very interesting.'

'Yes?'

'Here's an advance copy. Enjoy. In the quiet of your room look at pages three-fifty-five to three-sixty-two. See you tomorrow.'

* * *

In 2005 Baset al-Megrahi appointed a new solicitor, Tony Kelly. Kelly employed former policeman George Thompson, and then recruited several advocates who had worked for al-Megrahi's previous solicitor, Edward MacKechnie. At al-Megrahi's insistence, Thompson would continue to work with Kelly until the summer of 2007. Kelly also appointed John Ashton as a researcher. From then on Kelly led a drill-down investigation into the prosecution's trial evidence.

One of Kelly's several strategies was to examine Feraday's forensic reports and notebooks, and the words he recorded concerning fragment PT/35(b). In court, Feraday had conclusively stated that the fragment was, materially and structurally, 'similar in all respects' to the MST-13 timer boards supplied by Thüring as control samples for comparative purposes. If they were similar in all respects, then this was evidence to support the claim that Libya supplied the timer that triggered the bomb.

Feraday's conclusion went unchallenged throughout the trial, a first appeal, a four-year investigation by the Scottish Criminal Cases Review Commission and the opening stages of the second appeal.

Kelly's team noticed, however, in files handed over in early July 2009, two hand-written annotations by Feraday. Both were dated 1 August 1991, four months before he signed off on the forensic report prepared jointly with Dr Thomas Hayes. The first recorded that the protective layer covering the electronic circuit on PT/35(b) was 'pure tin'; the second stated that the protective layer on the MST-13 control sample boards was '70/30% tin/lead'.

The significance of the tinning process is this: in order to protect the copper tracks of an electronic circuit board a layer of 'tinning' is applied. Several methods can be used. During and before the 1980s the standard system used by Thüring and all commercial manufacturers was to apply an alloy – usually 70/30 per cent tin and lead – to cover the copper tracks. Homemade or non-commercial systems were sometimes used for electroplating. Prior to 1989 however, pure tin was used in a method called 'immersion tinning'.

John is unable to say for sure that the police and Crown were aware of the two Feraday hand-written annotations. The police labels on Feraday's notebook indicated that it was handed to the police in November 1999, six months before the commencement of the trial and eight years after Feraday wrote his final report.

The police had themselves investigated the fragment. One report they received was from New England Laminates, who removed three layers of the glass fibre laminate in order to conduct tests. Another was by Allan Worroll of Ferranti International who conducted tests on the structure and metallurgy. Further reports were by Doctors Wilkinson and Johnson of Strathclyde and Manchester universities who tested the metallurgy

In his examination of PT/35(b) Allan Worroll discovered the following:

- '[Small] tracks are coated with pure tin, probably from an electroless tin solution presumably to aid solderability.'
- 'Normal electronic grade solder 60–65% tin (remainder lead) has been used in the assembly of the device . . . Etch profile on copper pads and tracks

suggest the circuit could have been "home made" (although the machined radius suggest a commercial milling operation)'.[2]

Wilkinson and Johnson noted a metallurgical difference between PT/35(b) and the control Thüring samples. The two tracks on PT/35(b) were coated with pure tin, as Feraday himself had noted. The control sample tracks were coated with a 70/30 per cent alloy of tin and lead – again, as Feraday had observed. They speculated that the heat of the Lockerbie blast might have evaporated the lead content of the tracks leaving a covering of pure tin. Wilkinson advised that the hypothesis of heat-induced evaporation should be tested by experiment.

Unfortunately, no such tests appeared to have been done. There were no records in the police or Crown Office files of any testing or reports from tests. In addition, Kelly's team wondered if enquiries had been made of the manufacturers Thüring as to what form of 'tinning' they normally used during the years when MST-13 boards were being supplied to MEBO.

During the trial, the man responsible for the manufacture of circuit boards at Thüring, Urs Bonfadelli, had in his evidence used the word 'tin', but it was in answer to a question on another subject. The word 'tinning' was, and is, almost universally used to describe the process of applying a eutectic mixture, i.e. a combination of metals that allows further processes to take place without damaging the underlying copper circuitry.

John Ashton records the moment thus: On 23 October 2008 a member of Kelly's team finally put the crucial question to Bonfadelli: 'Was the circuitry of the MST-13 boards coated with pure tin or a tin/lead alloy?'

Bonfadelli's answer was clear and devastating: 'All were coated with an alloy of 70 per cent tin and 30 per cent lead.'

There was no mistaking this, as Thüring only ever made circuit boards this way. The use of pure tin required a completely different production process which the company never used and for which the company was not equipped.

The implications of Bonfadelli's statement meant that if the heat of the explosion had not changed the covering from an alloy to pure tin, then the fragment could not have come from a Thüring-made timer board.

So, had the heat of the explosion caused a change in the alloy? Kelly consulted two independent experts. Doctor Chris McArdle had many years' experience in the electronics industry in the design of circuit boards and was formerly a government adviser on microelectronics and nanotechnology. Dr Jess Crawley, a metallurgist with over thirty-five years' experience, was a former senior lecturer at Sheffield Hallam University.

The two scientists designed a series of experiments using boards with the same design and metallurgy as the Thüring boards supplied to MEBO. These were placed in a laboratory furnace at temperatures and over a period of time significantly exceeding the heat input to be expected in an explosion such as that in the Lockerbie attack. After removal from the furnace they retained an alloy of 70/30 per cent tin and lead.

The inevitable conclusion was that PT/35(b) could not have come from a Thüring board. It seemed to be a homemade version using as part of the construction a coating of pure tin. Indeed, when commenting on the metallurgy of the tracks of PT/35(b), Allan Worroll of Ferranti International used those very words: 'home made'. It therefore was not from one of the twenty boards provided to Libya in 1985.

When asked how PT/35(b) might have been made, McArdle and Crawley believed that its coating was probably done using the immersion tin process, an old method typical of non-commercial manufacture, and that it should not be confused with post-1989 commercial pure-tin methods. The Ferranti conclusion had been similar – 'an electroless tin solution'.

So where did the Lockerbie fragment come from? However and wherever it was made, it remains to this day a rogue piece of evidence unconnected to the batch provided in 1985 to Libya.

John's final comment was this: 'The strongest remaining element of the case against Abdelbaset [al-Megrahi] was destroyed and with it the case against his country. But it was all too late.'

The contrast between Feraday's hand-written entries and his assurance that the control samples and PT/35(b) were 'similar in all respects' remains to this day deeply puzzling. Did he perhaps assume al-Megrahi's guilt and extrapolate that there must have been a rational explanation, as yet undiscovered, for the difference between the fragment and the control samples? The question also arises as to whether Thomas Hayes was aware of Feraday's annotations when – acting in a consultancy role – he drafted sections of the final forensic report.

The story of fragment PT/35(b) appears to be a fascinating example of how miscarriages of justice can be brought about by organisational momentum – a 'group-think' of assumed guilt – and how evidence can be misinterpreted in support of that assumption.

* * *

The Edinburgh Book Festival's main tent is packed, several hundred seated, a few standing at the back and sides. I am on stage with John Ashton, Professor Hans Kochler, and interviewer, journalist and commentator Ruth Wishart.

John explains about the book, Hans discusses the United Nations view of the evidence and how it was presented. Ruth asks me for an opinion. Not too detailed, she hopes, perhaps short?

'I don't do short.' I didn't mean to make them laugh, but they do, and a few applaud. I tell them, 'I'm always saying this but it never seems to happen – I hope soon to step back from the front line of the quest for truth.'

Magnus Linklater, former editor of the *Scotsman* and current columnist for the Scottish edition of *The Times*, rises to address the gathering. 'This account is,' he stoutly asserts, 'an implication of the biggest conspiracy that has taken place in Europe since the Second World War. You are assuming collusion between several governments, their intelligence services, the entire Scottish police force and the Scottish Crown Office.'

Magnus has had a distinguished career and deserves the greatest respect, but all reasonably informed persons on the subject of Lockerbie are to this day puzzled that he draws it together like that. John's book assumes no conspiracy, no collusion. What he does question is the trial evidence and the provenance of PT/35(b), and quotes reliable scientific evidence to support his conclusion. As former CIA Middle Eastern specialist Robert Baer himself commented, once the supposedly key evidence had been found, for all those working on the case that was simply it; they could set about composing an indictment.

On this same morning of publication (27 February 2012), a Downing Street statement emerges on behalf of Prime Minister Cameron: 'This book is an insult to the Lockerbie dead and the bereaved relatives.' And simultaneously in Edinburgh, Crown and Scottish Office spokesmen release a statement that has become the government's mantra: 'Al-Megrahi was found guilty in a court of law and appeal court, based on evidence submitted to the trial.'

Copies of the book were unavailable prior to 9 a.m. that day. How could Downing Street and the Scottish Crown know its contents in any kind of detail, particularly the references to PT/35(b)? It has been publicly known for some years now that GCHQ Cheltenham and the US National Security Agency have monitored all phone calls and emails across the USA, the UK and other nations. It stretches credibility to believe that they would not have taken a close interest in an important book written by a close colleague of the Lockerbie campaigners. Did

Downing Street receive advance warning of the book's contents, drawn from reports by GCHQ? Is Cameron's brief but a cynical PR diversion to discredit all who doubt the official version of the tragedy? For the Lockerbie dead and their surviving relatives, in this sad and troubled world, that would be the greatest insult.

Spring 2021: Aftermath

THESE LINES ARE written after a third, posthumous appeal by the Megrahi family, led by Abdelbaset's son Ali. The appeal began on 24 November 2020 under a five-strong panel of judges led by Scotland's Lord Justice General, the Right Honourable Lord Carloway. He announced the panel's unanimous opinion on Friday 15 January 2021. The appeal was rejected.

Britain's history of mass murder by the use of bombs contains another most relevant trial and appeal. The Guildford Four and the Maguire Seven were the collective names of two groups whose convictions in English courts in 1975 and 1976 for the Guildford pub bombings of 5 October 1974 were eventually quashed after long campaigns for justice. The Guildford Four were wrongly convicted of bombings carried out by the Provisional Irish Republican Army (IRA), and the Maguire Seven were wrongly convicted of handling explosives found during the investigation into the bombings. The convictions of both groups were eventually declared 'unsafe and unsatisfactory' and reversed in 1989 and 1991 respectively after they had served up to 15–16 years in prison.

The impetus for an investigation into police and prosecution handling of the case was strengthened by a parliamentary inquiry by Sir John May. Sir John discovered that the concealment of evidence by a Dr Thomas Hayes – the same Dr Hayes who wrote the forensic report based upon which Abdelbaset Al-Megrahi was found guilty at the Zeist Lockerbie trial – and two RARDE colleagues, severely hampered the cross-examination of witnesses. Sir John concluded: 'The whole scientific basis upon which the prosecution was founded was so vitiated that on this basis alone the Court of Appeal should set aside the convictions.' An appeal was upheld. We refer to this in our chapter describing the first stages of the Lockerbie trial.

And so this basic principle of fair justice in British law – 'equality of arms' between prosecution and defence lawyers – was confirmed in a major criminal case in which bombs had been used to kill and maim British subjects. This principle has been reinforced in subsequent criminal cases under English jurisdiction.

But Scotland has long since followed its own uncertain path. And in the case of the Lockerbie third appeal, this guiding principle has been ignored. Lord Carloway and his colleagues have replaced a predictably forceful defence team interrogation of prosecution witnesses with their own conclusion. In paragraph 135 of their opinion, they maintain that the disclosure to defence advocates of a sequence of repeated demands by the sole prosecution identification witness for 'unlimited' rewards in exchange for evidence – later confirmed by $2 million for his evidence and $1 million to his brother –would not have made a difference to the guilty verdict. This principle would allow the Scottish Crown and Police in all future criminal trials to conceal, without sanction, any evidence which in their view might strengthen a defence case. The United Kingdom remains a member of the European Convention on Human Rights. A more obvious candidate for examination under that convention cannot be imagined.

Epilogue

FLORA'S MEMORIAL SERVICE on 8 February 1989 filled two churches. The service was relayed from Blackwell Methodist church to the Anglican church of St Catherine's. The Reverend Arnold Cooper took the service, a choir from Flora's senior school, King Edward's, sang 'God be in my head', and there were glowing tributes from her professors in Nottingham and London. Her godfather, Canon Eric James, read from T. S. Eliot's *Four Quartets* and later spoke of Flora and family on Radio Four's *Thought for the Day*. Obituaries followed in *The Times*, the *Guardian* and the *British Medical Journal*. Briefly, we shared our lovely girl with the wider world.

But Jane and I do not wish to end this narrative on a sad note. Both of us are in our eighties now and feel enormous love and gratitude towards our surviving children. Cathy and William bring us sustaining happiness with their warmth and kindness. We feel deep love, joy and pride when we see how they have overcome difficulties and setbacks in their lives to provide loving, happy and secure homes for their families. We witness amazing achievements by our grandchildren, Grace, Oscar, Sam and Lewis. We still have each other, and we encourage each other to keep walking and working. I have become a dedicated reader aloud of an eclectic choice of novels for Jane's enjoyment and still look after Flora's Wood at Caspidge, our old home in Bromsgrove. We still tend our garden. We are still able to travel and have wonderful holidays in our house in the

Isle of Skye and visit exotic places like Mustique, Eastern Europe, Russia and Scandinavia. Above all, we rejoice in our friends and family who have stood by us through the years and whose company, compassion and kindness have given us strength.

Jim and Jane Swire
April 2021

Notes

Into a New Existence
Chapter 1

1. Margaret Thatcher, *The Downing Street Years* (Harper Collins, 1993).
2. 'Who Could Do this? Victims were not told of bomb threat', *Daily Mirror*, 23 December 1988.
3. Information confirmed by Tiny Rowland to Alan Francovich during the filming of a 1994 documentary, *The Maltese Double Cross* (see Chapter 8).
4. Information via a source who wishes to remain anonymous.

Chapter 2

1. President of Palestine. Died in 2005.
2. The Israeli Intelligence Service.
3. The *Bundeskriminalamt*, the West German Federal Police, prior to the 1989 fall of the Berlin Wall.
4. Translation from the court proceedings.
5. Jargon for the Embassy office.
6. Release of Cabinet papers in 2018. *The Times* claimed that a further fifty documents existed to which they had been refused access. No reasons were given.
7. At the time of the bombing, the Machrihanish airbase was under the control of the US Navy. It was handed over to UK control in

1995. In a later chapter the helicopter is followed by cameras for the film *The Maltese Double Cross*.

8. Salinger appeared as a witness for the defence in the Lockerbie trial. After a distinguished career he died on 16 October 2004.

9. Appointed 24 July 1989.

CHAPTER 3

1. 4 August 1989.

2. https://www.cia.gov/library/readingroom/docs/CIA-RDP91B01306R000500010002-4.pdf. The fourth denial is most odd. The British Department of Transport and the German authorities were well aware of an intended attack, as the James Jack telexes and German police bomb brochure would demonstrate. Equally odd is that the release of documents spanning the years 1983 to 2016 and containing these denials has no other significant reference to the Lockerbie bombing, investigation and trial, other than that a 'staff' expert discovered the timer fragment PT/35(b).

3. Martin Cadman's statement repeated on camera in the film *The Maltese Double Cross*.

4. For the film *The Maltese Double Cross*, first screened in the UK in 1994.

5. Younger brother of Hafez Assad, former president of Syria.

CHAPTER 4

1. Copies of the two James Jack telexes and the BKA brochure are in our archive.

2. Helen, of Long Island, New York, lost her son Mark.

CHAPTER 5

1. This account is from Jim's diary and recollections. He was dismayed to discover that the minutes and report issued at the end of proceedings bore little relationship to his own records.

2. Peter Biddulph's recorded interview of John Mosey.
3. The term 'interline' refers to passengers and bags transiting from airlines other than Pan Am.

Two Guilty Men
Chapter 6

1. DIA combined message 22 December 1989. http://www.dia.mil/foia/panam103.pdf
2. DIA Terrorism summary 15 September 1990. http://www.dia.mil/foia/panam103.pdf
3. DIA Intelligence report February 1991. http://www.dia.mil/foia/panam103.pdf
4. Based on Jim's notes and diary of events.
5. We believed this at the time, basing our belief on news reports following the 1986 American bombing. In future years reports would emerge claiming that Hanna was not killed but remained alive and well. We never discovered if the reports were true.
6. At that time the BBC's chief correspondent.
7. Released from Beirut captivity 18 November 1991.
8. In 2014 Wikileaks traced two emails exchanged within America's largest intelligence contractor, Stratfor. These related to the dying al-Megrahi. One email threatened rendition for trial in the US, the second, assassination. We may assume that in the early days of the indictments similar expressions of intent were circulating. https://wikileaks.org/gifiles/docs/23/2358574_re-unique-t-line-idea.html and https://wikileaks.org/gifiles/docs/39/3984630_above-the-tearline-a-window-of-opportunity-for-a-rendition.html
9. William C. Chasey, *Foreign Agent 4221* (Bridger House Publishing, 1995). Gaddafi would honour that promise. In 1994, five years after this meeting, Chasey visited Gaddafi's former home. He writes that in Hanna's bedroom, upon the cracked wall of the shrine, hung side by side the photographs of Hanna and Flora.

Chapter 7

1. BBC television news, 22 December 1988.
2. Margaret Thatcher, *The Downing Street Years* (HarperCollins, 1993).
3. Ibid., pp. 747–8.
4. Ibid., p. 764.
5. Ibid., pp. 448–9.
6. Ibid., p. 792.
7. In 1988, Pan Am 103 accounted for 40 per cent of world casualties resulting from terrorism.
8. Margaret Thatcher, *Statecraft: Strategies for a Changing World* (HarperCollins, 2002).
9. *Mail on Sunday* (Scottish Edition), 17 August 2009.
10. Thatcher's knowledge of events was confirmed on 17 December 2009, in a *Yorkshire Post* column by her former Chief Press Secretary Sir Bernard Ingham. He describes the shock in Downing Street on the evening of the bombing, and a journey by Thatcher and her entourage to view the Lockerbie devastation.

Chapter 8

1. Died 17 April 1996. Achievements include the International Critics Award for best documentary at the 1980 Berlin Film Festival and the Leipzig Film Festival.
2. Winner 1980 FIPRESCI prize, Forum of New Cinema.
3. Nominated for 1988 Sundance Festival Grand Jury Prize.
4. 1995 Best Documentary Edinburgh International Film Festival.
5. One of our sources claims that US Intelligence boasted of $120 million to guarantee the film's banning in the US.
6. See also https://www.alternet.org/2014/12/truth-about-lockerbie -bombing-and-censored-film-dared-reveal-it/
7. Filmed interviews, *The Maltese Double Cross*.
8. All quotations are verbatim, apart from minor editing. Some quotations retain grammatical distortions. Space does not permit

the entire discussion, and we recommend a viewing of the film and debate for the full flavour of events. In 2017 they are available on YouTube and other sources.

9. This letter, dated 19 June 1993, continues, in a section that Francovich was diverted from reading, with: 'This is in addition to articles which we [Miller-Adams and Leppard] have written for our employers. They stirred interest but no action. There was no "smoking gun".'

10. South African Prime Minister Pik Botha, his chief of security and several others cancelled and rebooked for the earlier Pan Am 101. All his other staff cancelled their flight altogether.

11. Spiro and his entire family were massacred at their desert home in the USA. Police reports suggested a gangland contract, reasons and instigators unknown.

Chapter 9

1. *The Cook Report*, 1996.

2. In 2000 this is what the trial judges concluded, based on speculation and inference.

3. Mohamed Atta, the leader of the 11 September 2001 terrorists, chose Logan as a departure point prior to hijacking the aircraft that demolished the Twin Towers.

4. https://en.wikipedia.org/wiki/Bogdan_Dzakovic

Chapter 10

1. The following from recorded interviews with Robert Black.

2. US White House verbatim press release, including hesitations and laughter. To Rubin and the assembled journalists it had become a kind of game, at times a subject for humour.

3. Another 'terrorist' imprisoned to later become president, Mugabe was secretary general of the Zimbabwe African National Union (ZANU) during the 1960s conflict against the white government of Rhodesia.

4. Kate Adie once asked one of Gaddafi's inner circle why Gaddafi's close colleagues behaved this way: 'He said that the Colonel's rages were occasionally so terrible that many believed he might kill.' ('The Gaddafi I Knew', the *Guardian*, 2 March 2011.)

5. An intern at the White House working in the office of President Bill Clinton. There were allegations of sexual 'contacts' between her and Clinton.

CHAPTER 11

1. Shown December 1998 – *Justice for Flora*.

2. July 1986, the night-time bombing of Tripoli and Benghazi. Forty civilians were killed, many injured, in an obvious attempt to assassinate Colonel Gaddafi. Under international law this was state terrorism and a crime against innocent civilians and humanity.

3. In July 1998, at the age of eighty, after a prolonged illness.

4. This is a much-shortened version of the sermon.

THE TRIAL
CHAPTER 12

1. Sections of this account are from Jim's diary as related to Olgar Craig of the *Daily Telegraph*, May 2000, available at http://plane-truth.com/Aoude/geocities/swirediary1.html

2. John Donne, *Satire III*.

3. Trial transcript, 3 May 2001.

4. Trial transcript, p. 1.

5. Trial transcript, pp. 196–202.

6. Please note that there are two Gilchrists: DC Thomas Gilchrist as here, and Chief Superintendent James Gilchrist later.

7. Trial transcript, pp. 801–64.

8. Rt Hon. Sir John May, *Interim Report on the Maguire Case*, 12 July 1990, and *Second Report on the Maguire Case*, 3 December 1992. http://www.official-documents.gov.uk/document/hc8990/hc05/0556/0556.pdf

9. Trial transcript, pp. 2555–75.

10. Trial transcript, pp. 2326–783.

11. Trial transcript, p. 2593.

12. See also Allen Feraday's evidence concerning the items found with the alleged fragment from the MST-13 timer.

13. Trial transcript, p. 2781.

14. Feraday's confusion here is his own, and his words have been transcribed verbatim.

15. Trial transcript, pp. 3172–5.

16. Trial transcript, pp. 3690–4279.

17. Trial transcript, p. 7192.

18. At this time Germany was still divided by the Berlin Wall and Soviet occupation.

19. Chief Superintendent James Gilchrist, as distinct from the earlier DC Thomas Gilchrist.

20. Kamboj was a baggage scanner; Bedford was a baggage loader.

21. Trial transcript, pp. 6407–9.

22. Trial transcript, pp. 6469–79.

23. Trial transcript, p. 9306.

24. 'Airport Security Chief Concern at Megrahi Verdict', *Sunday Express* (UK), 11 March 2012. Shanks appears to be referring to Raymond Manly, who would give evidence in al-Megrahi's first appeal (see Chapter 14).

25. On camera interview, *The Maltese Double Cross*, 1994.

26. Trial transcript, pp. 6088–9.

27. Security tags added to lost baggage.

28. Gaelic name meaning 'Lair of the Seal'.

29. *The Sunday Times*, 5 November 1989.

30. This was Jim's understanding at the time. Since then this has been denied by the Crown office.

31. Trial transcript, pp. 8752–7.

32. Trial transcript, pp. 8743–97.

33. Trial transcript, pp. 3011–30.

34. Trial transcript, p. 9268.

35. Kenny MacAskill, *The Lockerbie Bombing: The Search for Justice* (Biteback, 2016).

Chapter 13

1. This section, up to the press conference in the Hilton Hotel, London, is from notes, diary entries and recollections of several relatives, David Ben Aryeah and Jim himself.
2. BBC News Scotland, 22 May 2000.

A Desperate Appeal
Chapter 14

1. 27 January 2002. The recording was by the defence team's legal investigator George Thompson.
2. The Lotto advice is recorded in Harry Bell's police diary.
3. *Daily Mirror*, 11 September 2001.
4. A period of time for further consideration of a judgment.
5. In 2003, this was increased on review to twenty-seven years.

Concealed Evidence, False Evidence
Chapter 15

1. Robert Baer, *See No Evil: The True Story of a Ground Soldier in the CIA's War on Terrorism* (Thorndike Press, 2002).
2. SCCRC officers claimed that this payment took place in 1987. We prefer Baer's first-hand knowledge of events.
3. Information supplied by a source with high-level contacts in the Middle East.
4. 'Lockerbie Trial was a CIA Fix', the *Herald*, 12 November 2006.
5. The main police recording system and database for criminal cases.
6. Extract from DCI Bell diary (Holmes version), 28/9/89 [SCCRC Appendix: Chapter 23/3], and subsequent entries in Bell's diaries and Holmes records.
7. Ibid. Extract from DCI Bell diary (Holmes Version) [SCCRC Appendix 23/3]

8. Ibid., p. 156. Record of discussion between Dana Bhiel of the US Department of Justice and DCI Harry Bell, concerning a $2 million reward to Majid Giaka, 8 February 1992.

9. Ibid., p. 168, potential for challenge of Gauci's credibility, para. 5.

10. Ibid. *Financial Interest and Reward Monies. Undisclosed Documents. Page 155.* Extract from Harry Bell diary (manuscript version) 26/02/91. We remain puzzled as to why Bell or some other person felt the need to redact the two locations. Were they places or properties connected with the police or Scottish government?

11. Ibid., pp. 60–230.

12. Ibid. Statement S4677N: CP466

13. Statement S4677Q: CP469.

14. Trial transcript, p. 7642.

15. SCCRC disclosures and Defence Team Submission, p. 143.

16. Ibid., pp. 141–8.

17. 'Fraser: My Lockerbie Doubts', *The Sunday Times*, 23 October 2005.

18. 'Lockerbie Twenty Years On', *The Times,* 19 December 2008.

19. 'How UK Government hid secret Lockerbie Report', the *Herald*, 1 June 2012.

20. 'Jack Straw admits Lockerbie bomber's release was linked to oil', *Daily Telegraph*, 5 September 2009.

21. 'Gordon Brown Denies Double Dealing Over Lockerbie Bomber', *The Guardian*, 2 September 2009.

22. 'The Avenger', *New Yorker Magazine*, 28 September 2015.

23. 'Wikileaks cables: Lockerbie bomber freed after Gaddafi "thuggish" threats', the *Guardian*, 7 December 2010.

CHAPTER 16

1. 'How Libyan "Regime Change" Lies Echo in Syria', https://www. consortiumnews.com/2016/09/25/how-libyan-regime-change-lies-echo-in-syria. Also, House of Commons Foreign Affairs

Committee: *Libya: Examination of intervention and collapse and the UK's future policy options. Third Report of Session 2016–17.*

2. 'Voices from Benghazi: "We have lived through the worst five years", Peter Oborne's letter from Libya', the *Spectator*, 2 January 2016.

3. NATO *Final Mission Statistics*, 2 November 2011.

4. On 3 March 2011, President Obama announced that Gaddafi 'must step down from power and leave'. Nineteen days later he ordered US Africa Command to cease all peace negotiations with Gaddafi.

5. Robert Parry, 'Three Deadly War Myths', Consortium News, 9 June 2011.

6. Classified memo, Sidney Blumenthal to Secretary of State Hillary Clinton, US Department Case no. F-2014-20439, doc no. CO5782401, 27 March 2011.

7. Written 1 November 2014. Libya is today a destroyed nation. The UN reports that hundreds of thousands have been forced to flee their homes, with millions of refugees travelling by boat to Italy in the hope of asylum in Europe and the UK.

8. 15 September 2011. 'Libya: Cameron and Sarkozy mobbed in Benghazi', bbc.co.uk/news/world-africa-14934352

9. 20October2011,www.cbsnews.com/news/clinton-on-qaddafi-we-came-we-saw-he-died/

10. http://www.wsj.com/articles/SB1000142405311190389590457654 7101159155100

11. The al-Saadi family, in 2012, settled the case on payment by the British government of £2.3 million.

12. In 2015 the Belhaj family agreed to settle for a token £1 and a public apology from Jack Straw and the British government. The offer was refused. On 16 January 2017 the UK Supreme Court ruled unanimously that Straw and Sir Mark Allen could be sued by Belhaj.

13. 'Libyan linked to Lockerbie welcome in the UK', *The Guardian*, 7 October 2001.

14. 'US: Torture and Rendition in Gaddafi's Libya', 6 September 2012, Human Rights Watch, http://www.hrw.org/news/2012/09/05/us-torture-and-rendition-gaddafi-s-libya

15. 'How Britain did Gaddafi's Dirty Work', the *Guardian*, 9 November 2017.

16. In December 2017 the Foreign and Commonwealth Office of the UK advised against all travel to Libya, and for any British nationals still in Libya to leave immediately: 'Terrorists very likely to carry out attacks within Libya. Kidnapping is rife. The British embassy remains closed. All airports are vulnerable to attack.'

17. 'The Avenger', *New Yorker Magazine*, 28 September 2015. Only in 2015, when Dornstein's interview with the *New Yorker* was published did Jim discover the attempt to clandestinely record the meeting. For Jim it would have been anathema and a breach of trust between Baset and himself. Dornstein's documentary, *My Brother's Bomber*, was broadcast on BBC4 on 2 November 2015, three weeks after the film's showing in the USA. The BBC's attitude contrasts strongly with that shown in 1994 when a well-researched documentary, *The Maltese Double Cross*, by award-winning director Alan Francovich was banned by the BBC and in the US. The Dornstein film supported the US/UK official line, the Francovich film challenged it.

18. John Ashton, *Megrahi: You Are My Jury* (Birlinn, 2012).

TRUTH WILL FIND A WAY
CHAPTER 17

1. John Ashton and Ian Ferguson, *Cover-up of Convenience: The Hidden Scandal of Lockerbie* (Mainstream, 2001).

2. Allan Worroll, Ferranti International, letter to Detective Inspector W. Williamson, 24 May 1990.

Acknowledgements

THESE ARE BUT a small selection of those who have helped our campaign over the last thirty years. Some of those named may not even feel that they have contributed; but they have, during the darkest hours, lifted the spirits or opened friendly doors. Some have by now passed away and we salute their memories.

There has been throughout a steady stream of supporting letters and emails. To my shame many have not received a response, yet their cumulative support has been a huge source of strength. If you are one of such and reading these words, I wish now to apologise and say that you helped me to feel always a member of the human race. I salute and thank you all.

I must also thank the American bereaved relatives, many of whom will have felt their 'closure' seriously threatened by our campaign to discover and reveal something of the truth about what really happened in the Lockerbie disaster. We are all in this tragedy together and time will hopefully smooth out differing opinions. Perhaps in the longer term we hope that the reward for all of us will be the opportunity to understand more of the truth behind this dreadful atrocity, for truth founded on fact has always been our goal.

Prominent among those who have helped are: Bernard Adamczewski, Kate Adie, the staff and reporters of Al Jazeera, Richard Anderson QC, David Ben Aryeah, David Benson, Jean and Barry Berkley, Ben Birnberg, Professor Robert Black QC, Harry Boggis-Rolfe, Professor Noam Chomsky, John Coates,

Robin Cook, John Cookson, Tam and Kathleen Dalyell, Carl Davies, Ian Ferguson, Barry Flick and UKF103, Laurie Flynn, Paul Foot and the staff of *Private Eye*, Robert Forrester and James Robertson of Justice For Megrahi (James knows that Fred Nilsen has still not called!), Alan Francovich, Christine Grahame SMP, Iain Hamilton QC, Richard Ingrams, Richard Jeffs, Professor Hans Kochler, Brenda Laugher, Nelson Mandela, Edward MacKechnie, Iain McKie, Cardinal Keith O'Brien, Cecil Parkinson, Gareth Peirce, Steven Raeburn, Tiny and Josie Rowland, Riki Schuurink, Jon Snow, Lord David Steel, Sir Teddy Taylor, Ingebourg van Teeseling, Rodney Wallis, Peter Watson and Professor Paul Wilkinson.

Special thanks too to the Scottish Criminal Cases Review Commission, labouring for several years to unearth new evidence and the momentous conclusion that that there may have been a miscarriage of justice and that a further appeal should be allowed. The Scottish Parliament's Justice Committee have agreed since 2010 to keep Petition e1370 active thus keeping open the possibility of an official inquiry into the Lockerbie events.

A special mention for my wife, Jane, and Lisa Mosey. Without their patient tolerance of our obsession all would long ago have sunk without trace. Nor must we forget John Mosey. He too lost a gifted daughter, Helga. His unwavering support has been a source of comfort and strength through the darkest of times. Especially too my thanks go to beloved daughter and son, Cathy and William, and – still walking beside me – Flora.

Finally, a special thanks to Baset al-Megrahi and family, his solicitor Tony Kelly, and currently Aamer Anwar, author John Ashton and dogged researcher George Thompson. Their untiring investigation into thousands of documents eventually extracted from the Crown prosecution archives revealed that the fragment of digital-timer circuit board known as PT/35(b) was incompatible with the type of timers supplied to Libya in 1985. This fragment was central to the prosecution case at Zeist.

Index

Abdel-Jalil, Mustafa, Libyan
    Minister for Justice 220, 221
Abu Nidal Group 6, 29, 205
Adamczewski, Bernard 39, 255
Adie, Kate 63
Al Ahram (Cairo newspaper) 56
Air Malta Flight KM 180 to
    Frankfurt 131
Albright, Madeleine 100
Alert Security 52
Aljadi, His Excellency Judge
    M' hammud 59–60, 63
Allen, Sir Mark 223
American relatives group 27, 34, 50,
    115, 130, 181, 182–3
    'bomb scare' among, Jim Swire
        and 42–3, 44
    hurt of Lockerbie for, Swire's
        letter to Thatcher concerning
        31–2
    trial demands by (and problems
        with) 87, 99, 106
American Victims of Pan Am 103
    150
Ammerman, Bert 27–8, 31, 42, 102,
    170, 211
Ancona Airport 90
Anderson, Jack 34
Anderson, Terry 64

Andover, Massachusetts 42
Andrew, Duke of York 118, 120
Angiolini, Elish, Lord Advocate 206
Annan, Kofi, UN Director-General
    102, 116, 117
Arab League 94, 96, 97, 103, 113,
    116
'Arab Spring' 218
Arafat, Yassar 24
Armstrong, Patrick 136
Aryeah, David Ben 34, 57, 59, 98,
    115, 169, 170, 181
    'Autumn Leaves,' message on
        operation from 38–9
    first newsman on scene at
        Lockerbie 28
    trial in neutral country, Robin
        Cook and news of possibility
        of 99–100, 109
Ashton, John 227, 231–2, 234, 236
Assad, Rifaat 37
Al-Assad, Bashar, President of Syria
    107
Azwai, Mohamed 223

Baer, Robert, CIA Middle East
    specialist 163, 187–8, 207, 237
Baker, James, US Secretary of State
    James 55–6

Bandler, Donald K 107–08

Bani-Sadr, Abul Hassan 81

Barlinnie prison, Glasgow 182, 187

Barr, US Attorney General William, indictment in Lockerbie case and 55

BBC 44, 75, 79, 118, 160, 171, 190
'Wisdom of Jim and Jane' on website 158

BBC Birmingham 74

BBC News 108, 198

BBC Panorama 112–13

BBC radio 70

BBC Scotland 109–10

BBC Six O' Clock News 198

BBC World Service 5, 100

Beckett, John 130

Bedford, John (Heathrow luggage loader) 51, 152, 177–8, 180

Bekaa Valley in Lebanon 37, 80, 84–5

Belhaj, Abdel Hakim 223

Bell, Detective Chief Inspector Henry Wood ('Harry Bell') 143–6, 157, 193–5, 195–7, 199

Berkley, Barry 170

Bernstein, Stephanie 106

Biddulph, Peter 91, 213

Biehl, Dana, US attorney 127, 157

Bin Laden, Osama 223, 226

BKA (German Central Criminal Investigation Agency) 24, 25, 40, 41, 145, 161–2, 164

Black QC, Professor Robert 203, 207
formula for trial in neutral country, final agreement on 108–9
formula for trial in neutral country, negotiations about 96, 97, 100, 103–04, 106, 107

legal impasse, forging key to 74, 93–5

meetings with Gaddafi in Libya 104–06, 114–15

miscarriage of justice letter, fundamental issues still to address 180–81

on payments to witnesses and credibility of evidence 195

sincere friend and wonderful travelling companion 94–5

Blackwell Methodist church 241

Blair, Prime Minister Tony 99, 101, 115, 120, 190
'Deal in the Desert' by government of 208–09, 222

delaying tactics from? 114

efforts to bring about trial, hyperdrive media and 117

transatlantic relationship and complex problem for government of 99

Westminster Abbey and 10th anniversary memorial service 117–18

Bollier, Edwin 140–43

Bonfadelli, Urs 234–5

Botha, Pik 7

Boult, Sir Adrian 158

Boyd QC, Colin, Solicitor General (later Lord Advocate) 121, 122, 154–5, 157, 159, 181, 202

Breakfast with Frost (BBC TV) 99, 113–14

British Airways 73

British government 29–30, 50, 51, 52, 103, 112, 210–11, 222
'Deal in the Desert' negotiations by 208–9
denial of anything that might embarrass them 181–2

hypocrisy of position of, exposure of 224
interference in Scottish trial process, accusation of 206–07
refusal of inquiry by 41
trial for Lockerbie suspects, prevarication on 95–6, 99–100, 102
British Medical Journal 241
British Petroleum 208, 212
British relatives group 36, 94, 97, 107, 177, 213–14
applause from Americans for 182–3
celebrities, headline news and 44–5
Dover House meeting with Boyd 122
Downing St visit for, trial possibilities and 117
Edinburgh meeting of, readiness for action in 98–9
Foreign Office meeting with Cook 166
government scrutiny of, *persons of interest* 173
Iranian involvement in Lockerbie, news for 55–6
powerlessness of 207
reliability of witnesses, assurance from Lord Advocate on 154
Bromsgrove 108, 151, 241
Caspidge House in 3
see also Caspidge House
Brown, Prime Minister Gordon 208–9
Buckley, William 86
Budd, Colin, Ambassador to Netherlands 181
Burns, William, US Assistant Secretary of State 223

Burns QC, David 130, 142
Burt, Alistair 166
Bush Jr, President George W. 174
Bush Sr, President George H.W. 18, 32, 34, 41, 44, 56, 73, 76, 83, 150
Byrne, DS 196–7
Byrne, Gay 72–3

Cadman, Martin 27, 36
Caithness, Earl of 71, 75, 89
Cameron, Prime Minister David 218, 221, 237–8
Campbell, Alastair (prosecution counsel) 122, 134, 137, 147–8, 155
Campbell QC, Colin 48
Cannistraro, Vincent (CIA) 8, 83, 84, 154, 167, 188
Carlos the Jackal 140
Carloway, Colin, Lord Justice General J.M.S. 239, 240
Caspidge House 3, 44, 94, 113, 125, 133, 191
BBC Birmingham at 74
Central TV at 19
distinguished footsteps at 158–9
'Flora's Wood' at 23, 241–2
home at, trial adjournment and August at 149–51
Nabil Nagameldin from *Al Ahram* at 56–7
Shelley Jofre at, family photographs and films dug out 110–11
winter at 22–3
CBS News 28, 222
Central TV 19–21
Channel 4 TV 79–80, 142, 188, 211
Channon, Paul 24–5, 26–7, 41
Chubim, Sharham 80, 86

CIA (US Central Intelligence
     Agency) 8, 24, 56–7, 73, 82–4,
     86, 143, 167, 190
  Company Business, Francovich's
     exposé of CIA activities 79–80
  drugs-for-hostages operation by
     35
  evidence from sources 'as good as
     it gets' 163–4
  evidence of CIA asset Majid
     Giaka 154–7
  former Middle East specialist
     Baer, Lockerbie investigation
     and 187–8, 207
  Libyan intelligence, regular
     dialogue with 222
  manipulation of Lockerbie trial,
     allegations against 191–2, 202
  misinformation from, media
     feeding on 174
  Pan Am and Frankfurt Airport
     management, investigation by
     41
  payments to witness Giaka,
     concerns about 195
  *President's Commission on
     Aviation Security,* briefing by
     35
  redactions of Giaka cables 159
Clark, General Wesley 217, 219
Clinton, President Bill 73, 107
Clinton, HUllary, US Secretary of
     State 211, 222
CNN 44, 181, 205
Cohen, Daniel, Susan, and
     Theodora 102, 121, 170, 211
Coleman, Lester 36–7
Commonwealth Heads of
     Government Meeting
     (CHOGM, Edinburgh 1997)
     98, 100–01

On Company Business (Allan
     Francovitch documentary) 79
Conlon, Gerard 136
Connelly, Clare 171–2
Cook, Robin, British Foreign
     Secretary 96, 97, 108, 113–14,
     120, 135
  British relatives meeting with 166
  'diplomatic activities being
     pursued' 102–03
  policy shift, thanks for Foreign
     Office help in 115–16
  trial in neutral country, possibility
     for 99–101
  Westminster Abbey, 10th
     anniversary memorial service
     in 117–18
Cook, Roger 89–92
The Cook Report (ITV) 89
Cooper, Rev. Arnold 241
Court of Appeal (UK) 136, 240
*Cover-up of Convenience: The
     Hidden Scandal of Lockerbie*
     (Ashton, J. and Ferguson, I.)
     231
  publication of, governments'
     criticism of 237–8
Crawley, Dr Jess 235
Crichton Hospital, Dumfries 15
Cullen, William, Lord Justice Clerk
     182
Cyprus 161
  pivot point for DEA operations
     85

Daily Express 7
Daily Telegraph 208
Dalkamoni, Hafez 161, 165, 188
Dalyell, Tam 8, 77–8, 203
Davidson QC, Jack 130, 152
'Deal in the Desert' 208, 222

Deerstalker (Saleh, Libyan official) 60–3

Delude-Dix, Elizabeth 27–8, 29

Democracy Now 217

'Desert Storm' 82

Dewar, Donald, First Minister of Scotland 96

Dextar warehouse, Lockarbie 134

Ditmas, Harry 173–4

Dix, Pam 99

Donahue, Steven 36–7, 80, 85

Dorda, Abuzed 96, 117

Dornstein, Ken 226

The Downing Street Years (Thatcher, M.) 75

Dryfesdale Parish church 16, 17, 27, 76

Duff, Alistair 130, 164

Duggan, Frank 80, 81, 85–6, 87, 211

Dumfries and Galloway Health Board 47

Dumfries and Galloway police 24, 198, 199, 200

Dunnabie farm, near Lockarbie 134

Dzakovic, Bogdan 91–2

On Eagles' Wings 43

Easterbrook Hall 47

Edinburgh Book Festival 236

Edinburgh High Court 207

Eliot, T.S. 241

European Convention on Human Rights 240

European Convention on Mutual Assistance in Criminal Matters 161

European Council (Rhodes, December 1988) 75

Express 126

Al Fatah (PLO armed wing) 160

Fatal Accident Inquiry (FAI, 1991) 47, 49, 51, 72, 89, 151, 173

Fattah-Younis, General Abdel 220

FBI (US Federal Bureau of Investigation) 7, 41, 73, 81, 84, 156, 161, 167

evidence of Special Agent Marshman 163–6

helicopters and personnel in Lockerbie search 28

Lockerbie bomb concealed in checked baggage 90

Lockerbie scene, speed of arrival on 8

manipulation of Lockerbie trial, allegations against 191–2

reports from, objections to revealing of 159

searches of Lockerbie scene, participation in 24

Federal Aviation Administration (FAA) 42, 44, 91–2

warning from 26, 29–30

Feraday, Allen 131, 138–9, 188, 200, 201, 232, 233, 234, 236

fragments of PT/35(b), falseness of evidence on 227

Ferguson, Ian 231

Ferranti International 233, 235

Fhimah, Khalifa 55, 56, 57, 59, 114, 130–31, 147, 154–7, 169, 191, 197, 204

Kamp van Zeist, trial at 114, 130–46, 154–7, 169, 202, 239–40

not-guilty verdict for 169

prosecution case against, key elements of 130–1

Fletcher, PC Yvonne 63, 64

Flick, Barry 42, 44

'Flowers of the Forest' (lament) 119

Flynn, Kathleen 177, 181, 183

Focus magazine 147, 193–4

Foreign and Commonwealth Office
(FCO) 70, 99, 113, 116, 117,
165, 166, 190, 206, 223–4
  trial in neutral country,
    negotiations about 97–8, 99,
    100–101, 106, 108–9

Four Quartets (Eliot, T.S.) 241

Fox, Liam, British Defence Secretary
219

Francovich, Allan 79, 80, 81, 82–6,
141

Frankfurt Airport 6, 24–5, 26, 35,
37, 41, 51, 52, 180
  trial at Kamp van Zeist, mentions
    during 131, 151–2, 155, 162,
    165

Fraser, Peter, Lord Advocate 15, 24,
26, 49, 63, 94, 96
  case against Libyans, beyond
    reasonable doubt 56
  doubts about Gauci testimony,
    admission of 202–03
  guilt of al-Megrahi and Fhimah,
    presupposition of 70

Fréchette, Louise, Deputy Secretary-
General of UN 101–02

Fulton, Professor R. Andrew 172

G7 summit in Birmingham (1998)
107

Gaddafi, Muammar 64, 113, 182,
183
  accusation of ordering Lockerbie
    bombing against 219–20
  Arab League and OAU pressure
    on 116
  Arch Satan, description as 16

balancing needs of, conflicting
  trial requirements and 94

Blair/Gaddafi Prisoner Transfer
  Agreement (PTA) 190, 205,
  208–09

bloody murderer, Susan Cohen on
  170

bombing of Tripoli and Benghazi,
  Thatcher's enthusiasm for 76

death of, conflict in Libya, fall of
  Tripoli and 221

demands on, United Nations and 87

disinformation by 81

dynasty of, fears for 189

former home (now derelict),
  Swire's visit to 64–5

former home in Tripoli,
  destruction of 225

international terrorism, 'sugar
  daddy' of 74

Libya 'in from the cold,' Blair's
  call to 190

Mandela's meetings with (and
  support for Libya) 98–9, 100

Moussa Koussa, closeness to 190

Nagameldin and suggestion of
  visit to 57–9

plot to assassinate by Libyan
  extremists 112

power of, friends and 70–71

release of suspects for trial,
  unlikeliness of 102–3, 107,
  108–09

Swire, first meeting with 66–8

Swire, fourth meeting with (in
  Benghazi) 211–13

Swire, second meeting with 104–6

Swire, third meeting with (at
  Sirte) 114–15

Swire's promise of fair trial for
  suspects to 135

trial in neutral country, turn
towards acceptance of 118
uprising against regime of
218–19
Gaddafi, Saif al-Islam 189, 205,
208, 210
Gauci, Tony 201–02
confusion and forgetfulness of
152
David Wright and doubts about
evidence of 198–200
evidence from, Bell's diary and
143–9, 193–6, 196–7
identification of al-Megrahi (and
concerns about) 146–9, 179–80
Megrahi's final comments on
evidence of 226–7
owner of Mary's House in Sliema
131
Scottish police and 'holidays in
Scotland' for 178
GCHQ Cheltenham 237–8
Ghanem, Chukri, Prime Minister of
Libya 190
Giaka, Abdul Majid 131, 143,
154–9, 191–2, 194–5
Gilchrist, Detective Constable
Thomas 133–5, 137, 139, 146,
195, 200
suspicions about testimony of
227
Gill QC, Brian 48–9
Gobel, Rainer 40, 161–2
Greenock prison 203, 209
Guantanamo Bay 223
Guardian 211, 224, 241
Guildford pub bombing (1974) and
Guildford Four 136, 193, 239

Hanna (daughter of Colonel
Gaddafi) 57, 60, 65, 67–8

Hardie QC, Andrew , Advocate
Depute (later Lord Advocate)
51, 89, 101, 121, 141, 151, 202
Hayes, Dr Thomas 131, 136–8, 139,
163, 188, 200, 239
suspicions about testimony of
227, 232–3, 236
Heathrow Airport 3. 5, 19, 26, 32,
45, 71, 131, 155, 201
aviation security at, Swire's test of
41–3
baggage container 14L at,
destined for Pan Am 103 24–5
controlled deliveries at 37
inspection of Pan Am systems at
Frankfurt and 41
instructions concerning
'suspicious devices' issued at
31
luggage container AVE4041
unsupervised at (21 December
1988) 151–2
Pan Am 103 at, security claims for
51
police station at 45–6
security at, deficiencies in 153,
178–80
Helsinki, warning from US embassy
in 29–30, 36, 88
Hendershot (FBI Special Agent)
161
Henderson, DCI Stuart 196, 210
Herald (Scottish) 165–6, 207
Hezbollah 85
Hill, Paul 136
Hogg, Douglas 27
Horgan, Joe 102
The Houses are Full of Smoke
(Allan Francovitch
documentary) 79
Human Rights Watch 222

Hurd, Douglas 27, 71
Hussein, Saddam 174, 189
King Hussein of Jordan 165

'ice-cube' timers 38, 40, 162, 170
International Court of Justice (ICJ)
    67, 97. 108
International Criminal Tribunal in
    The Hague 127
Iran Air 151, 152, 179
Iran-Contra scandal 73, 86
Ireland 72–3
Islamic Jihad 64

Jack, James 38, 45, 50
Jafaar, Khaled 7, 52, 80, 85
James, Canon Eric 19–21, 241
Jeliban, Omar 211
Jhoja, Havid (Megrahi defence
    lawyer) 182
Jibril, Ahmed 25, 34, 35, 38, 40, 80,
    81, 161, 164–5
Jofre, Shelley 109–11
John F. Kennedy Airport (JFK) 5,
    41, 42, 44, 131
John Paul II, Pope 100
Johnson, Carol 42
Johnson, Dr (metallurgist at
    Manchester) 233–4
Johnson, Glenn 42
Johnson, President Lyndon B. 29
Johnston, David 8
Justice Department (US) 127, 135,
    144, 149, 156–7, 192, 194
Justice Ministry in Libya 115

Kamboj, Sultash (Heathrow luggage
    loader) 152
Kamp van Zeist, Lockerbie trial at
    114–15, 127–47, 151–66, 202,
    239–40

prosecution case, key elements of
    130–1
Al-Kassar, Monzer 35, 37
Keen QC, Richard 130, 134, 137,
    138, 143, 161, 162
Kelly, Tony 192, 203–04, 206, 227
    drill-down investigation of
    prosecution trial evidence
    231–6
Kennedy, President John F. 29
Khalifa (interpreter in Tripoli) 59
Ayatollah Khomeini of Iran 34
Khreesat, Marwan (PFLP-GC bomb
    maker) 25, 38, 163–5
King Edward's High School for
    Girls 30, 241
Kochler, Professor Hans 236
Kohl, Chancellor Helmut 75
Koussa, Moussa 59–60, 190, 205,
    222, 223
Kreindler, Attorney Lee 105–06
Kretzmer, Michael 74–5
Kuwait invasion by Iraq (2003) 76

Larracoechea, Marina 47, 49, 52
The Late Late Show (RTE TV)
    72–3
Law Society of Scotland 172
Lebanon 24, 36, 84
    US hostages in 85
Leppard, David 80–1, 82, 83, 87,
    160
Libya
    Intelligence Service (JSO) of 154,
    156, 157
    international respectability, return
    to 188–9, 190
    Lockerbie committee of
    government of 94
    'New Libyan Coalition Council'
    in Benghazi 220

Provisional Libyan Government
225

Linklater, Magnus 237

Lockerbie 4, 5–6, 76–8
   dead of Flight 103 and town of
      9–15
   disaster, site, Wilson's find from
      47–8
   Dryfesdale Parish church,
      memorial service at (5 January
      1989) 16, 17, 18–19
   government decisions on, lack of
      ethical structure for 158–9
   ice rink as cold storage facility at
      16
   lost ones of 43
   public scrutiny of, problems for
      159
   Town Hall meeting, tea and
      biscuits (and rage at
      officialdom) 17–18

Lockerbie Air Disaster Group
   (LADG) 46, 47, 48, 50

Lockerbie Trial Briefing Unit 171–2

Logan International Airport in
   Boston 90

Long Walk to Freedom (Mandela,
   N.) 187

Lonrho 82

Lowenstein, Peter 102, 182

Luqa Airport, Malta 56, 131,
   155–6, 157, 197, 198

McArdle, Dr Chris 235

MacAskill, Kenny (Scottish Justice
   Minister) 165–6, 208, 209–10

McCain, Senator John 220

McClenny, Lee 106

McColm, Thomas 134

MacDonald, Flora 133

McDonald, Sheena 81, 84–5, 87–8

MacFadyen, Norman, Crown QC
   154, 181

McFarlane, Robert, US Security
   Adviser 86

Machrihanish, US Navy airbase at
   8, 28

Mack, Linda 29

MacKechnie, Edward 130, 164, 192,
   232

McKee, Major Charles (CIA) 8, 24,
   80

McLean, Hector 119

Macleod, Murdo 130

McNair, William (CIA) 154

McQueen, Marjorie 183

Maghur, Kamal 114

Maguire, Anne (and Maguire Seven)
   136, 239

Al Mahari Hotel, Tripoli 58, 63, 68,
   114

Maid of the Seas (Boeing 747-100,
   Pan Am 103) 7, 75, 182

Mail on Sunday 95, 178

Major, Prime Minister John 165

Malta 56
   Mary's House at Tower Road,
      Sliema 131, 143, 144–5, 193–5,
      196, 197, 198
   police headquarters in Floriana 144

The Maltese Double Cross (Allan
   Francovitch documentary) 36,
   79, 115, 141, 188

Manchester Airport 89

Mandela, Nelson 70–1, 98–9, 100,
   103, 116, 120–1
   meeting with al-Megrahi in
      Barlinnie 187
   speech on resolving Lockerbie
      issue 120–1

Manly, Raymond (Heathrow
   security officer) 178–9, 182

Marchioness disaster 29

Marquise, Richard (FBI) 210

Marshman, FBI Special Agent
    Edward 163–5

May, Sir John 136, 239–40

MEBO AG 131, 140, 201, 234, 235

Meehan, Patrick 203

Al-Megrahi, Abdelbaset ('Baset')
    55, 56, 57, 59, 173, 188–9, 190,
    191, 192–3

  appeal process at Kamp van Zeist
    (2002) for 177–83

  Bartlinnie prison, writing
    memoirs in 187

  compassionate release and return
    to Libya for 209–11

  destruction of case against (all
    too late) 236

  final meeting with Jim Swire and
    death of 226–8

  forensic report, injustice of guilty
    verdict based on 239–40

  Gauci's identification of (and
    concerns about) 146–9, 179–80

  guilt of, Thatcher's evidence for
    77

  guilty verdict for 168–9

  illness of 203–04

  Kamp van Zeist, trial at 114,
    130–46, 153–7, 165, 168, 173,
    239–40

  lawyers representing, dismissal of
    114

  legal representation at trial 130

  Mary's House, new evidence on
    purchase of clothes at 193–5,
    195–7, 197–9

  posthumous appeal on behalf of,
    rejection of 239–40

  prosecution case against, key
    elements of 130–1

US intelligence and threats to life
    of 225

Al-Megrahi, Aisha and family 204,
    226–8

Al-Megrahi, Ali 239

Al-Megrahi, Khaled 177, 226

*Megrahi: You Are My Jury – The
    Lockerbie Evidence* (Ashton,
    J.) 231–2

Meguid, Arab League Secretary
    General Dr Esmet 103

MI5 26–7, 29, 73, 112, 113

MI6 27, 59, 73, 103, 112–13, 172–3,
    190, 207, 222–3

Miliband, David, British Foreign
    Secretary 165, 206–7

Miller-Adams, Nathan 82

Mohtashemi, Ali Akbar, Iranian
    Interior Minister 56

Montassa, Libyan foreign affairs
    minister 104–5

Montreal Convention (1971) 63, 67

Moore, Peter 80

Mosey, Helga 30

Mosey, John 27, 30, 70, 166, 167,
    177, 181

  honesty and truth about
    Lockerbie, continuing search
    for 170

  Kretzmer interview with 74

  sermon in Westmenster Abbey
    119

  sinister pattern of events at
    Lockerbie site, experience of
    47–9

  trial at Kamp van Zrist,
    beginnings of 130

  Westminster Abbey, 10th
    anniversary memorial service
    at 117–20

Mosey, Lisa 30, 118, 181

Mosey, Marcus 119
Mossad 24
Mowat QC, Sheriff Principal John
    S. 47, 49, 50, 51, 52
MST-13 electronic timers 130–31,
    139, 200–01, 232, 234
Mueller, Robert, FBI Chief 210–11
Mugabe, Robert 100
Murdoch, Professor Jim L. 171–2
Murtagh, Brian US attorney 127,
    157

Nagameldin, Nabil 57–60, 61–2,
    63, 68, 75
National Commission on Terrorist
    Attacks 91
NATO (North Atlantic Treaty
    Organisation) 114, 127, 217,
    219–21, 224
New England Laminates 233
New York Times 220
New Yorker Magazine 226–7
Nidal, Abu 205
Norrie, Charles 170
North, Colonel Oliver 73, 80, 83,
    84, 86

Obama, President Barack 211, 220
Obeidi, Abdelati, Libyan Deputy
    Foreign Minister 205
Observer 82
'Operation Unified Protector' 219
Orbost House on Skye 110, 158,
    190–91
Organisation of African Unity
    (OAU) 96, 97, 100, 108, 116
Organisation of Islamic
    Cooperation (OIC) 96
Orr, Chief Superintendent John 24,
    49

Pan Am 103 30, 44–5, 102, 159, 191
    baggage container from Frankfurt
        on Pan Am 103A destined for
        24–5, 151–2, 157
    bereaved of, Swire speaking for 73
    bomb on, interline baggage
        system and 179–80
    bomb on, Khaled Jafaar and 52
    bomb on, Libyan intelligence
        officers and 55
    dead of Lockerbie town and 9–15
    detonators, operational sequence
        and initial flight phase of 162
    fall of, searches of Lockerbie site 24
    Fatal Accident Inquiry (FAI) into
        bombing of 47
    Gaddafi and, deadly myth about
        219–20
    international political event 74
    Khreesat and device responsible
        for bombing of 164
    Mandela and unlocking story of 98
    prominent people known to have
        cancelled flights on 83–4
    relatives of victims of, watch on
        26
    security at Heathrow, Hardie's
        claim for 51
    shock and confusion after
        destruction of 49
    shrine to deceased at Tundergarth
        graveyard 43
    story a twig of debris twisting
        upon a flood of deceit 224
    Thatcher at Lockerbie site 75
    Thatcher on Libyan involvement
        in bombing of 77
    'truth must be known' pin for 68,
        120, 125
    warning about threat to, denial of
        6–7

Pan Am 103A (Frankfurt–
 Heathrow) 24–5, 51, 151–2,
 162, 180
Pan American Airways 3, 6–7, 30,
 41, 50, 51–2, 71, 179
 dead of Flight 103 and town of
  Lockerbie 9–15
 flight 103 (Boeing 757-100, *Maid
  of the Seas*) 4–5, 7, 24–5, 26,
  30, 34, 35
 JFK, Pan Am desk at 5
Parkinson, Cecil 25, 26–7, 32–3, 41,
 44–5, 46, 118, 120
Parry, Robert 219–20
Parry, Emyr Jones , UN ambassador
 189
Parsons, Sir Anthony 70
PFLP-GC (Popular Front for
 Liberation of Palestine,
 General Command) 7, 24, 25,
 52, 86, 192, 207
 Abu Talb and evidence of PFLP
  bomb 161, 188
 bomb maker Khreesat and
  evidence of radio-cassette
  bombs 163–4
 King Hussein of Jordan and
  evidence on, concealment of
  165
 'ice-cube' timers and bombs made
  by 40, 162
 intelligence reports pointing
  finger at 34, 39
 investigation target 55–6
 Lockerbie bomb planted by, film
  claim of 80
 photographs of bombs by, DoT
  delay in issuing 50
Phillips, Richard, Dean of
 Hendricks Chapel, Syracuse
 University 118

plastic fragment (PT/35b) 136–7,
 138–9, 140, 141, 162, 188, 200,
 201, 227
 Kelly's examination of evidence
  concerning 232–3
 Miliband's public interest
  immunity against disclosure of
  evidence about 205–6
 Worroll's discovery about 233,
  235
Prescott, John 43, 118, 120, 166
*President's Commission on Aviation
 Security* 35, 80
Press Association (PA) 40, 44
Prisoner Transfer Agreement (PTA)
 190, 205, 207–8

Rasmussen, Anders, NATO
 Secretary General 219
Reno, Janet, US Attorney General 122
Reuters 44, 98, 105
Revell, Oliver 'Buck' 81, 82, 83–5,
 86–7, 88, 167
Ricardo, Ambassador Victor 77
Richardson, Carole 136
Richardson, William, US
 ambassador to UN 102
Rowland, Josie 118, 120
Rowland, Richard W. ('Tiny') 82,
 115, 118
Royal Armament Research and
 Defence Establishment
 (RARDE) 136, 239–40
Rubin, James 98
Rum, Isle of ('Crocodile Island')
 110
Rumsfeld, Donald 217
Rushdie, Salman 73

al-Saadi, Sami 223
St Andrews 50, 100

St Catherine's Anglican church 241

Salem, Mohammed 145

Salinger, Pierre 29

Sarkozy, President Nicolas 221

The Satanic Verses (Rushdie, S.) 73

Scanlan, Michael, President of Law Society of Scotland 172

Scharf, Michael, US State Department lawyer 191–2

Scicluna, Inspector of Maltese police 144–5, 147, 195, 196

Scotland Yard 7

Scotsman 95, 237

Scott QC, Margaret 206

Scottish Criminal Cases Review Commission (SCCRC) 144, 165, 180–1, 206, 232

report of 192–3

witness statements, offers of rewards and 193–95, 198–9, 200

Scottish Crown Office 70, 199, 200, 206, 234, 237

spin doctors at 165, 171

Scottish Executive 121

Scottish TV 115

Secret Intelligence Services (SIS) 113

See No Evil (Baer, R.) 187–8

Semtex (high explosive) 25, 38, 40, 41, 51

September 11, 2001 (9/11) 91, 174, 178, 217, 223

Sermon on the Mount 158–9

Shamis, Ashour 225

Shanks, Norman (head of security at Heathrow) 153

Shayler, David 112, 113, 114

Sherwood Crescent, Lockerbie 132

Shukra (Mary's House customer identified by Gauci in Malta) 145

Sirte, Gaddafi's home town 115, 221

Sky News 221

Skye, Isle of 3–4, 22, 67, 107–8, 111, 119, 125, 158, 171, 190–1, 242

South China News 40

Spiro, Brian 86

Sports Illustrated 90

Stasi (East German secret police) 140, 141, 142, 188

Statecraft: Strategies for a Changing World (Thatcher, M.) 77

Stephenson, Roland 132

Stockholm Syndrome 203

Strathclyde Police 178

Straw, Jack, British Home Secretary (later Foreign Secretary) 113, 172–4, 183, 208

Sun 95

Sunday Express 153

Sunday Times 80–1, 83, 160, 202

Sutherland, Lord Justice Ranald Iain 148, 160, 168

Sutherland, Tom 64

Swire, Catherine (Cathy) 4, 8, 20–1, 129, 133, 150, 153, 191, 213, 241

closeness to Flora, final memory and 111–12

family holiday on Skye for 110

with Flora at King Edward's High School for Girls 30

waving Flora goodbye at Heathrow 3

William and, loving relationship with Flora and 158

Swire, Flora 7, 15–16, 26, 27, 129, 132–3, 158, 212–13

Caspidge House, 'Flora's Wood' at 23, 241–2

Swire, Flora (*cont.*)
  Cathy and, closeness between
    111–12
  dead of Pan Am 103, listing
    among 14
  dental records, search for 8
  determination of father to
    discover facts on killer 159
  family visit to London bedsit 19
  father Jim and, endless moments
    between 16–17
  funeral of 21
  gift of Koran from Gaddafi,
    placing picture of Flora within
    67–8
  images of, thoughts and 21–2,
    125, 135, 149, 150–1
  inquisitive nature of 111
  Jane and, suffering at loss of 21–2
  last minute ticket on less than full
    aircraft 83
  Lockerbie disaster and death of,
    family and news of 3–5
  memorial service for (February
    1989) 241
  murder of, responsibility for still
    in question after 25 years
    227–8
  Pan Am 103 and death of,
    headline news after 19 months
    44–5
  Pan Am 103 passenger list check
    for 5
  photograph of (and strategic use
    of) 45, 60, 72, 103, 225
  portrait of, Skye backdrop to 125
  post-graduate medicine at
    Cambridge offer 19
  seat on Pan Am 103 (39D) 42
  thoughts of, images and 21–2,
    125, 136, 149, 150–1

truth and justice for, campaigning
    for 108–09
Swire, Jane 27, 56, 59, 128, 129–30,
    133, 136, 170, 181
  Caspidge house, family life at
    158–9
  Central TV, interview with
    19–21
  classified telexes, news of threats
    to aircraft security before
    Lockerbie in 38
  emergency code for, design of 57
  eternal pain of mother mourning
    112
  family and, dealing with
    campaigning 213–14
  fears for Jim of campaigning too
    much 69
  on Flora walking aboard Pan Am
    103 83–4
  Flora's ashes, returning home
    with 21
  Flora's place on London, visit to 19
  indictment in Lockerbie case,
    news of 55–6
  Jim's plan Jane won't like 41
  Kretzmer interview at Caspidge
    74–5
  letter posted on day of Lockerbie
    from 19–20
  much out of Jim's life lately 107
  positivity in ending narrative 241–2
  preparations for Kamp van Zeist
    trial 125–7
  Shelley Jofre and filming for BBC
    documentary 109–10
  Skye holiday (at last but short) for
    108
  Westminster Abbey, 10th
    anniversary memorial service
    at 118

Swire, Jim 55, 133, 135, 142–3, 158–9, 160
  '103 EXPLODED AFTER 38 MINUTES!' message to count 162
  Adamczewski, meetings with 39
  agreement between Libya and, 'working in private capacity' on 106
  airport security, Cecil Parkinson and 44–6
  American bereaved, relationship with 44
  American relatives, bomb prank revealed to 42–3
  Ammerman and Ben Aryeah, meeting on media interest with 28
  aviation security at Heathrow, test of 41–2, 45
  BBC website host 171
  BKA warning to Interpol, evidence of barometric bomb triggers 40
  Robert Black QC, relationship with 93–4, 94–5
  checking for Monica 105
  classified telexes, news of threats to aircraft security before Lockerbie in 38
  cross-examination of Prime Minister Thatcher, call for 49–50
  desert tent, meeting with Colonel Gaddaffi in 64–8
  detachment from reality of trial process 142–3
  determination to discover facts on Flora's killer 159
  dreams, thoughts and 149–50
  duped by Gaddafi, claims of

  bereaved 105–6
  final meeting with Al-Megrahi 226–8
  first meeting with Gaddafi 66–8
  Flora and, endless moments between 16–17
  Flora's place in London, visit to 19
  Flora's Wood, tidying up of 55
  Gaddafi, former home of (now derelict), visit to 64–5
  Gaddafi, fourth meeting with (in Benghazi) 211–13
  Gaddafi, meeting in Sirte with (third meeting) 114–15
  Gaddafi, second meeting with 104–06
  gift of Koran from Gaddafi and placing photograph of Flora within 67–8
  Greenock prison, visit to Al-Megrahi in 203–04
  indictment in Lockerbie case, news of 55–6
  irresistible drive within 27
  Shelley Jofre and filming for BBC documentary 109–10
  justice, dedication to pursuit of 31
  Justice Zawi, visit with 63
  Kretzmer interview at Caspidge 74–5
  letter to Margaret Thatcher seeking meeting (and reply) 31–2
  Libya visit, change as result for 70
  'The Man Who Does Not Give Up' 102–03
  media attention (again) 149
  momentum of campaigning, problems with 213–14

momentum of campaigning (*cont.*)
  murder, reflections on 9
  Nagameldin and suggestion of
    visit to Gaddafi 57–9
  national recognition for 27
  overnight flight to America,
    aviation security check and
    41–2
  permission to see Flora (by
    arrangement) 15–16
  positivity in ending narrative
    241–2
  post-trial media interviews
    (January 31 2001) 168–9
  post-verdict cutting slack for 171
  practical problems, effects of
    campaigning and 69–70
  preliminary hearing of trial,
    attendance at 127–8
  preparations for Kamp van Zeist
    trial 125–7
  press statement on doubts about
    Lockerbie trial 95
  promise of fair trial for suspects
    to Gaddafi 135
  prosecution falsehoods, reflections
    on 201
  publicity on 'bomb thing,' media
    frenzy over 44
  roller coaster to sadness and
    triumph for 109
  second meeting with Gaddafi
    104–06
  third meeting with Gaddafi (at
    Sirte) 114–15
  tree planting and 'Flora's Wood'
    22–3
  Tripoli, final visit to 224–6
  truth and justice, thoughts on 128
  uncertainty and anger of 153
  uneasiness at end of trial 167

verdict of trial, reaction to
    169–70
  Westminster Abbey, 10th
    anniversary memorial service
    at 117–20
  Whitehall speak, plans for
    counteracting (not the British
    way) 71–2
Swire, William 3, 8, 20–21, 129,
    133, 153, 169, 191, 213, 241
  Cathy and, loving relationship
    with Flora and 158
  Edinburgh degree for 93
  family holiday on Skye for 110
  grown to manhood and
    campaigning support from
    111–12
Swire family
  Caspidge house, family life at
    158–9
  comfort for each other in anguish
    and grief 8
  cruelty of events for, daily growth
    of 6–7
  21 December 1988, preparations
    for Christmas 3–4
  Shelley Jofre at Caspidge, family
    photographs and films dug out
    110–11
  Lockerbie disaster unfolds for 4–5
  John and Lisa Mosey, friendship
    with 30
  new existence for, first days of
    5–6
  personal memoir of day of
    remembrance (5 January 1989)
    18
  police inquiries of, intrusiveness
    of 8–9
  special kind of loneliness,
    surrounded by 7–8

'truth must be known' pin and 68, 120, 125

Symphony of Sorrowful Songs (Górecki) 118

Talb, Mohammed Abu 145, 146, 160–1, 180, 188

Taylor, Sir Teddy 80, 87

Taylor QC, William ('Bill') 130, 154–5, 157, 160–61, 162–3, 177, 179–80, 197

Teicher, Howard 86

Terrorism Watch 102

Thatcher, Dennis 18

Thatcher, Prime Minister Margaret 18, 30, 32, 56, 113, 150, 173

cross-examination of, Swire's call for 49–50

Lockerbie site, walking among bodies and debris 6, 75

memoirs of, publication of 75–8

reply to Swire's letter to, predictability of 32

security services of, Swire as 'person of interest' for 26

Swire's letter seeking meeting with 31–2

truth about Pan Am 103, playing down of 34, 95

warnings before Lockerbie disaster, claims about lack of 87–8

Thompson, George 232

Thought for the Day (Radio Four) 241

Thüring (manufacturers of MST-13 timers) 131, 139, 201, 232–3, 234–5

The Times 39, 202, 237, 241

Tobin, Helen 44

Toshiba bomb warning 40, 52, 88

Toshiba RT-SF16 'Bombeat' radio-cassette recorder 131, 163

TRANSEC (security section of DoT) 173

Transport Department (UK) 24–5, 26, 31–2, 38, 44, 50, 71, 90, 201

Travellers Club in Pall Mall 190

trial of Lockerbie suspects at Kamp van Zeist

end of 166–7

Fhimah, Khalifa and 114, 130–46, 154–7, 169, 239–40

Kelly's drill-down investigation of prosecution trial evidence 231–6

Lockerbie Trial Briefing Unit 171–3

manipulation of Lockerbie trial, allegations against CIA and FBI 191–2, 202

Al-Megrahi, Abdelbaset and 114, 130–46, 153–7, 165, 168, 173, 239–40

prosecution case, key elements of 130–1

Scots law, question of relevancy under 155

solemn judges, crimson and ermine-white row of 135

trial in neutral country, FCO negotiations about 97–8, 99, 100–01, 106, 108, 109

verdict 168–9

see also 'ice-cube' timers; plastic fragment; Toshiba radio-cassette recorder; unaccompanied baggage

Tsairis, Aphrodite and Peter 102, 150

Tundergarth church 43, 75

Tundergarth Mains farm 47–8, 75, 132

Turnbull QC, Alan (prosecution counsel) 122, 140–1, 154, 162, 179

El-Ubaidi, Abdel 209

UK Families Flight 103 campaign 27, 99

unaccompanied baggage 71, 72–3, 75, 80, 89–91, 174

tagging of 131

United Nations (UN) 16, 70, 87, 94, 96, 100, 108, 115, 173, 236

General Assembly 96–7, 100

Headquarters, New York 101–02

Security Council 96, 106, 116, 183, 189, 191, 219

Libyan address to (August 2003) 189

Urban, Mark 113

Uribe, Dr Alvaro 77

US Defense Intelligence Agency (DIA) 55–6

US Drug Enforcement Agency (DEA) 7, 36–7, 52, 80, 81, 84–5

US Federal Air Marshal programme 91

US Justice Department see Justice Department (US)

US National Security Agency (NSA) 237

reports from, objections to revealing of 159

US National Security Council 81, 84, 85, 86

US Presidential Commission on Aviation Security and Terrorism 80

US State Department 42, 98, 106, 107, 116, 191

warning from 6–7

US Transportation Security Administration 92

USAir 90

USS *Butte* 156

USS *Vincennes* 9, 81, 188, 210

UTA bombing (1989) 170

Van Teeseling, Ingebourg 126

Vassallo, Vincent 197

Waite, Terry 64

Washington Post 34

Watson, Peter 48

Westminster Abbey 19, 111, 117–20

Weston, Sir John 97

Whitehall, spin doctors in 165, 171

Wikileaks 211

Wilkinson, Dr (metallurgist at Strathclyde) 233–4

Wilkinson, Professor Paul 50, 74

Wilson, Jim (Tundergarth Mains farm) 47–8, 49

Winter, Oliver 80

Wishart, Ruth 236

Wolfowitz, Paul 217

World Trade Center 44, 223

Worroll, Allan 233, 235

Wright, David 197–200

Zawi, Justice Ahmed Tahev 63, 70